D1212775

WILLIAMS-SONOMA

Complete

Pasta Cookbook

WILLIAMS-SONOMA

Complete Pasta Cookbook

GENERAL EDITOR

CHUCK WILLIAMS

RECIPES

MICHELE ANNA JORDAN
KRISTINE KIDD
JOANNE WEIR

PHOTOGRAPHY

JOYCE OUDKERK POOL

WELDON OWEN

Originally published as Williams-Sonoma Pasta Collection:
*Pasta Soups & Salads; Pasta with Sauces; Ravioli & Lasagne;
Risotto* (all copyright © 1996 Weldon Owen Inc.)

WILLIAMS-SONOMA
Founder & Vice-Chairman: Chuck Williams
Associate Book Buyer: Cecilia Michaelis

PRODUCED BY
WELDON OWEN INC.
Chief Executive Officer: John Owen
Chief Operating Officer: Larry Partington
Vice President, International Sales: Stuart Laurence
Managing Editor: Jill Fox
Consulting Editors: Norman Kolpas, Sarah Putman
Copy Editor: Carolyn Miller
Art Directors: John Bull, The Book Design Company;
    Kari Perin, Perin+Perin
Production Manager: Christine DePedro
Production Editors: Linda M. Bouchard, Joan Olson
Proofreaders: Desne Border, Sharilyn Hovind
Indexer: Ken DellaPenta
Additional credits on page 304

The Williams-Sonoma Complete Cookbook Series
conceived and produced by Weldon Owen Inc.
814 Montgomery Street, San Francisco, CA 94133

Separations by Colourscan Overseas Co. Pte. Ltd.
Printed in China by Leefung-Asco Printers Ltd.

A Weldon Owen Production
Copyright © 1999 Weldon Owen Inc.
All rights reserved, including the right of
reproduction in whole or in part in any form.

First printed in 1999
10 9 8 7 6 5 4 3 2 1

Library of Congress
Cataloging-in-Publication Data:
Jordan, Michele Anna
    The Williams-Somoma Complete pasta cookbook/Chuck
Williams, general editor; Michele Anna Jordan, Kristine Kidd,
Joanne Weir, recipes; Joyce Oudkerk Pool, photography
        p.   cm. —
    Includes index.
    ISBN 1-892374-52-8 (hardcover)
    1. Cookery (Pasta) I. Kidd, Kristine. II. Weir, Joanne.
III. Williams, Chuck. IV. Title.
TX809.M17J665 1999
641.8'22—dc21   99-20376
                                CIP

A Note on Weights and Measures
All recipes include customary U.S., U.K. and metric measurements.
Conversions are based on a standard developed for these books and have
been rounded off. Actual weights may vary.

Contents

INTRODUCTION

FRESH PASTA

DRIED PASTA

RISOTTO

Introduction

&

Those of us who love pasta—and who doesn't?—usually like
to eat it often and in many forms. That love of pasta is the
simple inspiration behind this book, which compiles in a single
convenient volume a generous helping of recipes from
the original four-volume Williams-Sonoma Pasta Collection.

Throughout these fully illustrated pages, you'll find recipes
galore for fresh and dried pasta served with classic and contemporary
sauces. There are recipes for pasta soups, salads, side dishes and
entrees. You will find traditional favorites and exciting new ideas
whether your pleasure is noodles or shapes topped with sauces,
ravioli or other pasta with luscious fillings, or wonderful layered lasagne
or other baked pastas. As a bonus, there is an entire chapter
devoted to the pasta's cousin, the Italian rice dish known as risotto.

To help you gain the maximum benefit from all these recipes,
this introductory chapter includes comprehensive instructions
and step-by-step photographs for making fresh pasta, selecting dried
pasta, cooking pasta, making perfect risotto and serving any of
the dishes in this book with style. The goal in providing all of this
information, and the recipes it supports, is to make any meal
containing pasta an absolute pleasure.

ENJOYING PASTA AND RISOTTO

Culinary pleasures abound with filled pastas such as Wild Rice Ravioli with Walnut Butter Sauce (recipe on page 72). While versions of these delightful packages grace menus of the finest restaurants around the world, ravioli making can be mastered by the home cook with ease. Recipes for ravioli and other filled pastas begin on page 60.

Think of a meal featuring pasta and you'll likely find yourself smiling. So many of us rate these dishes high among our favorites, and with good reason. Regarded as ingredients on their own, pastas are like blank canvases, ready to be transformed by the cook's artistry into any of an endless number of different compositions. Versatile and generally inexpensive, pasta can be combined with fresh vegetables, spiced meats, grains and flavorful cheeses to elevate any meal to an extraordinary eating experience. Added to that, pasta and risotto recipes are generally easy to prepare, take little time to fix and can be adjusted for seasonally fresh ingredients with little trouble.

ꙏ Pasta can be light and delicate in nature or robust and satisfying. It can be casual enough to serve for an everyday family meal or possessed of an elegance befitting a formal dinner party. More often than not, you can put these recipes together for a quick weeknight supper, yet the elements have the ability to be transformed into dishes sufficiently elaborate and refined to offer to guests for a special-occasion celebration. These fine characteristics are also true of risotto, another traditional Italian meal base made from plump, medium-grain rice varieties.

ꙏ In short, pasta and risotto are quick-change artists of the pantry, ready and able to be transformed in any way you might require. The recipes in this book for soups, salads, appetizers, side dishes and entrees all reflect the myriad ways in which both pasta and risotto are capable of being enjoyed by you, your family and your guests.

Stocking the Pasta Pantry

Pasta and risotto meals become all the easier if you make the small effort to keep a selection of basic ingredients always on hand. You'll find a guide to many of these ingredients in the Glossary beginning on page 294.

ꙏ Chief among the items you should stock is, naturally, dried pasta itself. Include in your pantry a selection of several different types of dried semolina pasta: long strands or ribbons and assorted bite-sized shapes for use with sauces or in salads or soups; smaller shapes to includes in salads or soups; and broad ribbons, large shells or tubes for stuffing or baking. You'll find a comprehensive guide to common shapes on page 17. Fortunately, dried pasta stores well. Transfer it from opened packages to airtight glass containers, where it will keep for up to a year away from heat and light.

ꙏ Risotto rice, be it the Arborio, Carnaroli or Vialone Nano variety, also keeps well. Stored in an airtight container away from heat and light, it too will keep well for up to 1 year.

ꙏ If you like to make fresh pasta, at any given time you are likely to have most of the ingredients you need on hand: eggs, all-purpose flour, salt and water. This book, however, also recommends that you include semolina flour in fresh pasta dough to give it a firmer texture. You can find it in well-stocked markets, specialty food stores and Italian delicatessens. Store it as you would any other flour, in an airtight container away from heat and light.

ꙏ When it comes to sauces, toppings, fillings, dressings, soup ingredients or other elaborations to add to pasta or risotto, your pantry should, of course, reflect your own personal tastes.

ꙏ It makes sense to have extra-virgin olive oil on hand, since so many recipes begin with a few tablespoons of it. The same goes for unsalted butter. A wide complement of dried herbs and spices are also essential. So, too, are garlic and onions, which frequently provide a foundation of flavor.

Pasta soups offer heartiness and visual appeal. Making soups from dried pasta results in a quick starter or light entree that is high in nutritional values, easy to prepare and provides a good combination of foods. Although designed as a winter warm-up, you can prepare the Chicken and Farfalle Vegetable Soup (recipe on page 102) with various seasonal vegetables throughout the year. Recipes for pasta soups begin on page 102.

Tender, chewy noodles topped with a flavorful sauce is the way most of us first learned to enjoy pasta. This book celebrates the noodle in many forms, made from both fresh and dried pasta. Sauces for noodles are wonderfully adjustable as well. The Tagliolini with Asparagus (recipe on page 39) can be made with either artichoke hearts, as shown here, zucchini or yellow crookneck squash. Fresh noodle recipes begin on page 26.

❧ Several cans of good-quality tomatoes ensure that you can recapture the taste of summer at a moment's notice. You'll gain more versatility still if you include some that are whole and peeled, some diced, some crushed and some puréed to a sauce. Find canned tomatoes that taste good to you; many pasta cooks swear by the San Marzano variety, available imported from Italy.

❧ Broths are another important pantry staple, for use in sauces and soups alike. Chicken Stock (recipe on page 30), Fish Stock (recipe on page 145) and Vegetable Stock (recipe on page 238) each lend unique attributes to the recipes in this book. While you'll get the finest flavor from a homemade stock, it's easy today to find good canned or frozen chicken, seafood and vegetable broths in food stores. Check product labels to make sure that the brands

you buy are relatively low in salt, thus allowing you greater leeway in seasoning.

❧ If you like dairy-style pasta or risotto dishes, keep a selection of your favorite cheeses on hand in your refrigerator. Wrap them airtight (with the exception of blue cheeses, which do better loosely wrapped). As a rule, harder ripened cheeses will keep longer, staying good for weeks or even months; with soft or fresh varieties, keep a close eye on the "sell by" or "use by" dates on the packaging. Among the most versatile cheeses to keep on hand is a good Parmesan, bought in block form and ready to grate or shave freshly as needed.

❧ With such basics on hand, you should be able to put together many of these pasta and risotto dishes without even having to shop. On most occasions, though, a quick visit to the food store or farmers' market will provide you with all of the fresh vegetables or herbs, poultry, meat or seafood you will need to complete any of the recipes in this book.

Pasta and Good Health

Not so long ago, some people held the mistaken belief that pasta was a fattening food. Today, we view pasta and its cousin, risotto, in a clearer light, recognizing that the main ingredients themselves are remarkably healthful and nutritious.

❧ Both pasta and rice are classified among the complex carbohydrates that should provide a majority of the daily calories in a healthy diet. Both are relatively low in calories and extremely low in fat and sodium: A typical 1 cup (8 oz/250 g) of cooked dried semolina pasta has less than 200 calories (840 kilojoules), less than 1 gram of fat, no cholesterol and only 1 milligram of sodium. One cup (8 oz/250 g) of cooked rice is about 260 calories (1090 kilojoules), with less than 0.5 gram of fat, no cholesterol and no sodium. Even fresh pasta made with eggs is still very low in fat, with only 1.5 gram of fat in a 1-cup (8-oz/250-g) serving that provides about 180 calories (750 kilojoules). Pasta and rice are also good sources of fiber. Dietary fiber aids elimination and may help prevent heart disease, intestinal disorders and some cancers.

❧ Why, then, did pasta ever get a less-than-healthful reputation? The answer, of course, lies in what you put on it. Sauces rich with cheese or cream or robust with red meat are naturally more likely to be correspondingly high in calories, fat and cholesterol. For the most healthful pasta or risotto choices, opt for those that feature tomatoes or other vegetables, seafood or poultry; those based on light broths; or those made with olive oil, which is predominately a monounsaturated fat that has been found to help reduce blood cholesterol levels. Fresh herbs offer a healthful alternative to salt and plenty of interesting flavor without fat. If you are in general good health, even rich pasta and risotto dishes are fine to enjoy from time to time if you eat them in moderation and balance them with healthful dishes.

Relied on as the major source of sustenance by more than half the world's population, rice—not bread—deserves the pride of place as the true staff of life. Risotto, the traditional Italian rice dish, may well present the staple in its most glorious form. Cooked with onions, wine, cheese and herbs, risotto serves as an appetizer, side dish or entree. Clams with Fresh Lemon Risotto (recipe on page 267) marries the rice and citrus flavors of Northern Italy with fresh food from the sea for a delightful entree. Risotto recipes begin on page 232.

Making Fresh Pasta

You can make fresh pasta at home in about 10 minutes with common ingredients, using a food processor and a reasonably priced manual pasta machine. With just a bit more effort and time, you can make pasta by hand. For your own recipes and the recipes in this book, use the Egg Pasta ingredients and instructions as the basis for making all fresh pasta. To flavor the pasta, change ingredients as noted for each variation.

Pasta Ingredients

Semolina flour is made from the hardest wheat grown; for pasta making, buy finely ground rather than coarse semolina. The high-gluten semolina flour provides the elasticity necessary for kneading, cutting and shaping. All-purpose (plain) flour is a blend of wheat flours and has a finer consistency than semolina flour. While fresh pasta can be made with only all-purpose flour, the addition of semolina flour yields a firmer texture.

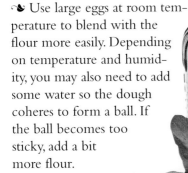

☙ Use large eggs at room temperature to blend with the flour more easily. Depending on temperature and humidity, you may also need to add some water so the dough coheres to form a ball. If the ball becomes too sticky, add a bit more flour.

Pound-and-a-Half Pastas

EACH RECIPE MAKES 1½ LB (750 G)

Serves 6–8 as an entree or 8–10 as a first course or side dish.

EGG PASTA
2 cups (10 oz/315 g) semolina flour
1 cup (5 oz/155 g) unbleached all-purpose (plain) flour, plus additional for dusting
½ teaspoon salt
3 eggs at room temperature
3 tablespoons water

BASIL PASTA
Replace the water with ¼ cup (½ oz/15 g) minced fresh basil.

BEET PASTA
Replace the water with ½ cup (4 fl oz/ 125 ml) cooked beet puree.

BLACK PEPPER PASTA
Add 1 tablespoon freshly ground pepper.

LEMON PASTA
Replace the water with 1 tablespoon fresh lemon juice and add ½ tablespoon grated lemon zest.

OLIVE PASTA
Replace the water with 3 tablespoons pitted olive puree or commercial or homemade tapenade (recipe on page 186), oil drained.

PUMPKIN PASTA
Replace the water with ½ cup (4 fl oz/ 125 ml) commercial pumpkin puree and ⅛ teaspoon ground nutmeg.

One-Pound Pastas

EACH RECIPE MAKES 1 LB (500 G)

Serves 4–6 as an entree or 6–8 as a first course or side dish.

EGG PASTA
1⅓ cups (7 oz/220 g) semolina flour
⅔ cup (4 oz/125 g) unbleached all-purpose (plain) flour, plus additional for dusting
¼ teaspoon salt
2 eggs at room temperature
1½ tablespoons water

BASIL PASTA
Increase the salt to ½ teaspoon, eliminate the water and add 3 tablespoons minced fresh basil.

BEET PASTA
Increase the salt to ½ teaspoon, eliminate the water and add ⅓ cup (3 fl oz/80 ml) cooked beet puree.

BLACK PEPPER PASTA
Add 2 teaspoons freshly ground pepper.

LEMON PASTA
Replace the water with 1½ tablespoons fresh lemon juice and add 1 tablespoon grated lemon zest.

OLIVE PASTA
Increase the salt to ½ teaspoon, eliminate the water and add 2 tablespoons pitted olive puree or commercial or homemade tapenade (recipe on page 186), oil drained.

PUMPKIN PASTA
Increase the salt to ½ teaspoon, eliminate the water and add ⅓ cup (3 fl oz/80 ml) pumpkin puree and ⅛ teaspoon ground nutmeg.

SAFFRON PASTA
Soak ⅛ teaspoon saffron threads in the 1½ tablespoons water for 30 minutes before using in forming the dough.

SPINACH PASTA
Replace the water with 1 cup (1 oz/30 g) loosely packed spinach leaves, steamed, squeezed dry and chopped.

TOMATO PASTA
Replace the water with 2 tablespoons commercial or homemade concentrated tomato paste.

Making Pasta by Machine

1. Gather the fresh pasta ingredients together. In the work bowl of a food processor fitted with the metal blade, combine all the ingredients. Pulse several times to fully incorporate the ingredients.

2. Using a rubber spatula, scrape down the sides of the work bowl. Pulse several times for a few seconds until the dough forms a ball. Dust the dough ball with flour. Cut the dough into 4 pieces.

3. Crank each piece through the pasta machine set at the widest setting. Dust it, fold it and pass it through again until it feels smooth and silky, 8–10 times. Cover and let rest for 1 hour.

4. Decrease the rollers of the pasta machine by 1 setting. Crank each piece of dough through the machine, reducing the roller opening, until the desired thickness is obtained. Dust with flour as needed.

5. Sprinkle a wooden board or a counter lined with waxed paper with flour. Place the pasta sheets on the flour and let rest until dry to the touch but still pliant, about 10 minutes.

6. For shapes, cut the sheets according to the individual recipes. For noodles, install the cutting attachment onto the manual pasta machine and pass the sheets through. Arrange the noodles to dry slightly before use.

Making Pasta by Hand

Although it takes slightly longer to make pasta by hand—that is, without using a pasta machine—the process is nonetheless easy and satisfying work. You will need a sturdy wooden or marble work surface, a good-quality rolling pin and a bit of elbow grease to work the dough by hand. For cutting pasta noodles by hand, use a knife and a metal straightedge. Follow these steps for good results every time.

1. On a work surface, combine the semolina and all-purpose flours and salt in a mound. Make a well in the center and break in the eggs. Add water or flavoring ingredients. Using a fork, blend the ingredients in the well, gradually drawing in the flour until all the ingredients are combined into a dough.

2. Dust a work surface with flour and transfer the dough to the surface. Using a dough scraper and the palm and heel of your hand, knead the dough, pushing it down and away from you and turning it repeatedly, until the dough feels smooth and satiny, 7–10 minutes. Sprinkle on flour if the dough becomes sticky or soft during kneading. Cut the dough into 4 pieces.

3. Place a piece of dough on a floured work surface. With your hand, flatten it into a rectangle. Using a floured rolling pin, roll the dough away from you, applying just moderate pressure. Turn the dough over and around. Repeat, adding flour if the dough becomes sticky, until the pasta reaches the desired thickness.

4. Line a table or counter with waxed paper or kitchen towels. Sprinkle the paper or towels lightly with flour. Place the pasta sheets on the paper or towels side by side and let rest until they are dry to the touch but still pliant, about 10 minutes.

CUTTING FRESH PASTA

Making fresh pasta dough as shown on the previous pages is only the first step in a wide variety of possible pasta dishes. Depending on how you treat the dough, you can easily produce all kinds of delightful pasta shapes, long pasta noodles of varying widths and thicknesses and inventive pastas filled with savory or sweet fillings.

❧ Whether you plan to make pasta shapes or filled pastas, begin by making the dough, following the recipes and instructions given on the previous pages, up to the point at which the dough is ready to be cut. Then, follow the cutting and shaping instructions here or in individual recipes.

Cutting Pasta Shapes

Prepare the pasta and roll into sheets using a pasta machine or rolling pin. Transfer the pasta sheets to a floured work surface and cut, following the instructions here.

❧ To store pasta shapes, refrigerate in a tightly covered container for several days. Or freeze by arranging the shapes in one layer on a baking sheet, not touching each other, and freeze until hard. Then transfer to a freezer bag. Well sealed, most pasta shapes can be frozen for several months. Be sure to indicate the pasta type, shape and freeze date on the freezer bag for future use in recipes. Do not defrost before cooking. Cook them directly from the frozen state.

FARFALLE Using a scalloped 2-inch (5-cm) cookie cutter, cut the pasta into circles. Pinch each round in the middle, pressing to secure it into a shape resembling a butterfly or bow tie. Set on waxed paper. Dry for 15–30 minutes before cooking.

FAZZOLETTI Cut the pasta into 4-inch (10-cm) squares. Dust the squares with flour. Set on waxed paper. Dry for at least 30 minutes before cooking.

GARGANELLI Cut the pasta into 1½-inch (4-cm) squares. Using a wooden pencil or a chopstick, roll each square diagonally around it, pressing slightly into the work surface to bond the pasta to itself. Slip the pasta off the pencil or chopstick and set on waxed paper. Dry for 15–30 minutes before cooking.

MALTAGLIATI Cut the pasta into 5-inch (13-cm) squares. Dust each square with flour and place in stacks of 3 or 5 squares. Cut the stacks into diagonal pieces, changing the direction of the knife back and forth so that they form irregular triangles measuring about 1 inch (2.5 cm) on their long sides. Separate the triangles and toss with flour. Set on waxed paper. Dry for 15–30 minutes before cooking.

QUADRUCCI Cut the pasta into 5-inch (13-cm) squares. Dust each square with flour and place in stacks of 3 or 4 squares. Cut the stacks into strips ½ inch (12 mm) wide, then cut the strips into ½-inch (12-mm) squares. Separate the squares and toss with flour. Set on waxed paper. Dry for 15–30 minutes before cooking.

Cutting Noodles

Prepare the pasta using the ingredients and instructions on pages 12–13.

❧ To cut noodles using a pasta machine, roll the pasta into sheets of the desired thickness. Secure the desired cutting attachment to the machine and crank the pasta sheets through the cutter. Dry the cut pasta for 15 minutes before cooking.

❧ To cut pasta noodles by hand, line a tabletop or counter with waxed paper or kitchen towels and dust with flour. Roll the pasta into sheets of the desired thickness and let rest until they are dry to the touch but still pliant, about 10 minutes. Roll each sheet into a cylinder. Using a small, sharp knife, cut the cylinder crosswise to the desired width. Unroll the ribbons, dust with flour and set on waxed paper. Dry for 15 minutes before cooking.

❧ To store fresh noodles, first form the flour-dusted ribbons into loose serving-sized mounds or nests. Pack in airtight plastic bags and refrigerate for up to 3 days. Or freeze and use within several months. Do not defrost before use; cook them directly from the frozen state.

FETTUCCINE Roll sheets ⅟₃₂ inch (1 mm) thick. Cut ribbons ¼ inch (6 mm) wide.

LINGUINE Roll sheets ⅟₁₆ inch (2 mm) thick. Cut ribbons ⅛ inch (3 mm) wide.

PAPPARDELLE Roll sheets $\frac{1}{32}$ inch (1 mm) thick. Cut ribbons 1¼ inch (3 cm) wide.

TAGLIATELLE Roll sheets $\frac{1}{16}$ inch (2 mm) thick. Cut ribbons ½ inch (12 mm) wide.

TAGLIOLINI Roll sheets $\frac{1}{32}$ inch (1 mm) thick. Cut ribbons ⅛ inch (3 mm) wide.

Making Ravioli

The most popular of filled pastas, ravioli are made from sheets of fresh pasta dough that are cut into circles, squares or other shapes, topped with a filling and then sealed around that filling. The step-by-step methods shown here explain how to make two of the most basic and versatile types of ravioli shapes: square and round. As you become proficient at them, allow your imagination to guide you in making other shapes, following the same basic guidelines.

❧ Make the fresh pasta and filling according to individual recipes.

❧ Dust a wooden work surface with flour.

❧ When making square ravioli, use a knife and ruler to trim a pair of pasta sheets to the exact same size.

❧ When making round ravioli, be sure to cut twice the number of pasta rounds as finished ravioli.

❧ Whatever type of filled pasta you make, it is essential to make sure that the edges of each individual piece are tightly sealed before you cook them; even a tiny opening will let some of the cooking water seep in and dilute the filling.

❧ After filling and sealing, place the ravioli on waxed paper dusted with flour, cover with a kitchen towel and dry slightly before cooking, about 30 minutes.

❧ To store ravioli, refrigerate in a tightly covered container for up to 2 days. To freeze ravioli, arrange them on a baking sheet, not touching each other, and freeze until hard. Then transfer them to a freezer bag. They can be frozen for several months. Do not defrost; cook them directly from the frozen state, adding an additional minute or so to their cooking time.

Forming Square Ravioli

1. Spread one pasta sheet on a floured surface. Using a pastry brush, lightly coat the sheet with water. Place about 1 teaspoon of filling in mounds approximately 2½ inches (6 cm) apart.

2. Gently place the matching sheet of pasta directly over the first sheet, carefully aligning the edges. Using your fingers, press the top sheet around the filling mounds, pushing out any air bubbles.

3. Using a special tool called a ravioli cutter, fluted pastry wheel or knife and ruler, cut the sheets into individual squares. Check that the seal is secure. Use a fork to press the edges together.

Forming Round Ravioli

1. Spread the pasta sheets side by side on a floured wooden work surface. Using a round cookie cutter, cut the desired shapes. Transfer half the rounds to waxed paper dusted with flour.

2. Using a pastry brush, lightly coat the remaining rounds with water. Place about 1 teaspoon of filling in the center of each round, leaving a border. Brush the border with water.

3. Top each round and filling with a reserved pasta round. Brush the border with water. Using a fork, carefully press the edges of the rounds together to secure the filling inside.

CHOOSING DRIED PASTA

The best dried pasta is manufactured entirely from semolina flour, which is ground from hard wheat. It is often referred to as durum wheat. *Durum* means "hard" in Latin. This variety of wheat is high in the elastic substance known as gluten, which gives the pasta its desired sturdiness, thus helping it maintain a desired chewy texture when drenched with a sauce, immersed in boiling-hot soup or coated with a salad dressing. It is also high in dietary fiber, low in fat, cholesterol-free and contains generous amounts of protein, making it a beneficial part of a balanced diet.

❧ Mixed with water in the factory, the semolina flour forms a paste that is extruded through metal dies to make strands, ribbons, tubes and other shapes, including those used in this book. The pasta is then dried in chambers that carefully control humidity and temperature.

❧ There are scores of different forms in which dried pasta is made, and you are likely to find the widest selection of these in well-stocked food stores and in Italian delicatessens. The latter are also likely to stock some of the imported Italian brands that pasta gourmets swear by. But plenty of good varieties of pasta are being made outside of Italy. To be sure you are using the finest dried pasta, check labels to make sure the pasta is made from 100 percent hard-wheat (semolina) flour.

❧ If you cannot find a specific pasta shape called for in a particular recipe, substitute a similarly sized shape, appropriate for the specific recipe, following the principles outlined here. Fresh pasta can also be substituted for many recipes, although an additional pleasure of dried pasta is its long shelf life, which allows you to make wonderful meals right from the pantry. Be sure to keep a good variety on hand at all times.

❧ Once you have opened a package of dried pasta, store it in a tightly covered glass container in a cool, dark place. Use the pasta within 1 year of purchase.

Choosing Pasta for Sauces

The pairing of dried pasta shapes and their sauces may at first seem arbitrary to the inexperienced cook. However, underlying the combinations is a sound logic based on the shapes themselves and the characteristics of the sauces that go with them.

❧ Generally speaking, the smaller or thinner the dried pasta, the better suited it is to sauces of comparable lightness or fine texture. Take, for example, the brothy, briny liquid that results when clams and mussels are steamed in white wine (page 176), perfectly complemented by the relatively delicate strands of linguine; or how well angel hair pasta goes with a poultry broth in which meatballs are simmered (page 196).

❧ By contrast, bite-sized shapes, tubes or broad ribbons of dried pasta better highlight sauces that have more body or contain larger pieces of ingredients. Consider how aptly wagon wheel–shaped ruote, for instance, match the shape and size of zucchini and Italian sausage slices (page 199); or the way in which curlicue fusilli seem an ideal choice for a pasta salad featuring squid (page 151). And pasta shapes that include deep ridges or crevices are frequently chosen to companion sauces that cling, the better to deliver their delicious flavor with every spoon or forkful; witness Creamy Shell Salad with Lobster (page 146) or cavatelli served with a buttery sauce of onions, shallots and leeks (page 190).

Choosing Pasta for Soups

The kind of pasta suitable for soup should be a size and shape that enables you to pick it up with a soup spoon and eat it without the pasta slipping or slithering back into the bowl. The pasta shapes chosen for the recipes meet that criteria. If the specific shape called for is not available, any of similar size or shape will work. Even lengthy pasta noodles may be used in a soup, provided you snap them into spoon-sized pieces before you cook them.

❧ In most cases, cook the pasta only until the first moment that it is al dente, since it will continue cooking briefly after it is added to the hot liquid. In some recipes, however, such as the Chicken and Farfalle Vegetable Soup (page 102), the pasta cooks right in the soup.

Choosing Pasta for Salads

Although ease of eating is not as critical a factor in the choice of pasta shapes for salad as it is for soup, it is still a matter of some consideration. If you plan to serve the salad for an elegant occasion, select a pasta size or shape that can be eaten easily. Casual events allow for pasta salads that require the dexterous twirling of pasta strands or balancing of larger pasta shapes.

❧ The other ingredients in the salad also play a factor in the choice of pasta you use. The sizes into which they are cut should be complemented by the size and shape of the pasta. Your choice of pasta can also add an element of wit to the salad, as with Creamy Shell Salad with Lobster (page 146), in which pasta shells are the perfect choice for a salad featuring seafood.

Dried Pasta Glossary

If a particular variety of pasta is unavailable, substitute any dried pasta of similar shape or size.

ANGEL HAIR Long, thin strands.
BUCATINI Hollow rods resembling spaghetti; also called perciatelli.
CAVATAPPI Short, spiral-shaped tubes.
DITALINI Little thimbles.
ELBOWS Small curved tubes.
FARFALLE Butterfly or bow tie shapes.
FARFALLINE Small farfalle.
FEDELINI Thin spaghetti.
FETTUCCINE Ribbonlike strands.
FUSILLI Short or long twisted strands, also called eliche or spirali, are rifled, like the inside of a rifle barrel, or "fusile" in Italian.
GARGANELLI Small, ridged, folded tubes.
GEMELLI "Twins," describing short, intertwined strands.
LASAGNE Long, wide ribbons with straight or fluted edges.
LINGUINE "Small tongues," thin, flat strands.
MANICOTTI "Muffs," short, wide tubes.
MOSTACCIOLI Mustachelike shapes, similar to penne.
ORECCHIETTE "Little ears," similar to small- to medium-sized shells.
ORZO Resembling grains of barley or rice.
PENNE Slender tubes with ends cut at an angle, resembling quill pens.
PENNE RIGATE Ridged penne.
PERCIATELLI Hollow spaghettilike rods. Also called bucatini.
RADIATORI "Radiators," medium-sized cubes.
RIGATONI Medium-sized ridged tubes.
RUOTE "Wheels"; also called rotelle.
SHELLS Conch shells are found in small, medium and large sizes.
SPAGHETTI Classic long, round strands.
SPAGHETTINI A slender spaghetti.
STELLINE Tiny star shapes.
TORTELLINI Little pies, ring-shaped and containing a filling.
TUBETTI Little tube shapes.
ZITI Long, slender tubes.

COOKING PASTA

If you can boil water and tell time, you can cook pasta perfectly. No special skills or equipment are required, and the basic method is the same whether the pasta you are cooking is fresh or dried, plain or flavored, simple or filled.

It is customary to add salt to the boiling water prior to adding the pasta. For the best taste, use kosher salt, which is slightly coarser in texture. It does not contain the anti-caking additives found in refined table salt and imparts more flavor. However, if you're following a low-sodium diet, you can leave out the salt completely without adversely affecting the finished dish.

Equipment Needed

For the best results when cooking pasta, choose a pot large enough to allow it to float freely while cooking, which will help prevent the pasta from sticking together. With two sturdy handles, the pot will be easier for you to pick up to drain the pasta.

Use a long-handled slotted spoon or cooking fork to stir pasta strands or shapes as they cook, thus helping to prevent them from sticking together. (This step should be omitted with filled pastas such as ravioli, to avoid damaging them and causing them to break open.) A pasta fork, also called a pasta puller, is a long-handled plastic or wooden tool that looks like a flattened spoon with teeth; it is particularly handy for lifting long pasta strands from the pot or serving bowl. A large slotted spoon or a wire-mesh skimmer is helpful to lift out ravioli when they are done. Two thick pot holders or oven mitts and a sturdy colander that can withstand the heat of a large quantity of boiling water are also good investments for cooking pasta safely and successfully. Of course, any well-stocked kitchen will already have such items on hand for a multitude of other cooking purposes.

If you cook pasta frequently, consider investing a small amount of money in a special pasta pot. This large pot includes a strainer insert that is fitted inside before the uncooked pasta is added to the water. When the pasta is done, you can then simply drain it by lifting the insert from the pot, thus eliminating the need for pouring the pasta and its cooking water into a colander. A pasta pot is especially helpful when cooking several batches of pasta, as you might when cooking for a crowd. Because the water remains hot in the pot, you lessen the time needed to bring the water to a boil before cooking successive batches.

Al Dente or Tender

The Italian term *al dente* has become universally accepted as a description of pasta cooked perfectly. Translated literally as "to the tooth," it describes pasta that offers a slight resistance when bitten into, an indication that it has reached a point at which it is tender while still being chewy in texture.

Technically, al dente is used only to describe the perfect cooked state of pasta that has been dried. Fresh pasta should be cooked just until "tender." In this case, tender means evenly soft but still chewy.

Either way, the best way to test for doneness is by biting into a single piece or strand of the pasta. Use a slotted spoon, a long-handled cooking fork or a pasta fork to fish it out of the still-boiling water at the earliest suggested time for doneness, as listed on the manufacturer's packaging or in the recipe you are using.

Blow on the pasta briefly to cool it before biting into it. Dried pasta should be tender but firm and chewy. It should not show any white undercooked portion at its center; al dente does not mean underdone. Fresh pasta should taste cooked, without any hint of the raw flavor of flour.

Cooking Filled Pasta

Taste-testing an individual piece of pasta is not as practical an option when you are cooking filled shapes such as ravioli. Fortunately, there is an easy visual cue to recognize when they are ready to be removed from the boiling water.

When they are slipped into boiling water, most filled shapes will sink to the bottom of the pot. Within a few minutes, they will rise to the surface as they cook through. Generally, ravioli and other filled shapes are done cooking about 1 minute after they rise to the surface, at which point they can then be lifted out with a slotted spoon or wire skimmer.

Cooking Pasta for Sauces

Once it is cooked, pasta for sauces should be served as soon as possible. If you must hold cooked pasta for a few minutes prior to serving, add a few tablespoons of sauce, olive oil or reserved cooking water to the drained pasta to keep it from sticking.

❧ If an individual recipe calls for the sauce to be mixed with the pasta, empty the cooked, drained pasta into the pan. You might want to reserve 2–3 tablespoons of the cooking water to add with the pasta to help it mix more easily. Stir gently but thoroughly to combine the pasta and sauce.

❧ Present the pasta as directed in the recipes, topping the sauce with additional grated cheese at the table, if desired. For an elegant look, garnish the finished dish with a fresh herb sprig or a wedge of fruit.

❧ Once cooked, any pasta will keep in the refrigerator for up to 12 hours, after which time its flavor will begin to sour.

Cooking Pasta for Soups

Pasta intended for use in a soup should be cooked in the same way as you would any other pasta, with one exception: It should be slightly undercooked, because it will then continue to cook slightly in the soup's hot liquid. Therefore, watch your cooking time, and cook soup pasta only until it is barely al dente, so that it will better retain its distinctive texture in the finished dish.

Cooking Pasta for Salads

When pasta is intended for use in a salad, cook it al dente as you would pasta that will be served with a sauce. Immediately after draining the pasta, transfer it to a large bowl. Drizzle the pasta with olive oil and toss to coat it well; this will lightly season the pasta while preventing it from sticking. Cool the oil-dressed pasta, uncovered, to room temperature; covering the hot pasta may cause it to sour. Once cooled, cover and refrigerate the pasta for at least 1 hour and up to 24 hours prior to mixing with other ingredients. This provides time for the pasta to absorb the flavor of the oil. For most salads, let the pasta return to room temperature before serving.

Preparing Pasta Perfectly

1. Start with sufficient water in a large enough pot to allow the pasta to circulate freely. Over high heat, bring the water to a full, rolling boil. If desired, cover the pot to shorten the time needed to bring it to a boil.

4. If using a pasta pot with a strainer insert, grasp the strainer's handles and lift it out. Otherwise, pour the contents of the pot into a sturdy colander set inside the sink. Shake the insert or colander until the water has drained.

2. When the water boils, add the salt. Do not add the salt before the water boils; doing so may cause an unpleasant aftertaste. When the water has returned to a boil, slowly add the pasta.

5. For sauced dishes, immediately transfer the pasta to the pan in which the sauce was cooked. For dishes to be baked, see individual recipes.

3. Cook the pasta, stirring occasionally, until it is al dente. Begin testing the pasta a minute before the earliest suggested time for doneness according to the recipe or the package directions.

6. Using a pair of wooden spoons or pasta servers, gently toss together the pasta and the sauce. When it is fully mixed, transfer it to an attractive bowl to serve.

MAKING RISOTTO

Archaeological evidence suggests that rice originated in India, was first cultivated in China about 7,000 years ago and was popularized in Europe by Alexander the Great. As its use spread, it became the pilaf of the Middle East, the paella of Spain and the risotto of Northern Italy. Today, risotto is used as a base for toppings featuring flavors from around the world

❧ An easy-to-follow formula for making risotto at its most basic, the Classic Risotto recipe at right employs principles that apply to any risotto or similar rice dish.

❧ First, choose a cooking vessel large and wide enough to allow for easy stirring and adequate evaporation of the cooking liquid.

❧ For the cooking liquid, chicken stock is the classic choice for risotto. But meat stock, vegetable stock or fish stock can be substituted in basic risotto. If you have no homemade stock on hand, and have no time to make it, use canned or frozen stock or bottled clam juice instead. Look for low-sodium versions and be sure to taste your dish before seasoning with any additional salt when you use commercial stocks or broths.

❧ Cook risotto with unsalted butter, which allows greater leeway in seasoning than salted versions. Be sure to heat the butter just until it melts and do not let it burn while you sauté the onion.

❧ Yellow onions were used in designing and testing the risotto recipes in this book, but any kind of onion can be used to make risotto. Slow cooking over moderate heat helps to develop the sugars naturally present in onions, bringing out a gentle, sweet flavor. You want the onion to be flavorful and translucent, not browned, before adding the rice.

❧ Any dry white wine fit to drink can be used in risotto. Never cook with wine that has soured or smells of vinegar, as that unpleasant flavor will be absorbed into the rice. Most of the alcohol will evaporate from the wine during simmering.

❧ After adding the cheese, do not cook the risotto too long. Stir in the cheese just until it melts. Prolonged cooking causes the casein in cheese to coagulate and separate from the water and fat, producing a stringy consistency and making the rice oily.

❧ To get the most flavor from the Parmesan, choose a good variety of that famous Italian cheese and store it properly before use. For the most flavor, freshly grate the cheese just before you add it to the dish. Provide more cheese and a grater at the table, so that guests can help themselves.

❧ Spices, from exotic saffron to basic black pepper, and culinary herbs each provide great flavor and visual appeal to risotto dishes. While the rice recipes in this book were designed using specific spices and herbs, you'll be able to create an incredibly varied range of dishes simply by substituting different spice and herb ingredients to your risotto. Fresh herbs are preferred over dried herbs in risotto dishes, for their more gentle flavor and visual interest. Stored properly, fresh herbs will keep for about a week. Most spices retain their flavor for six months.

❧ Perfectly made risotto will be quite creamy. If it cooks too fast or sits too long after cooking, it may become dry. If that happens, stir in more liquid to bring the rice to a creamy consistency.

Selecting a Rice

Only two species of rice have been cultivated by humankind: *Oryza glaberrima,* a species confined to West Africa, and the much more widespread *Oryza sativa,* of which approximately 120,000 different varieties are grown.

❧ All those varieties, however, may be divided into two main types: long-grain, which are less starchy and usually cook up into the fluffy, dry, separate grains of such dishes as pilafs; and medium- or short-grain, which have extra surface starch that yields the sticky rice favored in Japanese cuisine and the creamy sauce of risottos.

❧ The main type of rice used for risotto is a plump medium-grain variety known as Arborio. Two other hybrids can also be used: Carnaroli, prized for its firm texture; and Vialone Nano, which has shorter grains that yield a less creamy sauce and cook about 5 minutes more quickly.

Classic Risotto

MAKES 6 CUPS (30 OZ/940 G)

To make a perfect risotto in the classic style, use imported Arborio rice and be prepared to watch over it during the entire cooking process. The creamy results will be worth the effort. Once the grains are coated with butter, always add the hot liquid a little at a time to allow for even absorption. Adjust the heat so that the liquid simmers actively and stir the mixture almost constantly. Toward the end of the cooking time, the rice should be checked to see if it is al dente: tender but still firm and chewy. This method is shown in the photographs at right.

6 cups (48 fl oz/1.5 l) Chicken Stock
   (recipe on page 30)
2 tablespoons unsalted butter
1 onion, chopped
2½ cups (17½ oz/545 g) Arborio or
   medium-grain rice
⅔ cup (5 fl oz/160 ml) dry white wine
1¾ cups (7 oz/220 g) freshly grated
   Parmesan cheese
salt and freshly ground pepper

Cooking Risotto

1. In a small saucepan over high heat, bring the Chicken Stock to a simmer. Reduce the heat to low and keep the liquid hot.

4. Add the stock 1 cup (8 fl oz/250 ml) at a time, stirring constantly, until the rice starts to soften, about 10 minutes. Use three-fourths of the stock by this point.

2. In a heavy large saucepan over low heat, melt the butter. Add the onion and sauté, stirring frequently, until it is translucent, about 8 minutes.

5. Add the remaining stock ½ cup (4 fl oz/125 ml) at a time, stirring constantly, until the rice is tender and creamy, about 10 minutes longer.

3. Add the rice and stir until a white spot appears in the center of the grains, about 1 minute. Add the wine and stir until it is absorbed, about 2 minutes.

6. Add the Parmesan cheese and salt and pepper to taste. Stir to mix well. Remove from heat. To serve, spoon into bowls or plates as instructed in the recipes.

SERVING PASTA AND RISOTTO

As the wonderful range of recipes in this book demonstrates, pastas and risottos can be the stars of almost any course of a meal, from appetizers to soups and salads to all kinds of entrees and side dishes.

❧ The type of pasta or risotto you are preparing, and the role it will play in your menu, will help determine what kind of preparations you should make for serving it. Follow these general guidelines when planning your own menus and table settings.

Setting a Style

As you glance through the many photographs that accompany the recipes in this book, you'll find a wealth of ideas for serving pasta or risotto recipes with style.

❧ Some recipes naturally lend themselves to more elegant occasions that might call for your best china and silver. Others are more down-to-earth in nature, looking best in rustic pottery or earthenware dishes. Beyond such basic considerations, pay attention to the colors and shapes of the ingredients in any given recipe, letting them suggest pleasing pairings with particular serving pieces you might have.

❧ Let the style of the food and of the dishware you choose for serving it extend to the rest of your table as well. Choose napkins, for example, of a color or pattern that go with your serving pieces and the food. Bear in mind, however, that sauce-laden pasta dishes logically call for generously sized napkins that survive laundering well.

❧ Flowers in colors that complement the ingredients can also add a pleasing touch to your table, whether presented as informal posies or formally arranged bouquets. So, too, can beautiful, whole specimens of vegetables that are featured in the recipe, arranged in a bowl or basket to form a centerpiece. If the occasion warrants it (and most occasions do), add candlelight; but opt for dripless candles to make cleanup easier, and avoid candles with scents that can distract from your appreciation of foods or beverages.

Serving Pasta Entrees

The recipes in this book for both fresh and dried pastas with sauces were designed to be served primarily as entrees. Most of them can also be offered as first courses or side dishes, in which case the given ingredients will yield 2–4 more servings than the number listed.

❧ To present a sauced pasta at its very best, serve it piping hot. The easiest way to achieve this is to cook the sauce first, keeping it covered and warm while you boil the pasta. To the same end, warm the bowls or plates before serving. If they are ovenproof, you can heat them in the oven at its lowest setting; but if you are in any doubt, warm the dishes instead by filling them with hot tap water and then emptying and quickly drying them with a clean dish towel just before you put in the food.

❧ In most Italian homes, pasta noodles are served from a large, wide, relatively shallow bowl that allows them to be tossed with ease. The pasta is then divided among individual bowls that are smaller versions of the serving vessel. The wide shape of the bowl makes it easy for diners to twirl strands of pasta onto their forks, while helping to keep the pasta warm. Italian-style pasta bowls, both large and individually sized, may be found in any well-stocked kitchenware store.

❧ That is not to say, however, that such dishware is absolutely essential. Sauced pasta dishes may be served directly from any attractive serving bowl or from a platter with a raised rim. Shallow soup plates or standard dinner plates with a slightly raised rim will work well for serving individual portions of any recipes with sauces thick enough to cling to the pasta. Such containers also work perfectly well for serving baked and filled pastas, although the more substantial nature of many such recipes also allows them to be served on standard plates. For pasta served in more brothlike sauces, use soup plates or standard soup bowls.

❧ The cutlery you provide for guests should also suit the nature of both the pasta and its sauce. For most noodles coated with a sauce, a fork alone is sufficient. Italians traditionally use just forks, snaring a few strands with the tines, then holding the tines against the curved side of a shallow individual bowl as they twirl the fork to coil up a neat little mouthful. The same result can be accomplished by holding the tines inside the bowl of a soup spoon, although Italians would frown at the need for a second utensil. Forks can also be used for eating pasta shapes or chunkier sauces, although a soup spoon can also do an efficient job in such a case. Knives should only be employed for cutting large portions of baked or stuffed pastas. Never commit the sin of cutting pasta noodles with a knife!

Serving Pasta Soups

Shallow or deep bowls will, likewise, be the obvious choice for any of the recipes in this book in which pasta plays a featured role in a soup. If you like, present the soup at table in a large tureen, ladling up individual portions. Or, for an informal party, invite guests to serve themselves from a large soup pot simmering on the stove.

❧ One of the most intriguing aspects of serving pasta soups is the opportunity they provide for you to expand a simple-but-hearty bowlful into an entire meal. For a quick yet complete and satisfying repast, accompany

a pasta soup with a mixed green salad, a crusty loaf of bread or home-baked quick bread. Add fresh fruit or another favorite dessert and your choice of beverage.

Serving Pasta Salads

The introductory notes to the pasta salad recipes in this book offer useful ideas on the many roles they can play in a meal, from buffet or picnic food to side dish to entree. Quantities may easily be multiplied for larger gatherings, or halved for more intimate meals. And most pasta salads keep well, allowing you to enjoy them for more than one meal.

෴ In most cases, the pasta, cooked in advance and chilled in the refrigerator, is tossed with the dressing and other ingredients shortly before serving. Because the pasta will absorb the dressing and become softer over time, the salad, once tossed, will be at its best if it is eaten within 24 hours.

෴ Perhaps the most traditional way in which pasta salad is served is as a picnic food. Many of the salad recipes you will find here lend themselves well to travel. It's a good idea to pack the chilled pasta, the dressing and the other salad ingredients in three separate airtight containers, bringing along a large lightweight serving bowl or other container in which you can combine them once you've arrived at your destination. Use an ice chest or insulated bag and stack the salad containers between layers of reusable blue ice. All perishable picnic foods should be stored at a temperature lower than 42°F (6°C).

Serving Risotto

Risottos can be served efficiently in pasta bowls, in soup bowls or plates or on dinner plates. Depending on the style of the meal, you can present them at the table either in individual portions or dish them up from one large serving bowl. However you offer risotto to your guests, make sure to heat the bowls or plates before filling them, following the instructions given above for heating dishware for pasta with sauces.

෴ Forks and soup spoons make equally suitable utensils for eating risotto. Some people prefer spoons because of the soupy nature of certain recipes. When a risotto includes large chunks of other ingredients, however, or when it is served as an accompaniment to a main dish, a fork is a more sensible choice.

Beverages and Bread

The perfect finishing touch to many of these meals will be your selection of beverages and breads. Many people cannot resist the urge to mop up the delicious sauces with a slice of hearty bread. Sourdough or crusty Italian bread are good options. Bread sticks, both hard and soft, are an excellent choice with pasta salads and soups.

෴ When selecting a wine to accompany any pasta or risotto recipe, bear in mind that the main ingredient itself—namely, the pasta or rice—is relatively bland, acting as a blank canvas for a sauce or other ingredients that give the dish character. It makes sense, then, to let those other ingredients guide you in making your choice, following the basic principles that underlie most food-and-wine pairings.

෴ A good starting point is the tried-and-true notion of matching white wines with seafood, poultry or vegetables and red wines with meat or cheeses. Bear in mind, however, that you have a lot of leeway within those parameters, and you can make well-considered choices based upon matching up the corresponding flavors, textures and bodies of particular recipes and wines. A brisk red wine, for example, may be a better choice to accompany seafood in a robust tomato sauce, while an ample-bodied white wine may perfectly suit dishes featuring more delicate meats like veal or pork.

෴ In the end, your own personal preference should be the deciding factor. To help you in your selection, get to know a wine merchant near you who is sufficiently reliable and knowledgeable to help you pick wines that suit your taste and your budget. A lot of good wines from around the world are available today at reasonable prices.

෴ There are many nonalcoholic beverage options to pair with pastas and risottos as well. Many people will enjoy an Italian soda, which is a carbonated fruit blend, with these Italian-style meals. Sparkling apple juice is a good choice with pasta salads. Mineral water with a twist of lemon is refreshing with the hearty soups. Milk tastes great with many of the risotto dishes.

Fresh Pasta

❧

It's one of the most magical-yet-easy transformations any cook
can experience: Take flour, salt, eggs and water; mix them
together to form a dough; roll out the dough into thin sheets; and
cut the sheets to form your own fresh, flavorful, silken-textured
pasta. This simple process is just the starting point for a never-ending
journey of culinary discoveries. As the recipes in this chapter so
vividly demonstrate, fresh pasta dough can yield all manner of noodles,
shapes and filled creations, ready to receive quickly made sauces.
And, if time is short, you don't even need to expend the minimal effort
necessary to make your own fresh pasta. Sheets of fresh pasta are
available at specialty stores, and fresh ribbons and shapes are sold from
the refrigerated cases of well-stocked supermarkets. In addition,
many of the dishes that follow can be prepared with dried pasta.
All that remains for you to do is to cook the pasta,
complete the recipe and enjoy the meal.

Noodle Entrees

Few people can utter the word "noodles" without thinking "oodles" in the same instant. There's just something about the experience of eating a plate of fresh noodles that makes you want more. Whether they're familiar fettuccine, linguine and spaghetti or the more unusual pappardelle, tagliatelle and tagliolini, these ribbon shapes create a feeling of festivity at any meal. Satisfying, even sensuous to eat, they show off the tender-but-chewy texture of plain or flavored egg-and-semolina doughs. They also mix beautifully with a wide array of toppings.

On these pages you'll find dishes of utter simplicity designed for a quick meal and others worthy of being served at elegant dinner parties. While making fresh pasta noodles is not terribly time-consuming—especially using a pasta machine—if time is short, all of these noodle recipes can be made using dried pasta. Whatever your choice of noodles, you'll surely want to eat oodles.

OLIVE PAPPARDELLE WITH PROSCIUTTO AND PEAS

SERVES 8

A favorite Italian way of serving pappardelle, this sauce can also be used with any other fresh or dried broad noodles. Bear in mind that, other than during springtime when fresh English peas are at their peak of season, you are best off making this dish with frozen peas; look for a good brand of frozen petite peas, which should have excellent flavor and texture in the finished sauce. For a vegetarian version of the dish, feel free to leave out the prosciutto. In any case, you can make the sauce a day in advance, store it covered in the refrigerator and reheat it while the pasta cooks.

1½ lb (750 g) Olive Pasta
　(recipe on page 12)
1 cup (5 oz/155 g) fresh shelled peas
　or frozen peas, thawed
2 cups (16 fl oz/500 ml) heavy (double)
　cream
2 oz (60 g) prosciutto, minced
3 oz (90 g) aged Asiago cheese,
　freshly grated
8 qt (8 l) water
1½ tablespoons salt
freshly ground pepper

Make the Olive Pasta and cut it into pappardelle (see page 14).

🍃 In a medium saucepan of boiling salted water, cook the peas until tender, about 4 minutes.

🍃 In a small, heavy saucepan over medium heat, bring the cream and prosciutto to a simmer. Reduce the heat to low and simmer for 10 minutes. Add the peas and cheese and stir until the cheese melts. Keep warm.

🍃 In a large pot over high heat, bring the water to a boil. Add the salt and the pappardelle and cook until tender, about 3 minutes. Drain well.

🍃 In a large warmed bowl, combine the pappardelle and half of the cream mixture. Toss to mix well.

🍃 To serve, divide among individual warmed plates. Top each with an equal amount of the remaining sauce and a sprinkling of pepper to taste.

🍃 Serve hot.

FETTUCCINE ALFREDO

SERVES 8

For perfectly smooth and creamy results of this classic, never let the sauce come to a boil once you have added the egg yolks.

1½ lb (750 g) Egg Pasta
   (recipe on page 12)
4 tablespoons (2 oz/60 g) unsalted
   butter
3 cups (24 fl oz/750 ml) heavy (double)
   cream
ground nutmeg
2 egg yolks, lightly beaten
1 cup (4 oz/125 g) freshly grated
   Parmesan cheese
salt and freshly ground pepper
8 qt (8 l) water
1½ tablespoons salt
fresh flat-leaf (Italian) parsley sprigs

Make the Egg Pasta and cut it into fettuccine (see page 14).

❧ In a medium saucepan over medium heat, melt the butter. Add the cream, bring to a boil, reduce the heat to low and simmer until the cream is reduced by one-fourth, about 10 minutes.

❧ Add the nutmeg to taste and remove from the heat.

❧ Stir a generous spoonful of the reduced cream into the egg yolks, then return the mixture to the rest of the cream, stirring well. Add the Parmesan cheese and salt and pepper to taste.

❧ In a large pot over high heat, bring the water to a boil. Add the 1½ table- spoons salt and the fettuccine and cook until tender, about 2 minutes. Drain.

❧ To serve, combine the fettuccine and cream sauce in a warmed serving bowl. Toss to mix well. Garnish with the parsley.

❧ Serve hot.

BEET FETTUCCINE WITH ROASTED GARLIC SAUCE

SERVES 8

Cream, simmered with fresh herbs, moder- ates the flavor of the mild roasted garlic, providing a subtle complement to the beet- flavored pasta. Experiment with different herbs to change the flavor of this dish.

1½ lb (750 g) Beet Pasta
   (recipe on page 12)
2 cups (16 fl oz/500 ml) heavy (double)
   cream
3 fresh thyme sprigs
1 flat-leaf (Italian) parsley sprig
3 tablespoons Roasted Garlic Purée
   (see page 296)
1 tablespoon minced fresh flat-leaf
   (Italian) parsley
salt and freshly ground pepper
8 qt (8 l) water
1½ tablespoons salt
2 tablespoons chopped fresh thyme

Make the Beet Pasta and cut it into fettuccine (see page 14).

❧ In a medium pan over medium heat, combine the cream, thyme sprigs and parsley sprig and bring to a boil. Simmer until the cream is reduced by one-third, about 15 minutes. Remove from the heat.

❧ Remove and discard the thyme and parsley sprigs. Stir in the Roasted Garlic Purée, minced parsley and salt and pepper to taste. Keep warm.

❧ In a large pot over high heat, bring the water to a boil. Add the 1½ table- spoons salt and the fettuccine and cook until tender, about 2 minutes. Drain.

❧ In a large warmed bowl, combine the fettuccine and cream sauce. Toss to mix well.

❧ To serve, divide among individual warmed plates. Top with an equal amount of the chopped thyme.

❧ Serve hot.

Chicken Stock

MAKES ABOUT 3 QT (3 L)

Homemade stock adds wonderful flavor to many pasta and risotto recipes. If you must substitute, use low-fat, low-sodium canned or frozen broth. If you use leftover parts from a cooked bird, do not roast it with the vegetables.

1 yellow onion, peeled and cut into
   quarters
1 carrot, peeled and cut into large
   pieces
1 celery stalk, cut into large pieces
1 leek, white part and 2 inches (5 cm)
   green part
2 tablespoons pure olive oil
5 lb (2.5 kg) chicken parts (backs,
   necks, meaty carcasses and wings)
6 qt (6 l) water

Preheat an oven to 325°F (165°C).

❧ In a large bowl, toss the onion, carrot, celery and leek with the olive oil. Transfer the vegetables to a large roasting pan. Add the chicken parts. Roast until the vegetables are tender and just beginning to color, about 30 minutes.

❧ In a large pot over high heat, combine the vegetables, chicken, any pan drippings and the water and bring to a boil. Reduce the heat to medium-low and simmer, partially covered, until the liquid is reduced by half, about 3½ hours. Cool to room temperature.

❧ Using a strainer, strain the stock into a large bowl. Refrigerate until the fat on the surface solidifies. Before using, remove and discard the surface fat.

❧ Store in a tightly covered container in the refrigerator for up to 5 days, or the freezer for up to 3 months.

CREAMY LEMON FETTUCCINE AND LEEKS

SERVES 8

Leeks have a mild, sweet onion taste. Take care to follow the instructions on page 297 for cleaning leeks thoroughly.

1½ lb (750 g) Lemon Pasta
   (recipe on page 12)
2 tablespoons unsalted butter
1 tablespoon extra-virgin olive oil
1 lb (500 g) leeks, white parts and
   1 inch (2.5 cm) green parts, thinly
   sliced (see page 297)
¾ cup (6 fl oz/180 ml) Chicken Stock
¼ cup (2 fl oz/60 ml) fresh lemon juice
1½ cups (12 fl oz/375 ml) heavy
   (double) cream
salt and freshly ground pepper
8 qt (8 l) water
1½ tablespoons salt
1 tablespoon minced lemon zest
   (see page 295)

Make the Lemon Pasta and cut it into fettuccine (see page 14).

❧ In a large, heavy frying pan over medium heat, heat the butter and olive oil until the butter is melted. Reduce the heat to low, add the leeks and cook, stirring frequently, until they are wilted and tender, about 15 minutes.

❧ Add the Chicken Stock and lemon juice, increase the heat to medium and simmer until the liquid is nearly evaporated, 7–8 minutes. Reduce the heat to low, stir in the cream and simmer for 5 minutes. Add salt and pepper to taste. Remove from the heat and keep warm.

❧ In a large pot over high heat, bring the water to a boil. Add the 1½ tablespoons salt and the fettuccine and cook until tender, about 2 minutes. Drain.

❧ To serve, place in a warmed serving bowl. Top with the leek mixture. Toss to mix well. Garnish with the lemon zest.

❧ Serve hot.

A zester is a handy kitchen tool made specifically for removing the colorful, flavorful zest from citrus fruits, including oranges, lemons and limes. Remove only the colored outermost layer as the white part tastes bitter.

STRAW AND HAY PASTA WITH PARMESAN CHEESE

SERVES 8

Butter and cheese, one of the simplest of pasta sauces, traditionally highlights the beauty of this mixture of thin beige egg and green basil-flavored noodles, whimsically thought to resemble straw and hay. In place of the basil pasta, you could use fresh Spinach Pasta (recipe on page 12). Alternatively, make this dish with widely available store-bought straw and hay linguine or even with dried egg and spinach linguine.

1 lb (500 g) Egg Pasta
   (recipe on page 12)
1 lb (500 g) Basil Pasta
   (recipe on page 12)
12 qt (12 l) water
2 tablespoons salt
4 tablespoons (2 oz/60 g) unsalted
   butter at room temperature
salt
¾ cup (3 oz/90 g) freshly grated
   Parmesan cheese

Make the Egg Pasta and the Basil Pasta. Cut each pasta into tagliolini (see page 14).

❧ In each of 2 large pots over high heat, bring 6 qt (6 l) of the water to a boil. To each pot add 1 tablespoon of the salt and one of the pastas. Separately but simultaneously, cook the pastas until tender, about 2 minutes. Drain the pastas separately.

❧ In each of 2 large warmed bowls, combine one of the pastas, 2 tablespoons of the butter and salt to taste. Toss to mix well until the butter has melted and the pasta is evenly coated.

❧ To serve, place on a warmed platter. Top with the Parmesan cheese.

❧ Serve hot.

PUMPKIN TAGLIATELLE

SERVES 8

You can make this dish year-round using canned pumpkin in the pasta.

1½ lb (750 g) Pumpkin Pasta
(recipe on page 12)

2 cups (16 fl oz/500 ml) heavy (double) cream

7 fresh rosemary sprigs

6 oz (185 g) Gorgonzola cheese, crumbled

8 qt (8 l) water

1½ tablespoons salt

Make the Pumpkin Pasta and cut it into tagliatelle (see page 14).

❧ To make the Gorgonzola sauce, in a medium saucepan over medium heat, bring the cream and 1 of the rosemary sprigs to a boil, reduce the heat to low and simmer until the cream is reduced by one-third, about 15 minutes. Remove and discard the rosemary.

❧ Stir in the Gorgonzola cheese. Reduce the heat to low and stir until the cheese is completely melted.

❧ Remove from the heat but keep warm.

❧ In a large pot over high heat, bring the water to a boil. Add the 1½ tablespoons salt and the tagliatelle and cook until tender, about 2 minutes. Drain.

❧ In a large warmed bowl, combine the tagliatelle and the Gorgonzola sauce. Toss to mix well.

❧ To serve, divide among individual warmed plates. Garnish with the remaining rosemary.

❧ Serve hot.

BLACK PEPPER LINGUINE WITH RADICCHIO AND PANCETTA

SERVES 8

Sautéing tempers the slightly bitter taste of the leaf vegetable known as radicchio, which gives this dish a beautiful purple-red color and contrasts deliciously with the tangy goat cheese, salty meat, and earthy pine nuts. If you cannot find radicchio, feel free to substitute another bitter-tasting green such as Belgian endive (chicory/witloof). Pancetta, found in Italian delicatessens and well-stocked food stores, is a flat slab of seasoned pork belly that is rolled into a thick sausage shape. It is usually sold cut to order in thin, circular slices, which you can unwind into bacon-like rashers. You can also replace the pancetta with regular bacon, taking care to drain off excess fat after the bacon has been cooked. If time is limited, make this dish with dried linguine or with fresh linguine bought ready-made in your market's refrigerated case.

1½ lb (750 g) Black Pepper Pasta
    (recipe on page 12)

1 lb (500 g) radicchio

2 tablespoons extra-virgin olive oil

8 oz (250 g) pancetta, diced

½ cup (4 fl oz/125 ml) white wine
    vinegar

4 tablespoons (2 oz/60 g) unsalted
    butter

8 qt (8 l) water

1½ tablespoons salt

6 oz (185 g) fresh goat cheese, crumbled
salt

⅓ cup (3 oz/90 g) pine nuts, toasted
    (see page 297)

Make the Black Pepper Pasta and cut it into linguine (see page 14).

🍃 To prepare the radicchio, remove any wilted outer leaves, cut each head in half and cut out and discard the cores. Cut the radicchio crosswise into pieces ½ inch (12 mm) wide.

🍃 In a heavy frying pan over medium heat, heat the olive oil. Add the pancetta and cook until just crisp, about 10 minutes. Add the radicchio and vinegar and cook covered, until the radicchio is completely wilted, about 5 minutes.

🍃 Remove the lid and simmer until the liquid is reduced by half, about 3 minutes. Stir in the butter and remove from the heat.

🍃 In a large pot over high heat, bring the water to a boil. Add the 1½ tablespoons salt and the linguine and cook until tender, about 2 minutes. Drain.

🍃 In a large warmed bowl, combine the linguine, pancetta mixture, goat cheese and salt to taste. Toss to mix well.

🍃 To serve, divide among individual warmed plates. Top with the pine nuts.

🍃 Serve hot.

Basil, a culinary herb native to India, is a popular seasoning in Italian cooking. Basil pesto is a pungent uncooked sauce that will quickly become a favorite. Its great taste and stunning presentation belie the simplicity of its ingredients and preparation. Utilizing just basil, pine nuts, olive oil, garlic, butter, salt and Parmesan cheese and mixed with a mortar and pestle or in a food processor or a blender, the delicious sauce can be ready for the dining table in minutes.

CLASSIC TAGLIOLINI WITH PESTO SAUCE

SERVES 8

A classic sauce like this bright green pesto can be used on a variety of shapes or sizes of pasta, but noodles smaller than tagliolini should be avoided or there will not be enough surface area on the pasta for the pesto to cling to.

1½ lb (750 g) Egg Pasta
    (recipe on page 12)
Pesto Sauce
8 qt (8 l) water
1½ tablespoons salt
⅓ cup (1½ oz/45 g) freshly grated
    pecorino romano cheese
2 tablespoons pine nuts, toasted
    (see page 297)

Make the Egg Pasta and cut it into tagliolini (see page 14).

❧ Prepare the Pesto Sauce.

❧ In a large pot over high heat, bring the water to a boil. Add the salt and the tagliolini and cook until tender, about 2 minutes. While it is cooking, stir 3–4 tablespoons of the tagliolini cooking water into the Pesto Sauce and place the sauce in a large warmed bowl. Drain the tagliolini and add it to the bowl. Toss to mix well.

❧ To serve, divide among individual warmed plates. Top with an equal amount of the pecorino romano cheese and pine nuts.

❧ Serve hot.

Pesto Sauce

MAKES ABOUT 1 CUP (8 FL OZ/250 ML)

Pesto is the traditional welcome-home meal for Genovese sailors. Make this pungent sauce in summer, when basil is abundant and inexpensive. If made in advance, place in tightly covered jars and refrigerate for 1 week or freeze for 1 month. It is good over Classic Polenta (recipe on page 199) or as a dipping sauce for bread.

2 cups (2 oz/60 g) packed fresh
    basil leaves
6 garlic cloves, peeled
½ teaspoon salt
¼ cup (1 oz/30 g) pine nuts
½ cup (4 fl oz/125 ml) extra-virgin
    olive oil
3 tablespoons unsalted butter, softened
⅓ cup (1½ oz/45 g) freshly grated
    Parmesan cheese

In the work bowl of a food processor or in a blender, combine the basil and garlic. Pulse until the basil and garlic are very finely chopped.

❧ Add the salt and pine nuts and pulse several times. With the motor running, pour in the olive oil in a steady stream.

❧ Transfer the mixture to a small bowl. Using a spatula, fold in the butter and, when it has been incorporated smoothly, fold in the Parmesan cheese. Set aside until ready to use.

BLACK PEPPER PAPPARDELLE WITH WALNUTS

SERVES 8

Although the black pepper pasta contributes an intriguing dimension of flavor, you can use any fresh or dried broad noodle in the preparation of this dish. Try also substituting other favorite nuts for the walnuts, such as hazelnuts (filberts) or almonds. Serve the pasta on a menu with a highly seasoned accompaniment such as a spicy soup or a salad of bitter greens dressed with a mustard vinaigrette.

1½ lb (750 g) Black Pepper Pasta
    (recipe on page 12)
3 oz (90 g) Parmesan cheese, in
    one piece
8 qt (8 l) water
1½ tablespoons salt
⅓ cup (3 fl oz/80 ml) extra-virgin
    olive oil
ground nutmeg
6 tablespoons (1½ oz/45 g) coarsely
    chopped walnut pieces, toasted
    (see page 297)

Make the Black Pepper Pasta and cut it into pappardelle (see page 14).

❧ Using a vegetable peeler, cut 32 curls of Parmesan cheese and set them on a sheet of waxed paper.

❧ In a large pot over high heat, bring the water to a boil. Add the salt and the pappardelle and cook until tender, about 2 minutes. Drain.

❧ In a large warmed bowl, combine the pappardelle and olive oil. Toss to mix well. Add the nutmeg to taste and toss again.

❧ To serve, divide among individual warmed plates. Top with the walnuts and Parmesan cheese.

❧ Serve hot.

TAGLIOLINI WITH ASPARAGUS AND ZUCCHINI

SERVES 8

The trick to achieving excellent results with this dish is to cook the asparagus and the bell peppers (capsicums) long enough to draw out their flavors while cooking the zucchini (courgettes) only briefly to retain their firm texture. To add an extra dimension of color, try substituting yellow summer squash for one or both of the zucchini and a yellow bell pepper for one of the red peppers.

1½ lb (750 g) Egg Pasta
   (recipe on page 12)
¼ cup (2 fl oz/60 ml) Brown Butter
2 red bell peppers (capsicums), halved
   lengthwise, stemmed, seeded and
   deribbed (see page 298)
1 lb (500 g) fresh asparagus
2 small zucchini (courgettes)
1 tablespoon minced fresh ginger
1 teaspoon minced garlic
salt and freshly ground pepper
8 qt (8 l) water
1½ tablespoons salt

Make the Egg Pasta and cut it into tagliolini (see page 14).
❧ Make the Brown Butter.
❧ Cut each pepper into strips ¼ inch (6 mm) wide. Cut the strips in half. Cut the asparagus into pieces about 2½ inches (6 cm) long. If the stalks are thick, cut them in half lengthwise. Slice each zucchini lengthwise into ribbons ¼ inch (6 mm) thick, then slice each ribbon into strips ¼ inch (6 mm) wide. Cut the strips into pieces 2½ inches (6 cm) long.
❧ In a medium frying pan over low heat, heat the Brown Butter. Add the ginger and garlic and sauté for

2 minutes. Increase the heat to medium, add the red pepper strips and sauté, stirring frequently, until they are limp, about 8 minutes.
❧ Add the asparagus and continue to sauté until the asparagus is just tender, about 5 minutes. Add the zucchini and sauté, stirring frequently, until the zucchini is just barely tender, 3–4 minutes. Salt and pepper to taste and remove from the heat.
❧ In a large pot over high heat, bring the water to a boil. Add the 1½ tablespoons salt and the tagliolini and cook until tender, about 2 minutes. Drain.
❧ To serve, place in a warmed serving bowl. Top with the vegetables.
❧ Serve hot.

Brown Butter

MAKES 6 TABLESPOONS (⅓ CUP/3 FL OZ/90 ML)

Also called beurre noisette, *brown butter is amber colored with a nutty flavor. This butter is also delicious as a topping for poached fish and steamed vegetables.*

½ cup (4 oz/125 g) unsalted butter

In a small saucepan over medium-low heat, melt the butter, skimming off and discarding the foam that forms on the top. Continue until it is a deep golden brown. Remove from the heat.
❧ Transfer to a small container, discarding the solids at the bottom of the pan. Use immediately or refrigerate for up to 1 week.

Often used as a garnish to add a bit of color to a plate, parsley is also packed with nutrients. It contains significant amounts of vitamins A and C and the minerals calcium and iron as well as breath-sweetening chlorophyll. It is one of the easiest culinary herbs to grow in small garden containers both indoors and out.

OLIVE LINGUINE WITH SALSA VERDE

SERVES 8

The hardy olive tree is native to the Mediterranean, and its fruit is a common ingredient in pasta dishes. As an ingredient in the pasta itself, olives lend an extra dimension to this quick dish. There are dozens of different olive varieties and a different type will give this recipe a complete change in character. Whether an olive is green or black depends on if it is left on the tree to ripen. Green unripe, black ripe, both perfectly edible once they are cured.

1½ lb (750 g) Olive Pasta
    (recipe on page 12)
Salsa Verde
8 qt (8 l) water
1½ tablespoons salt
1 tablespoon grated lemon zest
    (see page 295)

Make the Olive Pasta and cut it into linguine (see page 14).
🕊 Prepare the Salsa Verde.
🕊 In a large pot over high heat, bring the water to a boil. Add the salt and the linguine and cook until tender, about 2 minutes.
🕊 While it is cooking, in a large warmed bowl, combine 2 tablespoons of the linguine cooking water and all but ¼ cup (2 fl oz/60 ml) of the Salsa Verde. Drain the linguine and add it to the bowl. Toss to mix well.
🕊 To serve, divide among individual warmed plates. Top with an equal amount of the remaining Salsa Verde and a sprinkling of the lemon zest.
🕊 Serve hot.

Salsa Verde

MAKES ABOUT 1¾ CUPS (14 FL OZ/430 ML)

The classic, pungent green parsley sauce goes well with any type of thin noodle, fresh or dried. Make the sauce up to 2 days ahead of time and store it in the refrigerator. Be sure to let the sauce come to room temperature before use.

4 cups (4 oz/125 g) flat-leaf (Italian)
    parsley, stemmed
5 garlic cloves, peeled
8 anchovy fillets in olive oil, drained
1 teaspoon salt
1 tablespoon Dijon-style mustard
¼ cup (2 fl oz/60 ml) fresh lemon juice
¾ cup (6 fl oz/180 ml) extra-virgin
    olive oil
¾ teaspoon freshly ground pepper

In the work bowl of a food processor with the metal blade or a blender, combine the parsley, garlic, anchovies and salt and pulse for 30 seconds.
🕊 Add the mustard and lemon juice and pulse to blend. With the motor running, slowly add the olive oil in a steady stream.
🕊 Transfer to a storage container or bowl and stir in the pepper. Set aside until ready to use.

To take parsley away from the cook would make it almost impossible for him to exercise his art.

—LOUIS BOSC D'ANTIC

CHICKEN AND FETTUCCINE WITH TOMATO CREAM SAUCE

SERVES 8

Prepare the chicken and the cream sauce very quickly to make this satisfying main course. If you don't have enough time to prepare the fresh pasta, substitute dried egg or spinach fettuccine.

1½ lb (750 g) Egg Pasta
   (recipe on page 12)
Tomato Cream Sauce
1 tablespoon pure olive oil
2 whole chicken breasts (2½ lb/
   1.25 kg), boned, skinned and cubed
salt and freshly ground pepper
8 qt (8 l) water
1½ tablespoons salt
6 sun-dried tomatoes packed in oil,
   drained and cut into strips
fresh thyme sprigs

Make the Egg Pasta and cut it into fettuccine (see page 14).

✽ Prepare the Tomato Cream Sauce.

✽ In a sauté pan or a wok over medium heat, heat the olive oil. Add the chicken and sauté, turning frequently, until it is cooked through, 7–8 minutes. Add the salt and pepper to taste. Remove from the heat and keep warm.

✽ In a large pot over high heat, bring the water to a boil. Add the 1½ tablespoons salt and the fettuccine and cook until tender, about 2 minutes. Drain.

✽ In a large warmed bowl, combine the fettuccine and Tomato Cream Sauce. Toss to mix well.

✽ To serve, divide among individual warmed plates. Top with an equal amount of the chicken and tomatoes. Garnish with a thyme sprig.

✽ Serve hot.

Tomato Cream Sauce

MAKES 2½ CUPS (20 FL OZ/625 ML)

Sun-dried tomatoes in oil are a flavorful addition to many dishes. However, they are high in calories. If you need to lessen the calorie count of this rich sauce, switch to water-packed tomatoes and half & half (half cream) rather than the oil-packed tomatoes and heavy (double) cream. The sauce will be thinner, but still good.

1½ cups (12 fl oz/375 ml) heavy
   (double) cream
1 fresh thyme sprig
1 cup (8 fl oz/250 ml) Chicken Stock
   (recipe on page 30)
10 sun-dried tomatoes packed in oil,
   puréed
salt and freshly ground pepper
½ teaspoon fresh thyme leaves

In a heavy, medium saucepan over medium heat, bring the cream and thyme sprig to a boil.

✽ Lower the heat and simmer until the cream is reduced by one-third, about 10 minutes. Remove from the heat and let sit 10 minutes.

✽ Remove and discard the thyme sprig. Return the cream to the heat, add the Chicken Stock and simmer for 5 minutes. Add the tomato purée and salt and pepper to taste. Remove from the heat, stir in the thyme leaves and keep warm until ready to use.

Botanically speaking, tomatoes are fruits of the tomato vine. However, people generally think of them as vegetables and they serve that purpose on the table. A member of the nightshade family, they are cousin to the eggplant, bell pepper and potato. All the many varieties of cultivated tomato belong to the genus Lycopersican, *or "wolf peach." Different categories of tomatoes shine in various culinary purposes. Round globe tomatoes (pictured), including beefsteaks and many popular heirloom varieties, are best for slicing. Plum tomatoes are best for cooking and for drying as they have a lower water content than slicing varieties. Small cherry tomatoes are great raw in salads or as a quick snack. A tomato allowed to ripen on the vine usually is sweeter than one picked green.*

LEMON TAGLIATELLE WITH LEMON SAUCE AND SCALLOPS

SERVES 8

When preparing this dish, be careful not to overcook the scallops, safeguarding their tender texture and mild, sweet flavor. If bay scallops are unavailable, substitute fresh sea scallops, cut in half, or small fresh shrimp.

1½ lb (750 g) Lemon Pasta
   (recipe on page 12)

1½ lb (750 g) bay scallops or sea
   scallops, halved

¼ cup (1½ oz/45 g) all-purpose (plain)
   flour

2 tablespoons grated lemon zest
   (see page 295)

salt and freshly ground pepper

5 tablespoons (2½ oz/75 g) unsalted
   butter

½ cup (4 fl oz/125 ml) fresh lemon
   juice

1½ cups (12 fl oz/375 ml) heavy
   (double) cream

3 tablespoons minced fresh flat-leaf
   (Italian) parsley

8 qt (8 l) water

1½ tablespoons salt

fresh flat-leaf (Italian) parsley sprigs

Make the Lemon Pasta and cut it into tagliatelle (see page 14).

❧ Rinse the scallops and pat them dry with paper towels. In a small plastic or paper bag, combine the flour, 1 tablespoon of the lemon zest and salt and pepper to taste. Shake to blend well. Add the scallops, close the bag tightly and shake to coat the scallops well. Transfer the scallops to a large dry sieve; shake them to remove any excess flour.

❧ To make the lemon cream sauce, in a small saucepan over low heat, melt 3 tablespoons of the butter with the lemon juice. Add the cream, stirring constantly, until the cream is hot but not boiling. Add the minced parsley. Stir to mix well. Keep warm.

❧ In a medium frying pan over medium-high heat, melt the remaining 2 tablespoons butter until foamy. Add the scallops and sauté, stirring frequently, until they are opaque, 4–5 minutes for bay scallops, 6–7 minutes for sea scallops. Using a slotted spoon, transfer the scallops to a small bowl. Pour half

of the lemon cream sauce over the scallops. Keep warm.

❧ In a large pot over high heat, bring the water to a boil. Add the 1½ tablespoons salt and the tagliatelle and cook until tender, about 2 minutes. Drain.

❧ In a large warmed bowl, combine the tagliatelle and the remaining lemon cream sauce. Toss to mix well.

❧ To serve, divide among individual warmed plates. Top with an equal amount of the scallops, sauce and remaining lemon zest. Garnish with a parsley sprig.

❧ Serve hot.

PEARS AND GORGONZOLA CHEESE OVER PAPPARDELLE

SERVES 8

The rich, sharp and tangy taste of Gorgon-zola cheese makes it a classic accompani-ment to fresh pears. It is essential to use fresh pasta in this dish; so, if time is short, buy it in sheets from a well-stocked food store or Italian delicatessen, then cut it into pappardelle at home. Alternatively, buy fresh pasta precut into other, more common ribbons such as fettuccine.

1½ lb (750 g) Egg Pasta
    (recipe on page 12)
4 tablespoons (2 fl oz/60 ml) Clarified
    Butter
2 ripe but firm pears, peeled, cored and
    cut into ¼-inch (6-mm) slices
1 lb (500 g) arugula, cut into crosswise
    strips 1 inch (2.5 cm) wide
8 qt (8 l) water
1½ tablespoons salt
3 oz (90 g) Gorgonzola cheese,
    crumbled
¾ cup (3 oz/90 g) walnut halves,
    toasted (see page 297)
salt and freshly ground pepper

Make the Egg Pasta and cut it into pappardelle (see page 14).

❧ Make the Clarified Butter.

❧ In a large frying pan over medium-high heat, melt 1 tablespoon of the Clarified Butter until it foams. Sauté the pears, turning once, until golden on each side, about 4 minutes. Transfer them to a plate and keep warm.

❧ In the same pan over medium-low heat, melt the remaining 3 tablespoons butter. Add the arugula and cook, stir-ring gently, until it wilts, about 2 min-utes. Transfer the arugula and butter to a large warmed bowl and keep warm.

❧ In a large pot over high heat, bring the water to a boil. Add the 1½ table-spoons salt and the pappardelle and cook until tender, about 3 minutes. Drain well and add to the bowl with the arugula and butter. Toss to mix well.

❧ To serve, divide the pappardelle mix-ture among individual warmed plates. Top with an equal amount of the pears, Gorgonzola cheese and walnuts. Add the salt and pepper to taste.

❧ Serve hot.

Clarified Butter

MAKES 6 TABLESPOONS (⅓ CUP/3 FL OZ/90 ML)

Also known as drawn butter, this is butter with the milk solids removed, and can withstand higher heat for cooking.

½ cup (4 oz/125 g) unsalted butter

In a small saucepan over medium-low heat, melt the butter, discarding the foam that forms on the top.

❧ Using a spoon, transfer the butter to a small container, leaving behind and discarding the solids at the bottom of the pan. Refrigerate for up to 1 week.

Shaped Entrees

The versatility of fresh pasta dough shines brightly when the dough is fashioned into all manner of shapes. Even more, the creativity of you, the home cook, enjoys one of its most delightful yet easy challenges. How often, after all, do you get to make butterflies or handkerchiefs when you cook? When using fresh pasta dough, such amusing projects are a matter of course, and all the more fun when they go by the Italian names of farfalle and fazzoletti. Kitchen playtime never produced more delicious results.

Shapes also extend the range of ingredients with which you can serve fresh pasta. While the recipes that follow are designed with specific toppings in mind, by matching these shapes to seasonal produce, you can extend your recipe options for year-round dining pleasure. Although few of these recipes can be made with dried pasta, if you haven't time to make pasta, look for sheets of fresh pasta at specialty stores and proceed from there.

WINDOWPANE PASTA WITH NASTURTIUM BUTTER

SERVES 6

Serve this pasta dish as either a light luncheon main course for a sunny spring or summer day, or as the appetizer preceding an elegant main course of seafood or poultry. The windowpane effect is achieved by sealing parsley leaves between two sheets of fresh pasta rolled so thinly that they are nearly translucent. In place of the parsley, try also making the windowpanes with other decorative, pleasant-tasting fresh herbs such as small basil leaves or little sprigs of chervil or dill. As shown in the photograph, edible violas and nasturtiums provide a colorful garnish. You might also want to try sealing some of their petals in between the sheets of pasta. Other edible flowers you can use include more of the yellow to bright orange to orange-red nasturtiums used in the sauce; orange to deep violet pansies; and bright purple borage blossoms. When using any edible flowers, buy them only from a source—such as a farmers' market stall or a specialty grower—that can assure you they have been grown free of pesticides or other potentially harmful additives. If you like, try growing the flowers yourself.

1 lb (500 g) Egg Pasta
   (recipe on page 12)
4 tablespoons (2 oz/60 g) Nasturtium
   Butter (recipe on page 294) at
   room temperature
60 fresh flat-leaf (Italian) parsley leaves
3 tablespoons fine yellow cornmeal
6 qt (6 l) water
1 tablespoon salt
⅓ cup (1½ oz/45 g) freshly grated
   Parmesan cheese
edible violas
nasturtium flowers and leaves

Make the Egg Pasta and roll it into sheets 4½ inches (11 cm) wide and 20 inches (50 cm) long.

❧ Make the Nasturtium Butter.

❧ On a work surface, place a strip of pasta and cut it in half crosswise. Arrange the parsley leaves in 2 rows on top of 1 sheet of pasta, spacing about 1 inch (2.5 cm) between leaves. Moisten the edge of the pasta slightly with water. Place the other sheet of pasta on top of the moistened one and press them together gently.

❧ Using a rolling pin or a manual pasta machine at the narrowest setting, roll the pasta until it is nearly translucent and the leaves are visible. The pasta and leaves will stretch considerably.

❧ Using a serrated pastry cutter, cut the pasta into 2-inch (5-cm) squares, trimming the outer edges as well as cutting between the squares. Set the completed squares on a sheet of waxed paper or a kitchen towel and sprinkle with the cornmeal. Repeat to make 60 pasta squares. Dry slightly before cooking, 15–30 minutes.

❧ In a large pot over high heat, bring the water to a boil. Add the salt and the pasta squares and cook, stirring frequently so they do not stick together, until they are tender, about 2 minutes. Drain carefully.

❧ In a large warmed bowl, combine the pasta squares and 2 tablespoons of the Nasturtium Butter and toss gently.

❧ To serve, arrange 10 squares on individual warmed plates. Top with the remaining Nasturtium Butter, Parmesan cheese, edible violas and nasturtium flowers and leaves.

❧ Serve hot.

PASTA TRIANGLES WITH TOMATOES AND BASIL

SERVES 8

Cutting this pasta into perfect little triangles, called maltagliati *in Italian, and pairing it with quartered cherry tomatoes gives this dish its strong visual appeal.*

1½ lb (750 g) Basil Pasta
   (recipe on page 12)
¼ cup (2 fl oz/60 ml) extra-virgin
   olive oil
1 tablespoon minced garlic
1½ lb (750 g) cherry tomatoes, cut
   into quarters
8 qt (8 l) water
1½ tablespoons salt
¼ cup (¼ oz/7 g) fresh basil leaves,
   cut into thin strips
⅓ cup (1½ oz/45 g) freshly grated
   aged Asiago cheese
fresh basil sprigs

Make the Basil Pasta and cut it into maltagliati (see page 14).

❧ In a large frying pan over low heat, heat the olive oil. Add the garlic and sauté until tender, about 2 minutes.

❧ Add the tomatoes and sauté, stirring gently, until just heated through, about 3 minutes. Keep warm.

❧ In a large pot over high heat, bring the water to a boil. Add the salt and the maltagliati and stir vigorously to separate the pieces. Cook until tender, about 2 minutes. Drain.

❧ In a large warmed bowl, combine the maltagliati, half of the cherry tomatoes and all of the basil strips. Toss to mix well.

❧ To serve, place on individual warmed plates. Top with an equal amount of the remaining tomatoes and Asiago cheese. Garnish with a basil sprig.

❧ Serve hot.

PASTA HANDKERCHIEFS

SERVES 10

*This version of pasta handkerchiefs—
fazzoletti in Italian—was designed for
entertaining. The sauce may be made
one or two days in advance and reheated.*

1 lb (500 g) Egg Pasta
   (recipe on page 12)
6 tablespoons (3 oz/90 g) unsalted
   butter
½ yellow onion, peeled and finely
   chopped
2½ lb (1.25 kg) plum (Roma) tomatoes,
   peeled, seeded and chopped
   (see page 299)
6 qt (6 l) water
1 tablespoon salt
2 tablespoons minced fresh flat-leaf
   (Italian) parsley
¾ cup (3 oz/90 g) freshly grated
   Parmesan cheese

Make the Egg Pasta and cut it into
30 fazzoletti (see page 14).

❧ In a large frying pan over medium-
low heat, melt 3 tablespoons of the
butter until it foams. Add the onion and
sauté until the onion is translucent,
about 8 minutes.

❧ Add the tomatoes, reduce the heat to
low and simmer until most of the liquid
has evaporated, about 15 minutes. Cut
the remaining 3 tablespoons butter into
small pieces and whisk them into the
tomatoes. Keep warm.

❧ In a large pot over high heat, bring
the water to a boil. Add the 1 tablespoon salt, 5 fazzoletti at a time, and
cook until tender, about 3 minutes.
Using a slotted spoon, carefully remove
each fazzoletto, drain it quickly and
dip it into the sauce so that each side is
thinly coated. Fold each fazzoletto in
half diagonally, then fold it again so that
it forms a small triangle.

❧ To serve, arrange on plates. Top with
the sauce, parsley and Parmesan cheese.

❧ Serve hot.

OLIVE PASTA TUBES WITH ANCHOVIES AND TOMATOES

SERVES 6

*This tangy sauce is a fresh version of the
traditional Italian* puttanesca *sauce. It
is delicious with these hand-rolled pasta
shapes called* garganelli *in Italian, but
you may also use dried penne.*

1 lb (500 g) Olive Pasta
   (recipe on page 12)
3 tablespoons extra-virgin olive oil
1 teaspoon minced garlic
4 anchovy fillets in olive oil, drained
   and chopped
2 cups (12 oz/375 g) cherry tomatoes
1 cup (5 oz/155 g) Kalamata olives,
   pitted and sliced
2 tablespoons capers, drained
2 tablespoons minced fresh flat-leaf
   (Italian) parsley
red pepper flakes
6 qt (6 l) water
1 tablespoon salt

Make the Olive Pasta and cut it into
garganelli (see page 14).

❧ In a medium frying pan over
medium-low heat, heat the olive oil
and sauté the garlic and anchovies for
2 minutes. Add the tomatoes, olives
and capers and cook until the ingredients are heated through, 3–4 minutes.
Add the parsley and red pepper flakes.

❧ In a large pot over high heat, bring
the water to a boil. Add the 1 tablespoon salt and the garganelli and cook
until tender, about 4 minutes. Drain.

❧ In a large warmed bowl, combine
the garganelli and three-quarters of
the tomato mixture. Toss to mix well.

❧ To serve, top with an equal amount
of the remaining tomato mixture.

❧ Serve hot.

POTATO GNOCCHI WITH SUMMER TOMATO SAUCE

SERVES 6

These classic dumplings go very well with a wide variety of sauces. Try them with a simple flavored butter (see page 294) or, for a more substantial meal, Pesto Sauce or Salsa Verde (recipes on pages 36 and 40).

Summer Tomato Sauce
2 lb (1 kg) russet potatoes
2 egg yolks, lightly beaten
4 teaspoons salt
2 cups (10 oz/315 g) all-purpose (plain) flour
4 qt (4 l) water

Make the Summer Tomato Sauce.
❧ Preheat an oven to 375°F (190°C).
❧ Using a fork, puncture the potatoes in several places and bake until tender, about 1 hour. Cool until easy to handle.
❧ Peel the potatoes, cut them into chunks, place in a bowl and mash them. Add the egg yolks and 2 teaspoons of the salt.
❧ Add the flour, ½ cup (2½ oz/75 g) at a time, mixing just until the dough is smooth but still just slightly sticky (some potatoes will take more flour than others). Divide the dough into pieces the size of a tennis ball.
❧ On a floured surface, form each piece of dough into a rope about ¾ inch (2 cm) thick. Cut each rope into ¾-inch (2-cm) pieces. Place one piece at a time on the inside curve of a fork. With the tip of the index finger pointing directly perpendicular to the fork, press the piece of dough against the prongs. While still pressing, flip it away from the prongs, toward the fork handle. Let it roll off and drop to the work surface.
❧ In a large pot over high heat, bring the water to a boil. Add the remaining 2 teaspoons salt and the gnocchi in batches. When they float to the surface, cook for an additional 15 seconds.
❧ Using a slotted spoon, transfer to a large warmed bowl. Drain any water collected in the bowl. Add the Summer Tomato Sauce and toss gently.
❧ To serve, divide among individual warmed plates.
❧ Serve hot.

Summer Tomato Sauce

MAKES ABOUT 1¾ CUPS (14 FL OZ/430 ML)

When fresh tomatoes are not available, substitute 48 oz (1.5 kg) of canned whole tomatoes in this easy topping.

6 tablespoons (3 oz/90 g) unsalted butter
1 yellow onion, peeled and cut into quarters
4 garlic cloves, peeled
3 lb (1.5 kg) tomatoes, halved
salt and freshly ground pepper

In a large, heavy frying pan over medium heat, melt 3 tablespoons of the butter. Add the onion, garlic and tomatoes, reduce the heat to low, cover the pan and simmer for 20 minutes.
❧ Remove the pan from the heat. Remove and discard the onion and garlic. Using a food mill or a blender, purée the tomatoes.
❧ Clean the frying pan and return the tomato purée to the pan. Place the pan over medium heat and simmer for 10 minutes. Add the remaining 3 tablespoons butter, 1 tablespoon at a time, stirring until the butter is incorporated. Add the salt and pepper to taste. Keep warm until ready to use.

The enticing aroma of a simple tomato sauce simmering on the stove may bring diners clamoring to your kitchen. Luckily this very basic pasta topping is easy to double or triple for a crowd. It is also an excellent choice for making ahead and refrigerating for up to a week or freezing for up to a month. Just reheat the sauce while the pasta cooks.

CRAB AND GARLIC BUTTER OVER FARFALLE

SERVES 8

Don't pass up this delicate dish just because handmade farfalle seem time-consuming. Once the fresh pasta is made, shaping and drying the butterflies doesn't take long. Of course, dried farfalle may be used instead.

1½ lb (750 g) Lemon Pasta
   (recipe on page 12)
⅓ cup (3 oz/90 g) unsalted butter
1 tablespoon minced garlic
1 tablespoon hot pepper sauce
2 tablespoons minced fresh flat-leaf
   (Italian) parsley
2½ cups (15 oz/450 g) freshly cooked
   crabmeat
salt
8 qt (8 l) water
1½ tablespoons salt
1 lemon, cut into 8 wedges

Make the Lemon Pasta and shape it into farfalle (see page 14).

❧ In a saucepan over medium heat, melt the butter. Add the garlic and hot pepper sauce and simmer for 2 minutes. Remove from the heat and add the parsley, crabmeat and salt to taste.

❧ In a large pot over high heat, bring the water to a boil. Add the 1½ tablespoons salt and the farfalle and cook until tender, about 2 minutes. Drain.

❧ In a large warmed bowl, combine the farfalle and crab mixture. Toss to mix well.

❧ To serve, divide among individual plates. Garnish with the lemon wedges.

❧ Serve hot.

PUMPKIN SQUARES AND SWISS CHARD SOUP

SERVES 6

A simple soup like this one benefits greatly from a flavorful homemade stock. Fresh pasta cut into little square shapes are called quadrucci *in Italian.*

1 lb (500 g) Pumpkin Pasta
　　(recipe on page 12)
8 cups (64 fl oz/2 l) Chicken Stock
　　(recipe on page 30)
1 lb (500 g) fresh Swiss chard
　　(silverbeet), large stems removed
2 tablespoons olive oil
1 teaspoon minced garlic
salt and freshly ground pepper
6 qt (6 l) water
1 tablespoon salt
⅓ cup (1½ oz/45 g) freshly grated
　　Parmesan cheese

Make the Pumpkin Pasta and cut it into quadrucci (see page 14).

❧ In a medium pot over low heat, bring the Chicken Stock to a simmer.

❧ On a work surface, cut the chard crosswise into 1-inch (2.5-cm) strips. In a medium frying pan or wok over medium heat, heat the olive oil. Add the garlic and sauté for 1 minute. Add the chard and sauté, stirring frequently, until it is wilted, about 5 minutes. Add the salt and pepper to taste. Keep warm.

❧ In a large pot over high heat, bring the water to a boil. Add the 1 tablespoon salt and the quadrucci and stir vigorously to separate the small pieces of pasta. Cook until tender, about 2 minutes. Drain.

❧ To serve, divide the quadrucci among individual warmed soup bowls. Top with an equal amount of the chard, stock and Parmesan cheese.

❧ Serve hot.

A selection of Mediterranean herbs planted in small containers makes a great decoration for garden, kitchen and table. Having your own plants around is also handy for pinching off a few leaves to season pasta and risotto recipes.

Sage is not hard to grow if you do not mind giving away your financial status: European superstition holds that it will not flourish if your money affairs are in bad order.

—WAVERLEY ROOT

SAGE SQUARES WITH SAGE AND SHALLOT BUTTER

SERVES 6

Here, fresh gray-green sage leaves are sealed between sheets of pasta to lovely effect. The same treatment will also produce strikingly beautiful and delicious results when made with fresh Pumpkin Pasta (recipe on page 12). If time is limited, feel free to begin with sheets of fresh pasta purchased at a well-stocked food store or Italian delicatessen. The dish makes an elegant first course before a traditional autumn main course such as roast turkey or baked ham. Or serve it as a light and simple main course, accompanied by a rustic loaf of crusty bread and a salad of bitter greens, fresh pears and crumbled blue cheese.

1 lb (500 g) Egg Pasta
   (recipe on page 12)
¼ cup (2 oz/60 g) Sage and Shallot
   Butter (recipe on page 294) at
   room temperature
¼ cup (2 fl oz/60 ml) plus 6 qt (6 l)
   water
60 fresh sage leaves, 1–1½ inches
   (2.5–4 cm) long
2 teaspoons cornmeal
1 tablespoon salt
2 tablespoons minced fresh sage

Make the Egg Pasta and roll it into sheets 4½ inches (11 cm) wide and 20 inches (50 cm) long.

❧ Make the Sage and Shallot Butter.

❧ On a work surface, place a strip of pasta and cut it in half crosswise. Using a pastry brush, coat the surface of 1 strip with some of the ¼ cup (2 fl oz/60 ml) water. Arrange the sage leaves in 2 rows on top of the moistened sheet of pasta, spacing about 1 inch (2.5 cm) between leaves. Place the other half sheet of pasta on top of the moistened one and press them together gently.

❧ Using a rolling pin or manual pasta machine at the narrowest setting, roll the pasta until it is nearly translucent and the sage leaves are visible. Both the pasta and the leaves will stretch considerably.

❧ Using a pasta cutter, cut the pasta into sixty 2-inch (5-cm) squares, trimming the edges and cutting between the squares. Set the completed squares on waxed paper or kitchen towels and sprinkle with the cornmeal. Dry slightly before cooking, 15–30 minutes.

❧ In a large pot over high heat, bring the 6 qt (6 l) water to a boil. Add the salt and the pasta squares and cook, stirring frequently so they do not stick together, until tender, about 2 minutes. Drain carefully.

❧ In a large warmed bowl, combine the pasta squares and the Sage and Shallot Butter and toss gently.

❧ To serve, arrange 10 squares on individual warmed plates. Top with an equal amount of the minced sage.

❧ Serve hot.

RIBBONS AND SQUARES WITH HERB CREAM SAUCE

SERVES 8

Because of the time involved in making two flavors of fresh pasta and cutting them into two different shapes, you might want to save this recipe for a special-occasion meal. But all of the work will be justified when you present the whimsical and delicious results of your efforts. Once you master the technique, prepare the two-toned ribbons and little squares, called quadrucci *in Italian, with different flavors of pasta.*

1 lb (500 g) Beet Pasta
   (recipe on page 12)
1 lb (500 g) Pumpkin Pasta
   (recipe on page 12)
¼ cup (2 fl oz/60 ml) plus 8 qt (8 l)
   water
Herb Cream Sauce
1½ tablespoons salt
1 tablespoon extra-virgin olive oil
salt and freshly ground pepper

Make the Beet and the Pumpkin Pasta.

✑ On a work surface, place a strip of Beet Pasta, brush lightly with some of the ¼ cup (2 fl oz/60 ml) water and top with a strip of Pumpkin Pasta.

✑ Using a rolling pin or a mechanical pasta maker on the narrowest setting, press the two pieces of pasta together, securing them firmly so that they become one sheet, beet on one side, pumpkin on the other. Cut all but 1 sheet into tagliatelle and the remaining sheet into quadrucci (see page 14).

✑ Prepare the Herb Cream Sauce.

✑ In a large pot over high heat, bring the 8 qt (8 l) water to a boil. Add the salt and the tagliatelle and cook for 1 minute. Add the quadrucci and cook until tender, about 2 minutes. Drain well, place in a large warmed bowl and toss immediately with the olive oil.

✑ To serve, divide the tagliatelle and quadrucci among individual warmed plates. Top with the Herb Cream Sauce and salt and pepper to taste.

✑ Serve hot.

Herb Cream Sauce

MAKES ABOUT 2 CUPS (16 FL OZ/500 ML)

The popularity of fresh herbs has taken them from specialty stores and farmers' markets right into most supermarket produce departments. The variety of fresh herbs used in this light sauce is often found bundled together for sale. If one of the group is out of stock, simply substitute an equal amount of one of the others until you achieve a taste you like.

2 cups (16 fl oz/500 ml) heavy (double)
   cream
2 flat-leaf (Italian) parsley sprigs
2 fresh thyme sprigs
2 fresh oregano sprigs
2 fresh marjoram sprigs
¾ cup (3 oz/90 g) freshly grated aged
   Asiago cheese
salt and freshly ground pepper

In a medium saucepan over medium heat, simmer the cream and the herb sprigs until the cream is reduced by one-third. Remove from the heat and steep for 10 minutes.

✑ Remove and discard the herb sprigs.

✑ Place over medium-low heat. Add the Asiago cheese and salt and pepper to taste. Cook, stirring constantly, until the cheese is completely melted. Keep warm until ready to use.

Large-scale terra-cotta dinner plates and heavy tumblers set the scene nicely for a casual pasta dinner. First, use the wide-rimmed plate as a charger under a smaller plate used for a first-course salad. Remove the salad plate and then use the larger plate to hold the entree.

Ravioli

Scholars tell us that the filled pasta known as ravioli evolved centuries ago in the northwestern Italian city of Genoa, where local sailors would wrap galley scraps, *rabiole*, inside sheets of pasta. Today, ravioli have evolved far beyond a matter of rough-and-ready kitchen economy to become specialties, including both hearty, rustic classics and refined, contemporary examples.

The recipes featured here were especially designed to interweave the flavor of the fresh pasta and its filling along with that of the sauce or topping.

As shown on page 15, forming ravioli is an easily mastered cooking technique. However, if making fresh ravioli is overwhelming, try these toppings with purchased ravioli for fine results as well. You can also fill sheets of premade fresh pasta to make ravioli or use Asian wonton wrappers, which are made from a dough similar to fresh pasta, as a pasta substitute in many ravioli recipes. These shortcuts will make your forays into Genovese tradition all the easier.

POTATO AND GARLIC RAVIOLI WITH BROWN BUTTER

SERVES 6

When mashing the potatoes for this filling, be sure to use just a fork or a classic manual potato masher. Do not be tempted to use a food processor to purée the mixture, because the speed and agitation of its blades will give the potatoes an unappetizingly gummy consistency. The potato filling, rich with the flavors of garlic, chives and lemon juice, is also delicious served on its own, and the ravioli or the filling alone will make an excellent accompaniment to robust main courses of grilled or roasted beef, lamb or pork. The quantity of garlic may be reduced by half, if desired, and still yield a good flavor. If made with a little sautéed onion in place of the garlic, the ravioli will resemble in flavor the Eastern European potato dumplings called pierogi, *and they may even be enjoyed as a breakfast or luncheon dish accompanied by generous helpings of sour cream and apple sauce in place of the brown butter and chives.*

1 lb (500 g) Egg Pasta
    (recipe on page 12)
6 tablespoons (3 fl oz/90 ml) Brown
    Butter (recipe on page 39)
3 large russet potatoes
4 tablespoons (2 fl oz/60 ml)
    extra-virgin olive oil
6 garlic cloves, peeled and minced
3 tablespoons minced fresh chives
2 tablespoons fresh lemon juice
salt and freshly ground pepper
6 qt (6 l) water
1 tablespoon salt

Make the Egg Pasta and Brown Butter.

✤ Preheat an oven to 375°F (190°C).

✤ Using a fork, puncture the potatoes in several places and bake until tender, about 45 minutes. Cool to the touch. Cut in half, scoop out the insides, place in a bowl and mash. Discard the skins.

✤ To make the filling, in a small frying pan over medium heat, heat 1 tablespoon of the olive oil. Add the garlic and sauté for 1 minute. Add to the potatoes and stir to mix well. Add the remaining 3 tablespoons olive oil, 1 tablespoon of the chives, the lemon juice and salt and pepper to taste. Stir to mix well.

✤ Form the pasta and filling into thirty-six 2½-inch (6-cm) round ravioli (see page 15).

✤ In a large pot over high heat, bring the water to a boil. Add the 1 tablespoon salt and the ravioli in batches and cook until they rise to the surface, about 3 minutes, then cook for 1 minute more. Drain.

✤ To serve, divide among individual warmed plates. Top with an equal amount of melted Brown Butter and remaining chives.

✤ Serve hot.

SMOKED SALMON RAVIOLI WITH LEMON CREAM SAUCE

SERVES 6

Serve these luxurious ravioli at an elegant supper. For an extra-special touch, garnish with additional fresh chives.

1 lb (500 g) Black Pepper Pasta
    (recipe on page 12)
Lemon Cream Sauce
6 oz (185 g) sliced smoked salmon
1 tablespoon minced lemon zest
1 tablespoon sliced fresh chives
salt and freshly ground pepper
1 egg, lightly beaten
1 cup (8 oz/250 g) whole-milk ricotta
    cheese
⅓ cup (1½ oz/45 g) grated Parmesan
    cheese
6 qt (6 l) water
1 tablespoon salt

Make the Black Pepper Pasta.

❧ Prepare the Lemon Cream Sauce.

❧ To make the filling, in a food processor with the metal blade or in a blender, combine the salmon, lemon zest, chives and salt and pepper to taste. Pulse to combine.

❧ Transfer to a medium bowl. Add the egg, ricotta cheese and Parmesan cheese. Stir to mix well. Cover and refrigerate for 1 hour.

❧ Form the pasta and filling into thirty 3-inch (7.5-cm) round ravioli (see page 15).

❧ In a large pot over high heat, bring the water to a boil. Add the 1 tablespoon salt and the ravioli in batches and cook until they rise to the surface, about 3 minutes, then cook for 1 minute more. Drain.

❧ To serve, divide among individual plates. Top with the Lemon Cream Sauce.

❧ Serve hot.

Lemon Cream Sauce

MAKES ABOUT ½ CUP (4 FL OZ/125 ML)

Tangy crème fraîche is cultured cream that is thicker than whipping cream but thinner than sour cream, which can be substituted.

6 tablespoons (3 oz/90 g) crème fraîche
    or sour cream
1 tablespoon fresh lemon juice
1 teaspoon grated lemon zest
1 teaspoon minced fresh chives
salt and freshly ground pepper

In a medium bowl, whisk together the crème fraîche or sour cream, lemon juice, zest, chives and salt and pepper to taste. Serve at room temperature.

LEMON RAVIOLI WITH PUMPKIN FILLING

SERVES 6

These festive ravioli will help ring in the winter holidays.

1 lb (500 g) Lemon Pasta
   (recipe on page 12)
2 cups (16 fl oz/500 ml) pumpkin
   purée
2 tablespoons candied ginger, minced
2 tablespoons candied lemon peel,
   minced
3 tablespoons currants, soaked in brandy
   or water for 30 minutes and drained
1 tablespoon white mustard seed
salt and freshly ground pepper
ground nutmeg
ground cloves
6 qt (6 l) water
1 tablespoon salt
6 tablespoons (3 oz/90 g) unsalted
   butter at room temperature
6 tablespoons (1½ oz/45 g) grated
   Parmesan cheese

Make the Lemon Pasta.

❧ To make the filling, in a medium bowl, combine the pumpkin, ginger, lemon peel, currants, mustard seed and salt, pepper, nutmeg and cloves to taste.

❧ Form the pasta and filling into thirty 3-inch (7.5-cm) round ravioli (see page 15).

❧ In a large pot over high heat, bring the water to a boil. Add the 1 table-spoon salt and the ravioli in batches and cook until they rise to the surface, about 3 minutes, then cook for 1 minute more. Drain. Place on a large warmed platter. Top with half of the butter and toss gently.

❧ To serve, top with the remaining butter and the Parmesan cheese.

❧ Serve hot.

CRAB RAVIOLI WITH HOT LEMON BUTTER

SERVES 6

When preparing ravioli seems too time-consuming, use this crab filling for cannelloni made with the same fresh pasta dough, or in dried manicotti, and serve with the same sauce. Garnish the ravioli or filled tubes, if you like, with sprigs of parsley or with finely chopped fresh chives.

1 lb (500 g) Lemon Pasta
   (recipe on page 12)
Hot Lemon Butter
1 tablespoon unsalted butter
¼ cup (1½ oz/45 g) minced onion
½ cup (2½ oz/75 g) finely diced celery
9 oz (280 g) fresh crabmeat
2 teaspoons Dijon-style mustard
2 tablespoons heavy (double) cream
1 egg, lightly beaten
2 tablespoons fresh lemon juice
2 tablespoons minced fresh flat-leaf
   (Italian) parsley
¼ cup (½ oz/15 g) dried bread crumbs
   (see page 294)
salt
red pepper flakes
6 qt (6 l) water
1 tablespoon salt
1 lemon, cut into 6 slices

Make the Lemon Pasta.
❧ Prepare the Hot Lemon Butter.
❧ In a small frying pan over medium-low heat, melt the butter until it foams. Reduce the heat to low, add the onion and celery and sauté, stirring frequently, until tender, about 15 minutes.
❧ To make the filling, in a medium bowl, combine the crabmeat, mustard, cream, egg, lemon juice, parsley, bread crumbs and salt and red pepper flakes to taste. Add the sautéed onion and celery and toss to mix well.

❧ Form the pasta and filling into thirty-six 2½-inch (6-cm) square ravioli (see page 15).
❧ In a large pot over high heat, bring the water to a boil. Add the 1 tablespoon salt and the ravioli in batches and cook until they rise to the surface, about 3 minutes, then cook for 1 minute more. Drain.
❧ To serve, divide among individual warmed plates. Top with an equal amount of the Hot Lemon Butter and garnish with a lemon slice.
❧ Serve hot.

Hot Lemon Butter

MAKES ABOUT ½ CUP (4 OZ/125 G)

Adding a bit of citrus juices gives melted butter a zesty new dimension of flavor. Unsalted butter is preferable for this recipe, as it lets the lemon flavor shine through clearly. If you are cutting back on sodium, by the way, lemon juice and zest are both good choices for highlighting the taste of foods without adding salt.

½ cup (4 oz/125 g) unsalted butter
4 garlic cloves, peeled and minced
1 tablespoon fresh lemon juice
2 teaspoons hot pepper sauce
1 teaspoon grated lemon zest

In a small saucepan over medium-low heat, melt the butter and skim off the foam that forms on top. Add the garlic and simmer for 2 minutes.
❧ Stir in the lemon juice, hot pepper sauce and zest. Reheat before serving.

Knowest thou the land where the lemon trees bloom?

—JOHANN WOLFGANG VON GOETHE

The bright tart taste of lemon juice and lemon zest enlivens any number of dishes. When purchasing lemons, look for ones that are firm and heavy for their size, which indicates more juice inside. Refrigerated, lemons will keep for up to a month. Although their life span may be slightly shortened without refrigeration, lemons displayed in a bowl make a beautiful addition to your table or kitchen counter and give up their juice more readily than cold lemons.

THREE-CHEESE RAVIOLI

SERVES 6

The cheeses and beaten egg produce a fluffy filling for vivid beet pasta.

1 lb (500 g) Beet Pasta
 (recipe on page 12)
4 oz (125 g) whole-milk ricotta cheese
6 oz (185 g) fresh mild goat cheese
1 cup (4 oz/125 g) grated pecorino
 romano cheese
2 eggs, lightly beaten
2 lb (1 kg) beet greens or Swiss
 chard (silverbeet), stemmed and
 cut into strips
3 tablespoons water, plus 6 qt (6 l) water
1 tablespoon salt
⅓ cup (3 fl oz/90 ml) extra-virgin
 olive oil
⅓ cup (1½ oz/45 g) walnut pieces,
 toasted (see page 297)

Make the Beet Pasta.

❧ To make the filling, in a small bowl, combine the ricotta, goat and pecorino romano cheeses and eggs.

❧ Form the pasta and filling into thirty-six 2½-inch (6-cm) square ravioli (see page 15).

❧ In a heavy frying pan over medium heat, place the greens and the 3 tablespoons water, cover and cook until the greens wilt, about 5 minutes.

❧ In a large pot over high heat, bring the 6 qt (6 l) water to a boil. Add the 1 tablespoon salt and the ravioli in batches and cook until they rise to the surface, about 3 minutes, then cook for 1 minute more. Drain.

❧ To serve, divide the wilted greens among individual warmed plates. Top with the ravioli, olive oil and walnuts.

❧ Serve hot.

Common table beets are a root vegetable with an edible wine-colored bulb and green leaves. Less common varieties have golden and white flesh. People who have eaten only commercial canned or pickled beets may be pleasantly surprised at the sweet taste of fresh beets, served raw in salads or cooked in pasta sauces. Look for smooth, firm bulbs and tender crisp leaves. For long storage, remove the leaves and keep the bulbs in the refrigerator for up to 1 month. Store beet greens in a plastic bag in the refrigerator for up to 5 days.

PORK AND DRIED APRICOT RAVIOLI WITH APRICOT AND WINE SAUCE

SERVES 6

Sweet apricots find a perfect flavor counterpoint in both this pork filling and spiced wine sauce. Using the dried version in the filling and jam in the sauce brings a taste of summer to a dish you can make any time of year.

1 lb (500 g) Egg Pasta
   (recipe on page 12)
Apricot and Wine Sauce
3 tablespoons olive oil
1 yellow onion, peeled and finely diced
5 garlic cloves, peeled and minced
1 lb (500 g) ground (minced) pork
¾ cup (3 oz/90 g) dried apricots,
   finely diced
6 tablespoons (2 oz/60 g) pine nuts,
   toasted (see page 297)
salt
ground cumin
ground cinnamon
ground cloves
6 qt (6 l) water
1 tablespoon salt

Make the Egg Pasta.

❧ Prepare the Apricot and Wine Sauce.

❧ To make the filling, in a medium frying pan over medium heat, heat the olive oil. Add the onion and sauté, stirring frequently, until tender and fragrant, about 15 minutes. Add the garlic and sauté for 2 minutes. Add the pork and cook, breaking it up with a fork, until it is no longer pink, about 5 minutes. Drain off any excess fat and return the pan to the heat. Add the apricots, half the pine nuts, and salt, cumin, cinnamon and cloves to taste. Stir to mix well.

❧ Form the pasta and filling into thirty 3-inch (7.5-cm) round ravioli (see page 15).

❧ In a large pot over high heat, bring the water to a boil. Add the 1 tablespoon salt and the ravioli in batches and cook until they rise to the surface, about 3 minutes, then cook for 1 minute more. Drain.

❧ To serve, top with the Apricot and Wine Sauce and remaining pine nuts.

❧ Serve hot.

Apricot and Wine Sauce

MAKES ABOUT 2½ CUPS (20 FL OZ/625 ML)

The ginger and multiple spices serve as a savory counterpoint to the sweet jam in this flavorful sauce, which can be made ahead and refrigerated in a tightly sealed jar for several days.

2 tablespoons olive oil
1 small yellow onion, peeled and
   minced
4 garlic cloves, peeled and minced
1 teaspoon minced fresh ginger
½ cup (5 oz/155 g) apricot jam
1½ cups (12 fl oz/375 ml) dry
   white wine
ground cloves
ground nutmeg
ground cinnamon

In a small frying pan, heat the olive oil over medium heat. Add the onion and sauté, stirring frequently, until the onion is transparent, about 10 minutes. Add the garlic and sauté for 2 minutes.

❧ Add the ginger, jam and wine and cloves, nutmeg and cinnamon to taste. Stir to mix well. Simmer until the sauce is fragrant, about 15 minutes. Reheat before serving.

Pork is the real hero of the feast. Like a passionate youth it puts on different disguises on different occasions.

—NIKITA VSELOLZHSKY

SPINACH RAVIOLI WITH SUMMER TOMATO SAUCE

SERVES 6

This classic dish features both ricotta and Parmesan cheeses mixed with spinach as a filling for round ravioli. They are topped with a simple tomato purée that is also delicious on pasta noodles.

1 lb (500 g) Egg Pasta
   (recipe on page 12)
1¾ cups (14 fl oz/435 ml) Summer
   Tomato Sauce (recipe on page 53)
2 tablespoons extra-virgin olive oil
4 garlic cloves, peeled and minced
2 lb (1 kg) fresh spinach, stemmed
   and chopped
1 teaspoon minced lemon zest
½ cup (4 oz/125 g) ricotta cheese
½ cup (4 oz/125 g) freshly grated
   Parmesan cheese
salt
6 qt (6 l) water
1 tablespoon salt

Make the Egg Pasta.

❧ Prepare the Summer Tomato Sauce.

❧ To make the filling, in a small frying pan over medium-low heat, heat the olive oil. Add the garlic and sauté for 1 minute. Add the spinach, cover and cook until the spinach is wilted, 3–4 minutes. Cool to room temperature and add the lemon zest, ricotta and Parmesan cheeses and salt to taste. Stir to mix well.

❧ Form the pasta and filling into thirty-six 2½-inch (6-cm) round ravioli (see page 15).

❧ In a large pot over high heat, bring the water to a boil. Add the 1 table-spoon salt and the ravioli in batches and cook until they rise to the surface, about 3 minutes, then cook for 1 minute more. Drain.

❧ To serve, divide among individual warmed plates. Top with an equal amount of the Summer Tomato Sauce.

❧ Serve hot.

CHICKEN RAVIOLI WITH MARSALA CREAM SAUCE

SERVES 6

The filling for these ravioli resembles fresh chicken sausage. If you can find sausages, feel free to use them in place of the filling mixture, removing the casing and sautéing the mixture for about 5 minutes.

1 lb (500 g) Egg Pasta
   (recipe on page 12)

3 tablespoons olive oil

1 yellow onion, peeled and finely diced

1 pippin apple, peeled, cored and
   finely diced

1 lb (500 g) ground (minced) chicken

1 tablespoon curry powder

ground cardamom

2 cups (16 fl oz/500 ml) half & half
   (half cream)

2 tablespoons unsalted butter

2 tablespoons minced onion

1 tablespoon curry powder

ground cardamom

¾ cup (6 fl oz/180 ml) dry Marsala
   wine

salt

cayenne pepper

6 qt (6 l) water

1 tablespoon salt

Make the Egg Pasta.

❧ To make the filling, in a medium frying pan over medium heat, heat the olive oil. Add the onion and sauté, stirring frequently, until tender and fragrant, about 15 minutes.

❧ Add the apple and chicken, breaking it up with a fork, and cook until the chicken is no longer pink, about 5 minutes. Add the curry and cardamom to taste. Stir to mix well.

❧ Form the pasta and filling into thirty-six 2½-inch (6-cm) round ravioli (see page 15).

❧ To make the Marsala cream sauce, in a medium saucepan over medium heat, cook the half & half to reduce by one-third, 12–15 minutes. In a small frying pan over medium heat, melt the butter until it foams. Reduce the heat to medium-low, add the onion and sauté, stirring frequently, until fragrant, about 10 minutes. Add the curry and cardamom to taste and cook for 2 minutes.

❧ Increase the heat to medium, stir in the wine and simmer until it is reduced to 3 tablespoons, about 15 minutes. Reduce the heat to medium-low, add the reduced half & half and simmer for 5 minutes. Add salt and cayenne to taste.

❧ In a large pot over high heat, bring the water to a boil. Add the 1 tablespoon salt and the ravioli in batches and cook until they rise to the surface, about 3 minutes, then cook for 1 minute more. Drain.

❧ To serve, divide among individual warmed plates. Top with an equal amount of the wine sauce.

❧ Serve hot.

WILD RICE RAVIOLI WITH WALNUT BUTTER SAUCE

SERVES 6

Though it may seem unusual to fill pasta with rice, these festive ravioli, full of autumn flavors, make a perfect first course before a holiday roast.

1 lb (500 g) Egg Pasta
 (recipe on page 12)
Walnut Butter Sauce
½ cup (3 oz/90 g) wild rice
2 cups (16 fl oz/500 ml) water
1 teaspoon plus 1 tablespoon salt
¾ cup (3 oz/90 g) chopped walnuts,
 toasted (see page 297)
¼ cup (1 oz/30 g) dried cranberries,
 soaked in warm water for 30 minutes
 and drained
3 tablespoons minced fresh flat-leaf
 (Italian) parsley
2 tablespoons unsalted butter, melted
freshly ground pepper
6 qt (6 l) water

Make the Egg Pasta.

❧ Prepare the Walnut Butter Sauce.

❧ In a small saucepan over medium heat, combine the rice, water and the 1 teaspoon salt and bring to a boil. Reduce the heat to medium-low, cover and cook until the rice is tender, about 40 minutes. Drain any excess water.

❧ To make the filling, in a medium bowl, combine the rice, walnuts, cranberries, parsley, butter and pepper to taste and toss again.

❧ Form the pasta and filling into thirty 3-inch (7.5-cm) square ravioli (see page 15).

❧ In a large pot over high heat, bring the water to a boil. Add the 1 tablespoon salt and the ravioli and cook until they rise to the surface, about 3 minutes, then cook for 1 minute more. Drain. Top with half of the Walnut Butter Sauce. Toss to coat well.

❧ To serve, divide among plates. Top with the remaining sauce.

❧ Serve hot.

Walnut Butter Sauce

MAKES ABOUT 1 CUP (8 FL OZ/250 ML)

Toasting brings out the full flavor of walnuts, an ancient food popular in all Mediterranean cuisines. This buttery sauce is a variation of a traditional Italian sweet sauce made from walnuts and cream. For a variation, substitute toasted hazelnuts (filberts) for the walnuts. Before chopping them, rub them while still warm to flake off their brown skins.

⅓ cup (3 oz/90 g) unsalted butter
¼ cup (1 oz/30 g) grated Parmesan
 cheese
¼ cup (1 oz/30 g) chopped walnuts,
 toasted (see page 297)
1 tablespoon minced fresh flat-leaf
 (Italian) parsley
salt and freshly ground pepper

In a small saucepan over low heat, melt the butter. Add the Parmesan cheese, walnuts, parsley and salt and pepper to taste. Mix well. Reheat before serving.

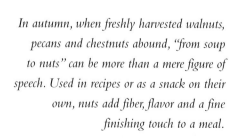

In autumn, when freshly harvested walnuts, pecans and chestnuts abound, "from soup to nuts" can be more than a mere figure of speech. Used in recipes or as a snack on their own, nuts add fiber, flavor and a fine finishing touch to a meal.

TURKEY AND SAGE RAVIOLI WITH SAGE CREAM SAUCE

SERVES 6

The natural affinity between turkey and sage produces an especially flavorful pasta filling. If you cannot locate the fresh herb, substitute 1 tablespoon of dried but not ground sage. For an unusual and delicious variation, substitute ground pork for all or part of the uncooked turkey or finely chopped ham for all or part or the cooked turkey. No matter what combination of meats you use, a spoonful of cranberry sauce made with whole cranberries makes a delightful accompaniment to each serving.

1 lb (500 g) Egg Pasta
    (recipe on page 12)
Sage Cream Sauce
3 tablespoons olive oil
1 yellow onion, peeled and finely
    chopped
1 shallot, peeled and minced
1 celery stalk, finely chopped
1 lb (500 g) ground (minced) turkey
2 tablespoons minced fresh sage
salt and freshly ground pepper
6 qt (6 l) water
1 tablespoon salt
fresh sage sprigs

Make the Egg Pasta.

❧ Prepare the Sage Cream Sauce.

❧ To make the filling, in a large, heavy frying pan over medium heat, heat the olive oil. Add the onion, shallot and celery and cook until they are tender, about 15 minutes.

❧ Add the turkey and cook, breaking it up with a fork, until it is no longer pink. Add the minced sage and salt and pepper to taste. Stir to mix well. Cool to room temperature.

❧ Form the pasta and filling into thirty-six 2½-inch (6-cm) square ravioli (see page 15).

❧ In a large pot over high heat, bring the water to a boil. Add the 1 tablespoon salt and the ravioli in batches and cook until they rise to the surface, about 3 minutes, then cook for 1 minute more. Drain.

❧ To serve, divide among individual warmed plates. Top with the Sage Cream Sauce. Garnish with a sage sprig.

❧ Serve hot.

*Turkey
is certainly one of
the handsomest gifts the
New World made to the Old
World…, the most tasty of our
domestic birds.*

—JEAN-ANTHELME BRILLAT-SAVARIN

Sage Cream Sauce

MAKES ABOUT 1 CUP (8 FL OZ/250 ML)

From ancient times, sage has been credited with increasing mental capacities. In fact, the word for the herb comes from the Old English for a "wise person," still widely in use in contemporary English. While this cream sauce may not increase your brain power, its great taste should provoke enthusiastic dinner conversation about your wise choice of menu ingredients.

2 tablespoons unsalted butter
1 shallot, peeled and minced
2 tablespoons minced fresh sage
2 cups (16 fl oz/500 ml) heavy (double)
    cream
3 fresh sage sprigs
salt and freshly ground pepper

In a small saucepan over medium-low heat, melt the butter until it foams. Add the shallot and minced sage and sauté until the shallot is tender, about 5 minutes.

❧ Add the cream and sage sprigs and simmer until the cream is reduced by half, about 15 minutes.

❧ Cool for 10 minutes. Remove and discard the sage sprigs.

❧ Strain the sauce into a clean saucepan and add salt and pepper to taste. Reheat before serving.

75

TWO-TONED RAVIOLI WITH PESTO SAUCE

SERVES 6

This distinctive-looking dish is made by forming the ravioli from two pastas. To serve six, make 1 lb (500 g) of each pasta and, after kneading, store the extra in a covered container in the refrigerator for up to 1 week. It makes a lovely presentation, but you can make it from one.

8 oz (250 g) Tomato Pasta
   (recipe on page 12)
8 oz (250 g) Spinach Pasta
   (recipe on page 12)
1 cup (8 fl oz/250 ml) Pesto Sauce
   (recipe on page 36)
3 oz (90 g) ricotta cheese
4 oz (125 g) fresh mild white goat
   cheese at room temperature
2 oz (60 g) Parmesan cheese, grated
6 qt (6 l) water
1 tablespoon salt
2 tomatoes, peeled, seeded and chopped
   (see page 299)
2 tablespoons pine nuts, toasted
   (see page 297)

Make the Tomato and Spinach Pastas.
❧ Prepare the Pesto Sauce.
❧ To make the filling, in a medium bowl, combine the ricotta, goat and Parmesan cheeses and ¼ cup (2 fl oz/60 ml) of the Pesto Sauce. Stir to mix well.
❧ Form the pastas and filling into thirty-six 2½-inch (6-cm) square ravioli (see page 15).
❧ In a large pot over high heat, bring the water to a boil. Add the 1 table-spoon salt and the ravioli in batches and cook until they rise to the surface, about 3 minutes, then cook for 1 minute more. Drain. Place on a large warmed platter.

❧ In a small bowl, thin the remaining Pesto Sauce with 3 tablespoons of the pasta cooking water. Add half of the thinned Pesto Sauce to the ravioli and toss gently.

❧ To serve, divide among individual warmed plates. Top with an equal amount of the remaining thinned Pesto Sauce, tomatoes and pine nuts.
❧ Serve hot.

CURRIED-POTATO AND PEA RAVIOLI WITH YOGURT SAUCE

SERVES 6

The filling for these ravioli was inspired by one used in samosa, *traditional deep-fried Indian vegetarian turnovers. If you like, substitute other vegetables such as carrots or zucchini (courgettes), diced, for all or some of the peas.*

1 lb (500 g) Saffron Pasta
    (recipe on page 12)
¼ cup (2 fl oz/60 ml) Clarified Butter
    (recipe on page 45)
2 russet potatoes
1 cup (5 oz/155 g) shelled fresh peas
    or frozen peas, thawed
½ yellow onion, peeled and diced
1 tablespoon curry powder
1 teaspoon ground cumin
½ teaspoon ground turmeric
¼ teaspoon ground cardamom
cayenne pepper
salt
1 tablespoon unsalted butter
2 teaspoons curry powder
¾ cup (6 oz/185 g) plain yogurt
6 qt (6 l) water
1 tablespoon salt
6 tablespoons (1½ oz/45 g) Major
    Grey's chutney

Make the Saffron Pasta.

 Prepare the Clarified Butter.

 Preheat an oven to 375°F (190°C).

 Using a fork, puncture the potatoes in several places and bake until tender, about 45 minutes. Cool to the touch. Cut in half, scrape out the insides, place in a medium bowl and mash. Discard the skins.

 In a small saucepan of boiling salted water, cook the peas until just tender, about 4 minutes. Drain.

 To make the filling, in a small frying pan over low heat, heat the Clarified Butter. Add the onion and sauté, stirring frequently, until tender and fragrant, about 15 minutes.

 Add the curry, cumin, turmeric, cardamom and cayenne and salt to taste and cook for 2 minutes. Add to the potatoes. Add the peas and stir to mix well.

 Form the pasta and filling into thirty-six 2½-inch (6-cm) round ravioli (see page 15).

 To make the yogurt sauce, in a small saucepan over medium-low heat, melt the butter until it foams. Stir in the curry and cook, stirring continuously, for 2 minutes. Reduce the heat to low, add the yogurt and stir until it is just warmed through.

 In a large pot over high heat, bring the water to a boil. Add the 1 tablespoon salt and the ravioli in batches and cook until they rise to the surface, about 3 minutes, then cook for 1 minute more. Drain.

 To serve, divide among individual warmed plates. Top with an equal amount of the sauce and chutney.

 Serve hot.

Other Filled Pastas

Whoever said that filled pastas had to follow the narrow path defined by simple ravioli? Certainly not lovers of fresh pasta, who enjoy vast creative license when filling and fashioning the dough. As the recipes that follow show, virtually no roadblocks stand in your way. You can halve circles of dough around a filling, casually fold them handkerchief style, or stack rounds into individual casseroles. You can roll the dough into tubes around a filling or wind it jellyroll-fashion.

So versatile are such filled dishes, in fact, that you don't even have to use pasta. Witness the recipes beginning on page 92 based on *crespelle,* the Italian version of French crepes. The fillings are versatile, too, featuring ingredients for every palate: including cheeses, vegetables, seafood, poultry and meat. Once the filling and folding is through, a classic or contemporary sauce completes the dish.

Like ravioli, these filled dishes are designed with all elements in mind. The flavors of the pasta, filling and topping have been chosen to enhance each other as well as your dining enjoyment.

SPINACH PASTA ROLLS WITH SUMMER TOMATO SAUCE

SERVES 6

The spiral-patterned green-and-white slices of this pasta roll make a festive presentation when paired with a bright red tomato sauce. Top the slices with a sprig of fresh flat-leaf (Italian) parsley for even more visual interest. These rolls make a wonderful choice for a dinner party because they can be filled several hours in advance and then cooked on the stovetop in less than 30 minutes. You need cheesecloth (muslin) and cotton string for forming the rolls.

1 lb (500 g) Spinach Pasta
   (recipe on page 12), rolled by
   hand into two rectangles
   10 by 14 inches (25 by 35 cm)
1¾ cups (14 fl oz/435 ml) Summer
   Tomato Sauce (recipe on page 53)
3 tablespoons olive oil
1 tablespoon minced garlic
2 lb (1 kg) spinach, stemmed and
   chopped
2 eggs, lightly beaten
½ cup (2 oz/60 g) chopped walnuts,
   toasted (see page 297)
1 cup (4 oz/125 g) grated Parmesan
   cheese
2 cups (1 lb/500 g) whole-milk ricotta
   cheese
salt and freshly ground pepper
6 qt (6 l) water
1 tablespoon salt
fresh flat-leaf (Italian) parsley sprigs

Make the Spinach Pasta.
❧ Prepare the Summer Tomato Sauce.
❧ To make the filling, in a large frying pan over medium heat, heat the olive oil. Add the garlic and sauté until tender, 2 minutes. Add the spinach, reduce the heat to medium-low, cover and cook until it wilts, about 4 minutes.

Remove the lid, increase the heat and simmer until all of the liquid has evaporated, about 4 minutes. Cool to room temperature.
❧ Place the spinach in a medium bowl. Add the eggs, walnuts, Parmesan and ricotta cheeses and salt and pepper to taste. Stir to mix well.
❧ Place the pasta on a floured work surface. Using a rubber spatula, spread half of the filling evenly over 1 sheet of the pasta, leaving a 1-inch (2.5-cm) margin on all sides. Roll the pasta tightly lengthwise. Wrap with 2 thicknesses of cheesecloth (muslin). Tie the ends securely with cotton string. Repeat with the second sheet of pasta.
❧ In a large wide pot over high heat, bring the water to a boil. Add the 1 tablespoon salt, carefully place the pasta rolls in the water and cook for 20 minutes. Remove from the water and cool for 5 minutes. Using a sharp knife, cut and remove the cheesecloth. Slice each roll.
❧ To serve, divide the pieces among individual warmed plates. Top with an equal amount of Summer Tomato Sauce. Garnish with a parsley sprig.
❧ Serve hot.

CANNELLONI PRIMAVERA WITH PEPPER SAUCE

SERVES 6

Primavera, *Italian for springtime, aptly describes the mixture of asparagus, zucchini (courgettes) and peas used in the pasta filling. At other times of year, use other seasonal vegetables. Carrots and green beans make a flavorful winter version of this dish.*

Pepper Sauce
8 oz (250 g) Lemon Pasta
   (recipe on page 12)
1 cup (5 oz/155 g) fresh shelled peas
   or frozen peas, thawed
3 tablespoons unsalted butter
1 lb (500 g) asparagus, cut into pieces
   2 inches (5 cm) long
2 small zucchini (courgettes), cut into
   thin strips
2 tablespoons minced fresh mint
salt and freshly ground pepper
4 qt (4 l) water
1 tablespoon salt
fresh mint sprigs

Prepare the Pepper Sauce.
❧ Make the Lemon Pasta and cut it into twelve 4-by-5-inch (10-by-13-cm) rectangles.
❧ Preheat an oven to 350°F (180°C). Coat the inside of a 9-by-13-inch (23-by-33-cm) baking dish with olive oil.
❧ In a medium saucepan of boiling salted water, cook the peas until tender, about 4 minutes. Drain.

❧ To make the filling, in a medium frying pan over medium-low heat, melt the butter until it foams. Add the asparagus and sauté until tender-crisp, about 8 minutes. Add the zucchini and sauté for 3 minutes. Add the peas, mint and salt and pepper to taste. Cool to room temperature.
❧ In a large pot over high heat, bring the water to a boil. Add the 1 table-spoon salt and the pasta rectangles and cook until tender, about 2½ minutes. Drain and set individually on a work surface.
❧ Spoon an equal amount of the filling in the center of each pasta rectangle. Roll the short side and place in the baking dish. Top with the Pepper Sauce.
❧ Bake until heated through, about 10 minutes.
❧ To serve, divide among individual plates. Garnish with a mint sprig.
❧ Serve hot.

Bell peppers (capsicums) provide more than their wonderful color and flavor to recipes. Although the exact amount varies according to the pepper's color, bell peppers provide more vitamin C per serving than citrus fruit. When cooking with peppers, experiment with various colors and the distinct spark each supplies to a given recipe.

Pepper Sauce

MAKES ABOUT 1½ CUPS (12 FL OZ/375 ML)

This smooth-textured, robust-tasting sauce can be used to top plain pasta noodles, rice or steamed vegetables and can be served as a bread-dipping sauce as well.

1 tablespoon olive oil
1 large shallot, peeled and minced
2 garlic cloves, peeled and minced
⅓ cup (3 fl oz/80 ml) dry white wine
1½ cups (12 fl oz/375 ml) Chicken
   Stock (recipe on page 30)
2 large red bell peppers (capsicums),
   roasted, peeled, seeded, deribbed and
   diced (see page 298)
1 tablespoon minced fresh mint leaves
salt and freshly ground pepper

In a medium saucepan over medium heat, heat the olive oil. Add the shallot and sauté until tender, 5 minutes.
❧ Add the garlic and sauté for 2 minutes. Add the wine, increase the heat to medium and simmer until almost completely evaporated, about 10 minutes.
❧ Add the Chicken Stock and simmer until it is reduced to 1 cup (8 fl oz/250 ml), about 10 minutes. Stir in the peppers and simmer for 8 minutes.
❧ Add the mint and salt and pepper to taste.
❧ Using a food mill or a blender, purée the sauce. Set aside until ready to use.

PAPPARDELLE WITH SUMMER TOMATO SAUCE

SERVES 8

This delicate baked dish calls for a gentle hand in assembling and serving.

Summer Tomato Sauce (recipe on
    page 53)
1½ lb (750 g) Egg Pasta
    (recipe on page 12)
4 small zucchini (courgettes), cut
    lengthwise into ribbons
8 qt (8 l) water
1½ tablespoons salt
8 oz (250 g) prosciutto, thinly sliced
¾ cup (3 oz/90 g) grated aged
    Asiago cheese
fresh flat-leaf (Italian) parsley sprigs

Prepare the Summer Tomato Sauce.

🕊 Make the Egg Pasta.

🕊 Preheat an oven to 325°F (165°C).

🕊 To cut the pappardelle, roll the pasta sheets into cylinders and cut crosswise into slices 1¼ inch (3 cm) wide. Unroll the ribbons and dry 15–30 minutes before cooking.

🕊 In a medium pot of boiling water, blanch the zucchini ribbons for 1 minute. Drain well.

🕊 In a large pot over high heat, bring the 8 qt (8 l) water to a boil. Add the 1½ tablespoons salt and the pappardelle and cook until tender, about 2 minutes. Drain well and place in a large bowl.

🕊 Spoon ½ cup (4 fl oz/125 ml) of the Summer Tomato Sauce over the pappardelle and toss to coat well.

🕊 In a low-sided 3-qt (3-l) gratin dish, layer half the pappardelle, half the zucchini ribbons and half the prosciutto slices. Pour on half of the remaining Summer Tomato Sauce. Add a second layer of the remaining pappardelle, zucchini and prosciutto. Top with the remaining Summer Tomato Sauce and Asiago cheese. Bake until the cheese is completely melted, about 15 minutes.

🕊 To serve, cool for 5 minutes. Garnish with a parsley sprig.

🕊 Serve warm.

STACKED PASTA ROUNDS WITH LAMB AND EGGPLANT

SERVES 6

Think of this dish as individual lasagne rounds. If you do not have fresh rosemary, substitute fresh oregano or tarragon. Try the technique with various fillings and sauces for an unusual presentation.

1 lb (500 g) Tomato Pasta
   (recipe on page 12)
6 tablespoons (3 fl oz/80 ml)
   extra-virgin olive oil
1 large eggplant (aubergine), halved
2 tablespoons minced garlic
1½ lb (750 g) ground (minced) lamb
2 teaspoons minced fresh rosemary
2 lb (1 kg) tomatoes, peeled, seeded
   and chopped (see page 299)
6 qt (6 l) water
1 tablespoon salt
3 red bell peppers (capsicums), roasted,
   peeled, seeded, deribbed and cut
   into thin strips (see page 298)
1 cup (5 oz/155 g) Kalamata olives,
   pitted and sliced
8 oz (250 g) fresh mozzarella cheese,
   thinly sliced
fresh rosemary sprigs

Make the Tomato Pasta and cut it into eighteen 4-inch (10-cm) rounds.

❧ Preheat an oven to 375°F (190°C). Line a heavy baking sheet with waxed paper and coat it with 1 tablespoon of the olive oil.

❧ Brush the cut surfaces of the eggplant with 1 tablespoon of the olive oil, place them in a baking dish and bake until very soft, about 40 minutes. Cool to the touch. Scoop out the insides and place in a small bowl. Add 2 tablespoons of the olive oil and 1 tablespoon of the garlic and mash well.

❧ In a medium frying pan over medium heat, cook the lamb, breaking it up with a fork, until it is no longer pink, about 7 minutes. Add the remaining garlic and the rosemary and remove from the heat.

❧ In a small bowl, combine the tomatoes with the remaining olive oil.

❧ In a large pot over high heat, bring the water to a boil. Add the 1 tablespoon salt and the pasta rounds and cook until tender, about 2 minutes. Drain carefully and separate the rounds.

❧ Place 6 pasta rounds on the baking sheet. On each, layer the eggplant mixture, lamb mixture, another pasta round, peppers, olives and mozzarella cheese. Top with a third pasta round and the tomato mixture. Bake for 15 minutes.

❧ To serve, divide among individual plates. Garnish with the rosemary.

❧ Serve hot.

BEET FAZZOLETTI WITH ORANGE VINAIGRETTE

SERVES 6

Bright colors, tastes and fragrances give this sweet-and-sour dish a winning character. An ideal accompaniment to the pasta is beet greens, quickly sautéed.

1 lb (500 g) Beet Pasta
   (recipe on page 12)
Orange Vinaigrette
¾ lb (12 oz/375 g) beets, about 3 beets
2 tablespoons chopped walnuts, toasted
   (see page 297)
1 tablespoon minced orange zest
½ teaspoon minced fresh tarragon
salt and freshly ground pepper
6 qt (6 l) water
1 tablespoon salt
fresh tarragon sprigs

Make the Beet Pasta and cut it into twenty-four 4-inch (10-cm) squares called fazzoletti. Let dry 15–30 minutes before cooking.

✤ Preheat an oven to 375°F (190°C).

✤ Prepare the Orange Vinaigrette.

✤ To make the filling, place the beets in a small ovenproof dish and bake until tender, 30–50 minutes, depending on the size of the beets. Cool to the touch. Peel, finely chop and place in a small bowl. Add the walnuts, orange zest, tarragon and salt and pepper to taste. Toss to mix well.

✤ In a large pot over high heat, bring the water to a boil. Add the 1 tablespoon salt and the fazzoletti and cook until tender, about 2 minutes. Drain.

✤ Spread them out on a work surface. Place about 2 tablespoons of the filling in the center of each fazzoletto, fold in half diagonally and then bring the bottom corners together to form a small triangle.

✤ To serve, divide among individual warmed plates. Top with an equal amount of the Orange Vinaigrette. Garnish with a tarragon sprig.

✤ Serve hot.

Orange Vinaigrette

MAKES ABOUT ¾ CUP (6 FL OZ/375 ML)

Warm, this citrus vinaigrette is wonderful over the beet pasta and beet greens. Chilled, it's great over lettuce greens or a combination of greens, pasta shapes and orange sections for a stunning salad.

⅓ cup (3 fl oz/80 ml) fresh orange juice
1 tablespoon white wine vinegar
1 small shallot, peeled and minced
½ teaspoon minced fresh tarragon
½ cup (4 fl oz/125 ml) walnut oil
1 tablespoon chopped walnuts, toasted
   (see page 297)
salt and freshly ground pepper

In a small saucepan over medium heat, simmer the orange juice, vinegar, shallot and tarragon, stirring, until the liquid is reduced to ¼ cup (2 fl oz/60 ml), about 5 minutes.

✤ Remove from the heat and add the walnut oil, walnuts and salt and pepper to taste. Reheat before serving.

Fresh-squeezed orange juice adds a tangy sweetness and vivid color to vinaigrettes and sauces. With a good-quality juicer, the process of extracting citrus juice can go quite quickly, and is certainly worth the effort. Hamlin, Jaffa and Valencia oranges are among the best varities for juicing.

Swiss Chard Fazzoletti with Shallot Vinaigrette

SERVES 6

The fresh pasta in this simple, delicate dish is filled and folded after cooking. If you like, use Egg Pasta instead of the black pepper variation. The light vinaigrette dressing makes the dish ideal for a lunch or a summer supper.

1 lb (500 g) Black Pepper Pasta
   (recipe on page 12)
Shallot Vinaigrette
3 tablespoons olive oil
1 shallot, peeled and minced
2 lb (1 kg) Swiss chard (silverbeet),
   leaves and stems chopped separately
5 garlic cloves, peeled and minced
6 qt (6 l) water
1 tablespoon salt
fresh flat-leaf (Italian) parsley sprigs

Make the Black Pepper Pasta and cut it into twenty-four 4-inch (10-cm) squares, called fazzoletti (see page 14). Let dry 15–30 minutes before cooking.
❧ Prepare the Shallot Vinaigrette.
❧ To make the filling, in a medium frying pan over medium heat, heat the olive oil. Add the shallot and chopped chard stems and sauté until tender, 5 minutes. Add the garlic and sauté for 2 minutes. Add the chopped chard leaves and cook, stirring frequently, until they wilt, about 8 minutes. Remove from the heat.
❧ In a large pot over high heat, bring the water to a boil. Add the 1 tablespoon salt and the fazzoletti and cook until tender, about 2 minutes. Drain.
❧ Spread them out on a work surface. Place about 2 tablespoons of the filling in the center of each fazzoletto, fold in half diagonally and then bring the bottom corners together to form a small triangle.
❧ To serve, divide among individual warmed plates. Top with an equal amount of the Shallot Vinaigrette. Garnish with a parsley sprig.
❧ Serve hot.

Shallot Vinaigrette

MAKES ABOUT 1 CUP (8 FL OZ/250 ML)

The mild member of the onion family, shallots are small bulbs sheathed in red or yellow skin that is easily removed. Shallots are a key ingredient in French cuisine, most notably beurre blanc, *the inspiration for this vinaigrette.*

3 tablespoons Clarified Butter
   (recipe on page 45)
2 tablespoons finely chopped pancetta
3 shallots, peeled and minced
⅓ cup (3 fl oz/80 ml) white wine
   vinegar
1 tablespoon minced fresh flat-leaf
   (Italian) parsley
salt and freshly ground pepper
½ cup (4 fl oz/125 ml) extra-virgin
   olive oil

In a small saucepan over medium-low heat, heat the Clarified Butter. Add the pancetta and sauté until it is just crisp, about 8 minutes.
❧ Add the shallots and sauté until tender, 5 minutes.
❧ Add the vinegar, parsley and salt and pepper to taste and simmer for 1 minute. Add the olive oil and immediately remove from the heat. Reheat before serving.

…the onion tribe is prophylactic and highly invigorating, and even more necessary to cookery than parsley itself.

—GEORGE ELLWANGER

SPINACH TORTELLINI WITH GORGONZOLA CREAM SAUCE

SERVES 6

Rich, tangy Gorgonzola cheese flavors both the filling and the sauce in this memorable recipe. Tortellini must be made from fresh pasta, but you can prepare them up to 2 days in advance and refrigerate.

1 lb (500 g) Spinach Pasta
   (recipe on page 12)
Gorgonzola Cream Sauce
4 oz (125 g) fresh mild white goat
   cheese, crumbled
3 oz (90 g) Gorgonzola cheese at room
   temperature
¾ cup (3 oz/90 g) grated pecorino
   romano cheese
3 oz (90 g) thinly sliced prosciutto,
   minced
1 egg, lightly beaten
1 teaspoon minced fresh flat-leaf
   (Italian) parsley
1 teaspoon minced fresh chives
½ teaspoon freshly ground pepper
6 qt (6 l) water
1 tablespoon salt
fresh chives

Make the Spinach Pasta.

❧ Prepare the Gorgonzola Cream Sauce.

❧ To make the filling, in a bowl, blend the cheeses, prosciutto, egg, parsley, minced chives and pepper.

❧ Using a 2-inch (5-cm) cookie cutter, cut the pasta into 72 circles. Working with one at a time, using a pastry brush, coat each circle lightly with water. Place about ¾ teaspoon of the filling in the center. Fold over, lining up the edges; pinch the edges together. Pull the ends together, wrapping the pasta around the tip of your finger and pinching the ends together. Let dry for 30–60 minutes before cooking.

❧ In a large pot over high heat, bring the water to a boil. Add the 1 tablespoon salt and the tortellini in batches and cook until they float to the top, about 3 minutes, and cook for 1 minute more.

❧ Spoon a small amount of the Gorgonzola Cream Sauce into a large bowl. Using a slotted spoon, transfer the tortellini to the bowl with the sauce and toss to coat.

❧ To serve, divide among individual warmed plates. Top with an equal amount of the remaining Gorgonzola Cream Sauce. Garnish with the chives.

❧ Serve hot.

Gorgonzola Cream Sauce

MAKES ABOUT 1½ CUPS (12 FL OZ/375 ML)

Cheeses are often classified by the process with which they are made. Gorgonzola is a moist, creamy member of the blue-veined group of cheeses, named for the way the mold spores produce lines of color on the interior of the cheese. Another cheese in the same classification could be substituted.

1 cup (8 fl oz/250 ml) heavy (double)
   cream
6 oz (185 g) Gorgonzola cheese, cut
   into pieces
1 tablespoon minced fresh chives
freshly ground pepper

In a medium saucepan over medium heat, bring the cream to a simmer. Reduce the heat to medium-low, add the Gorgonzola cheese and stir until the cheese melts.

❧ Remove from the heat. Add the chives and pepper to taste. Reheat before serving.

SAGE-SCENTED SEMOLINA GNOCCHI WITH MOZZARELLA

SERVES 6

This typically Roman pasta dumpling, known as gnocchi, uses coarse-ground semolina—not the flour used to make fresh pasta—as the basis for the dough. Look for the pale ivory grain in Italian markets. Placed in an airtight container in a cool dark place, semolina will keep for up to a year.

8 tablespoons (4 oz/125 g) unsalted butter
2 cups (16 fl oz/500 ml) milk
4 cups (32 fl oz/1 l) water
2 fresh sage sprigs
1⅔ cups (8 oz/250 g) semolina
3 egg yolks
1 cup (4 oz/125 g) grated aged Asiago cheese
1 tablespoon salt
4 oz (125 g) smoked mozzarella cheese, thinly sliced into 48 pieces
48 fresh sage leaves
freshly ground pepper

Preheat an oven to 425°F (220°C). Coat the sides and bottom of a 13-by-17-inch (33-by-43-cm) baking sheet with sides and a 9-by-13-inch (23-by-33-cm) baking dish with 2 tablespoons of the butter.

❧ In a medium saucepan over medium heat, bring the milk, water and sage sprigs to a simmer. Remove from the heat and cool for 15 minutes. Remove and discard the sage sprigs. Place the liquid over medium-low heat. Whisk the semolina into the milk. Continue whisking until it thickens, 4–5 minutes. Remove from the heat.

❧ In a small bowl, mix the egg yolks with 2 tablespoons of the cooked semolina. Then, add the egg mixture to the semolina in the saucepan. Quickly stir in the Asiago cheese, 4 tablespoons (2 oz/60 g) of the butter and the salt.

❧ Pour onto the baking sheet, using a spatula to spread it evenly. Cool in the refrigerator for at least 30 minutes or up to 1 hour.

❧ Using a 2-inch (5-cm) round cookie cutter, cut the semolina into 48 gnocchi. Top each with 1 slice of smoked mozzarella and 1 sage leaf. Place in the baking dish, overlapping them slightly. Cut the remaining 2 tablespoons butter into small pieces and scatter over the top. Add pepper to taste.

❧ Bake for 10 minutes. Increase the heat to 475°F (250°C) and bake until the gnocchi just begin to brown, about 10 minutes longer.

❧ To serve, divide among individual warmed plates.

❧ Serve hot.

Many different kinds of cheeses can add interest to recipes or be served as appetizers. Shown here (clockwise from top left) are blue cheese, sharp Cheddar, Danish fontina, herb-coated goat cheese, striped Cheddar-and-blue Huntsman and a black peppercorn-flavored Havarti.

Cheese is probably the friendliest of foods. It endears itself to everything and never tires of showing off to great advantage.

—JAMES BEARD

Crespelle

MAKES 24 CRESPELLE

The Italian version of crepes, crespelle, are very easy to make once you get the hang of it. You'll need a 6-inch (15-cm) frying pan or crepe pan. Be sure to measure the bottom of the pan to ensure that it is the proper diameter. Most recipes for 6 people call for 12 crespelle. Remaining crespelle can be stacked, wrapped and frozen.

1 cup (5 oz/155 g) unbleached
   all-purpose (plain) flour
¾ teaspoon salt
4 eggs, lightly beaten
2 cups (16 fl oz/500 ml) milk
6 tablespoons (3 fl oz/90 ml) pure
   olive oil

In a medium bowl, using a whisk or an electric mixer, mix the flour, salt, eggs, milk and 4 tablespoons (2 fl oz/60 ml) of the olive oil until smooth.

❧ Coat a 6-inch (15-cm) frying pan with some of the remaining 2 tablespoons olive oil and heat it over medium-high heat. Add 2 tablespoons of the batter and distribute it evenly by swirling the pan quickly. Cook until the crespella is set, about 30 seconds. Using a narrow spatula, turn it over and cook for 5 seconds. Remove from the pan and place it on waxed paper.

❧ Repeat until all the batter has been used, adding more of the remaining olive oil to the pan as necessary. When the crespelle have cooled to room temperature, they may be stacked.

❧ Use immediately or wrap in plastic and refrigerate for up to 3 days.

SWEET POTATO CRESPELLE WITH WALNUT SAUCE

SERVES 6

Sweet potatoes can be extremely sweet, making this hearty vegetarian main course seem almost like dessert. To cut the sweetness, use half sweet potatoes and half russet potatoes.

12 Crespelle
Walnut Sauce
3 sweet potatoes (3 lb/1.5 kg)
2 tablespoons unsalted butter, melted
1 cup (4 oz/125 g) grated Parmesan
   cheese
2 tablespoons chopped walnuts
1 tablespoon minced fresh flat-leaf
   (Italian) parsley
salt and freshly ground pepper
fresh flat-leaf (Italian) parsley sprigs

Make the crespelle.

❧ Preheat an oven to 350°F (180°C).

❧ Prepare the Walnut Sauce.

❧ Coat the inside of a 9-by-13-inch (23-by-33-cm) baking dish with olive oil.

❧ To make the filling, using a fork, puncture the sweet potatoes in several places and bake until tender, about 45 minutes. Cool to the touch. Cut in half, scoop out the insides, place in a medium bowl and mash. Add the butter, Parmesan cheese, walnuts, minced parsley and salt and pepper to taste. Stir to mix well.

❧ Fill the crespelle with equal amounts of the filling, roll and place in the baking dish. Bake until heated through but not brown, about 20 minutes.

❧ To serve, divide among individual warmed plates. Top with an equal amount of the Walnut Sauce. Garnish with a parsley sprig.

❧ Serve hot.

Walnut Sauce

MAKES ABOUT 2 CUPS (16 FL OZ/500 ML)

When you're not in the mood for pasta, stir this nutty cream sauce into mashed sweet potatoes for an interesting side dish. Use the same technique with pecans rather than walnuts.

3 tablespoons butter
3 tablespoons chopped walnuts
¾ cup (6 fl oz/180 ml) heavy (double)
   cream
½ cup (2 oz/60 g) grated Parmesan
   cheese
1 tablespoon minced fresh flat-leaf
   (Italian) parsley
freshly ground pepper

In a small saucepan over medium-low heat, melt the butter until it foams. Add the walnuts and sauté for 2 minutes.

❧ Add the cream, Parmesan cheese, parsley and pepper to taste. Bring to a simmer. Reheat before serving.

SEAFOOD CRESPELLE WITH CHERRY TOMATOES

SERVES 6

No cheese or cream is used to bind together this seafood mixture, so take care to handle these crepes as gently as possible to keep the filling from falling out. Vary the seafood mixture according to availability.

12 Crespelle (recipe on page 92)
8 tablespoons (4 oz/125 g) unsalted butter
12 oz (375 g) medium shrimp (prawns), peeled and deveined (see page 299)
8 oz (250 g) bay scallops or sea scallops, halved
1 shallot, peeled and minced
¼ cup (3 oz/90 g) balsamic vinegar
¼ cup (3 oz/90 g) honey, warmed
salt and freshly ground pepper
18 cherry tomatoes, quartered
¼ cup (¼ oz/7 g) thinly sliced fresh mint leaves
fresh mint sprigs

Make the Crespelle.

❧ Preheat an oven to 325°F (165°C). Coat the inside of a 9-by-13-inch (23-by-33-cm) baking dish with olive oil.

❧ To make the filling, in a medium frying pan over medium-low heat, melt 3 tablespoons of the butter until it foams. Add the shrimp and sauté until they pink and curl, about 4 minutes. Using a slotted spoon, remove the shrimp, reserving 12 for garnish and placing the rest into a medium bowl.

❧ To the pan, add another 1 tablespoon of the butter, melt it until it foams, add the scallops and sauté until opaque, about 5 minutes. Transfer to the medium bowl with the shrimp.

❧ To the pan, add 2 tablespoons of the butter, melt it until it foams, add the shallot and sauté, stirring frequently, until soft, about 5 minutes. Add the vinegar, honey and salt and pepper to taste. Reduce the heat to low and whisk in the remaining butter.

❧ Reserve one-third of the cherry tomatoes. Add the remaining tomatoes, sliced mint and 3 tablespoons of the shallot mixture to the filling. Mix well.

❧ Fill the Crespelle with equal amounts of the filling, roll and place in the dish. Bake until heated through, 7–8 minutes. Heat the remaining shallot mixture.

❧ To serve, divide the Crespelle among individual warmed plates. Top with an equal amount of the reserved tomatoes and remaining shallot mixture. Garnish each with a mint sprig and 2 reserved shrimp.

❧ Serve hot.

CHEESE CRESPELLE WITH SWEET TOMATO SAUCE

SERVES 6

A delicate egg-and-goat-cheese mixture fills these oven-baked crepes. The goat cheese is feta, a crumbly textured white cheese traditionally made in Greece and Turkey, of which domestic versions are widely available. The tomato sauce in this recipe complements them with its subtle combination of sweet and spicy seasonings. If you'd prefer a slightly tamer version, omit the red pepper flakes from the sauce.

12 Crespelle (recipe on page 92)
1½ cups (12 fl oz/375 ml) Béchamel
 Sauce at room temperature
Sweet Tomato Sauce
3 egg yolks, lightly beaten
1 lb (500 g) feta cheese, crumbled
1½ cups (6 oz/185 g) grated
 Parmesan cheese
¼ cup (⅓ oz/10 g) minced fresh
 flat-leaf (Italian) parsley
1 tablespoon minced fresh oregano
 leaves
freshly ground pepper
fresh oregano sprigs

Make the Crespelle.
❧ Prepare the Béchamel Sauce.
❧ Prepare the Sweet Tomato Sauce.
❧ Preheat an oven to 375°F (190°C). Coat the inside of a 9-by-13-inch (23-by-33-cm) baking dish with olive oil.
❧ To make the filling, in a medium bowl, combine the Béchamel Sauce and egg yolks. Add the feta and Parmesan cheeses, the parsley, the oregano and pepper to taste. Stir to mix well.
❧ Fill the Crespelle with equal amounts of the filling, roll and place in the baking dish. Bake until the filling is completely hot, 12–15 minutes.

❧ To serve, divide the Sweet Tomato Sauce among individual warmed plates. Top with 2 Crespelle. Garnish with an oregano sprig.
❧ Serve hot.

Béchamel Sauce

MAKES ABOUT 3 CUPS (24 FL OZ/750 ML)

This version of the traditional white sauce can be used as the basis for a rich pasta filling, as it is in the crespelle recipe at left. It is also often layered in baked lasagne, and appears as a pasta topping or as a base for other sauces. You can make the sauce less rich, if you wish, by using half & half (half cream) in place of the heavy (double) cream. The quantities given below are easily cut in half when less sauce is needed.

¼ cup (2 oz/60 g) unsalted butter
2 shallots, peeled and minced
¼ cup (1½ oz/45 g) all-purpose (plain)
 flour
2 cups (16 fl oz/500 ml) milk
1 cup (8 fl oz/250 ml) heavy (double)
 cream
salt
ground white pepper

In a medium saucepan over medium-low heat, melt the butter. Add the shallots and sauté until they are soft, about 5 minutes.
❧ Add the flour and cook, stirring frequently, for 3 minutes. Do not let it brown. Using a whisk, slowly mix in the milk and cream.
❧ Reduce the heat to medium-low and simmer, stirring frequently, until the sauce thickens, about 8 minutes.
❧ Remove from the heat and add salt and pepper to taste. Use at once or cover and refrigerate for up to 1 day.

Sweet Tomato Sauce

MAKES ABOUT 3 CUPS (24 FL OZ/750 ML)

Cinnamon and honey impart a touch of North African flavor to this chunky sauce. They provide balance to the peppery spice, turning this into an interestingly textural tomato accompaniment rather than an overwhelming hot sauce. If time is scarce, you can substitute a mild bottled salsa.

2 tablespoons olive oil
1 small yellow onion, peeled and diced
1 lb (500 g) tomatoes, peeled, seeded
 and chopped (see page 299)
1 teaspoon dried oregano
ground cinnamon
red pepper flakes
2 teaspoons honey
salt

In a medium saucepan over medium heat, heat the olive oil. Add the onion and sauté, stirring frequently, until tender and fragrant, about 15 minutes.
❧ Add the tomatoes, oregano and cinnamon and red pepper flakes to taste. Simmer for 15 minutes. Add the honey and salt to taste. Stir to mix well. Reheat before serving.

AGNOLOTTI FLOATING IN MUSHROOM BROTH

SERVES 6

Mushroom-lovers will especially like this delicate, flavorful recipe. You can also make the agnolotti with cremini or portobello mushrooms; just make sure that you sauté the mushrooms long enough that no excess moisture remains in the frying pan. For even more complexity of flavor, add some diced prosciutto to the mushroom mixture. Or try adding a splash of dry sherry to each serving at the table. If time is at a premium, feel free to substitute wonton wrappers for the fresh pasta. You'll find them in Asian markets as well as in well-stocked food stores, usually sold in cellophane-wrapped packages in the refrigerated case.

1 lb (500 g) Egg Pasta
    (recipe on page 12)
8 oz (250 g) shiitake mushrooms
¼ cup (2 oz/60 g) unsalted butter
1 shallot, peeled and minced
4 tablespoons (⅓ oz/10 g) minced
    fresh chives
salt and freshly ground pepper
8 cups (64 fl oz/2 l) Chicken Stock
    (recipe on page 30)
¼ oz (7 g) dried porcini mushrooms
2 fresh flat-leaf (Italian) parsley sprigs
2 fresh thyme sprigs
1 teaspoon whole black peppercorns
6 qt (6 l) water
1 tablespoon salt

Make the Egg Pasta.

❧ Remove and reserve the shiitake mushroom stems. Mince the caps.

❧ To make the filling, in a frying pan over medium-low heat, melt the butter until it foams. Add the shallot and sauté until tender, about 10 minutes. Reduce the heat to low, stir in the minced mushrooms, cover and cook until tender and limp, 10–15 minutes. Add 2 tablespoons of the chives and salt and pepper to taste. Stir to mix well.

❧ To make the agnolotti, using a 2-inch (5-cm) cookie cutter, cut the pasta into 60 circles. Working with one at a time, using a pastry brush, coat each pasta circle lightly with water. Place about ¾ teaspoon of the filling on one side of each circle. Fold over, lining up the edges, and pinch the edges together. Dry 30–60 minutes before cooking.

❧ To make the broth, in a large saucepan over medium heat, combine the Chicken Stock, reserved shiitake mushroom stems, dried porcini mushrooms, parsley, thyme and peppercorns and bring to a boil. Reduce the heat to low and simmer, partially covered, for 15 minutes.

❧ Remove from the heat and cool for 15 minutes. Strain into a saucepan. Reheat before serving.

❧ In a large pot over high heat, bring the water to a boil. Add the 1 tablespoon salt and the agnolotti in batches and cook until they float to the surface, about 2 minutes, and then cook 1 minute more.

❧ To serve, ladle the agnolotti and broth into individual warmed soup bowls. Top with the remaining chives.

❧ Serve hot.

Recent advances in growing techniques and increased consumer interest have greatly extended the types of mushrooms readily available in markets. Shiitake and porcini are two of the most popular. Along with adding texture, mushrooms are high in minerals and fiber. Although sometimes these varieties are called "wild" in recipes, consume only mushrooms obtained from a reputable merchant; never eat mushrooms gathered in the wild.

Dried Pasta

❧

As the recipes in the following chapter so deliciously demonstrate, the many different shapes and sizes of dried semolina pasta available in stores today open up a wide world of possibilities for the creative home cook. Want to turn an ordinary soup into a robust bowlful? Add your choice of tiny or bite-sized pasta shapes. In search of a salad to bring distinction to a special luncheon, dinner or picnic? Try basing it on pasta, adding a flavorful dressing and fresh herbs and elaborating it with your choice of vegetables, seafood, meat or poultry. Need a quick, easy and satisfying entree to serve for dinner tonight? Look no further than that box of dried pasta in your pantry, ready to be boiled in a matter of minutes and then transformed with a simple sauce or layered and baked to form a hearty lasagne or other robust casserole. With an almost unlimited variety of dried pastas to choose from, the opportunities for creativity are as limitless as your imagination.

Pasta Soups

When you include pasta in a soup recipe, you elevate that soup from a possibly ordinary bowlful of broth into a hot dish sustaining enough to be served as a main course. Indeed, pasta soups that also contain beans or lentils are especially good entree choices because the combination of grain and bean provides a well-balanced portion of protein and fiber while being low in fat yet still delicious.

In addition, pasta soups with chicken or seafood nicely present the meat flavor in the small portions recommended for a healthful diet. Both hearty soups and more delicate combinations of pasta in broth with a scattering of herbs have an uncanny power to satisfy.

Serve pasta soups as a first course or paired with a salad and bread for a lunch or light supper. As an entree, consider the quantity of each recipe as yielding 4 generous servings rather than the 6 first-course servings designated.

CHICKEN AND FARFALLE VEGETABLE SOUP

SERVES 6

You can use many different kinds of vegetables in this soup, selecting whatever is at peak of season. Good options include asparagus, snow peas, sugar snap peas, Swiss chard (silverbeet) and young carrots in springtime; zucchini, yellow crookneck squashes, wax beans, purple beans or such fresh shell beans as cranberry beans in summer; and leeks or small florets of broccoli in autumn and winter. In place of the farfalle, try other medium-sized pasta shapes such as elbows or orecchiette. For a quicker version of the soup, start by cooking boneless, skinless chicken breasts in good-quality canned or frozen chicken broth.

1 small chicken (3 lb/1.5 kg), quartered
   and skin removed
2½ qt (2.5 l) water
1 large yellow onion, peeled and
   coarsely chopped
1 carrot, peeled and coarsely chopped
6 parsley sprigs
1 teaspoon finely chopped fresh thyme
2 bay leaves
3 celery stalks with leaves, trimmed and
   cut diagonally into ½-inch (12-mm)
   pieces
½ small head (6 oz/185 g) Savoy cabbage, coarsely chopped
8 oz (250 g) green beans, cut diagonally
   into 1-inch (2.5-cm) pieces
6 oz (185 g) dried farfalle
¼ cup (⅓ oz/10 g) finely chopped
   fresh parsley
1 tablespoon fresh lemon juice
salt and freshly ground pepper
¾ cup (3 oz/90 g) grated Parmesan
   cheese

In a large pot over high heat, combine the chicken, water, onion, carrot, parsley, thyme and bay leaves and bring to a boil. Reduce the heat to medium-low and simmer, covered, until the chicken falls from the bone, about 1 hour.

🍂 Remove the chicken from the broth and cool. Strain the remaining broth and return it to the pot. Discard the vegetables. Remove the chicken from the bone and discard the bones.

🍂 Tear the meat into 1-inch (2.5-cm) pieces and reserve the meat separately from the broth.

🍂 To the pot, add the celery, cabbage, green beans and farfalle and simmer, covered, until the farfalle is al dente, 10–12 minutes. Add the chicken, parsley, lemon juice and salt and pepper to taste. Heat, stirring occasionally, until the chicken is warm.

🍂 To serve, ladle into individual bowls and top with the Parmesan cheese.

🍂 Serve hot.

ONION BROTH WITH ORECCHIETTE

SERVES 6

Onions, leeks, garlic and balsamic vinegar build a heady aroma in a light soup made hearty with ear-shaped orecchiette or other pasta shapes. Garnish the soup with garlic toasts.

1 tablespoon extra-virgin olive oil
4 oz (125 g) pancetta, cut into
 ¼-inch (6-mm) dice
6 large yellow onions, peeled and
 thinly sliced
2 leeks, 2 inches (5 cm) of the green
 part and white part, thinly sliced
7 cups (56 fl oz/1.75 l) Chicken Stock
 (recipe on page 30)
6 oz (185 g) dried orecchiette
6 slices country-style bread
2 garlic cloves, peeled
3 tablespoons balsamic vinegar
salt and freshly ground pepper

In a large pot over medium heat, warm the olive oil. Add the pancetta, onions and leeks and sauté, stirring occasionally, until the onions and leeks are soft, about 15 minutes. Add the Chicken Stock and simmer, covered, for 15 minutes. Add the orecchiette and continue to simmer, covered, until the orecchiette is al dente, 12–15 minutes.
❧ To make the garlic toast, in a toaster or under a broiler (griller), toast the bread until golden. Rub the toast on one side with the garlic cloves.
❧ To the pot, when the orecchiette is al dente, add the vinegar and salt and pepper to taste. Stir to mix well.
❧ To serve, ladle into individual bowls and float 1 piece of garlic toast in each.
❧ Serve hot.

PASTA IN BROTH WITH CHIVES

SERVES 6

In Italy, this pungent soup is called pasta in brodo. *Nice and light, it makes a wonderful first course. For added color and flavor, try adding green beans, fresh herbs, peas, Swiss chard (silverbeet) or spinach.*

2 lb (1 kg) chicken parts (necks and
  backs), fat removed
1 small onion, quartered
1 small carrot, peeled and coarsely
  chopped
⅛ teaspoon dried thyme
2 qt (64 fl oz/2 l) water
5 oz (155 g) dried soup pasta
  (stelline, ditalini or farfalline)
1 tablespoon minced fresh chives
salt and freshly ground pepper
½ cup (2 oz/60 g) grated Parmesan
  cheese

In a large pot over high heat, combine the chicken parts, onion, carrot, thyme and water and bring to a boil. Reduce the heat to low and simmer, uncovered, for 3 hours. Periodically add water to the pot to maintain the original level.

❧ Strain the broth and discard the bones. Skim the fat and discard.

❧ In a large clean soup pot over medium-high heat, reheat the broth, adding water if necessary, to make 2 qt (2 l). Add the pasta and cook according to the package directions or until al dente, 2–3 minutes. Add the chives and salt and pepper to taste. Stir to mix well.

❧ To serve, ladle into warmed individual soup bowls and sprinkle with the Parmesan cheese.

❧ Serve hot.

ITALIAN-STYLE CLAM SOUP WITH PASTA SHELLS

SERVES 6

For a complete meal, serve this quick sea-food soup with slices of toasted bread that you've rubbed with cut garlic cloves and spread with mayonnaise flavored with puréed garlic and a dash of cayenne. Or use the Sage Croutons on page 110. Try to find small clams, about the same size as the pasta.

3 qt (3 l) plus 2 cups (16 fl oz/500 ml) water

2 teaspoons salt

4 oz (125 g) dried small pasta shells

1 tablespoon extra-virgin olive oil

3 cups (24 fl oz/750 ml) Fish Stock (recipe on page 145)

1 cup (8 fl oz/250 ml) dry white wine

2 tomatoes, peeled, seeded and chopped (see page 299), or 2 cups (12 oz/ 375 g) chopped canned tomatoes

4 garlic cloves, peeled and minced

6 parsley sprigs, tied together

½ teaspoon chopped fresh thyme

2 bay leaves

cayenne pepper

4 lb (2 kg) clams, scrubbed well

3 tablespoons finely chopped fresh parsley

salt and freshly ground pepper

In a large pot over high heat, bring the 3 qt (3 l) water to a boil. Add the 2 teaspoons salt and the pasta shells and cook according to the package directions or until al dente, 12–15 minutes. Drain the pasta and toss it immediately with the olive oil.

❧ In a large pot over high heat, combine the Fish Stock, wine, the 2 cups (16 fl oz/500 ml) water, tomatoes, garlic, parsley sprigs, thyme, bay leaves and cayenne to taste and bring to a boil. Reduce the heat to medium-low and simmer, covered, for 15 minutes.

❧ Remove and discard the parsley and bay leaves.

❧ Discard any clams that do not close to the touch. Add the clams to the pot and simmer, covered, shaking the pot periodically, until they open, 3–5 minutes. Discard any unopened clams.

❧ Using a slotted spoon, remove the clams and let them cool slightly. Remove the clams from the shell and discard the shells.

❧ Return the clams to the pot. Add the pasta, chopped parsley and salt and pepper to taste. Simmer until the pasta is heated through, about 1 minute.

❧ To serve, ladle into individual bowls.

❧ Serve hot.

ORZO IN TOMATO BROTH WITH A CHEESE CRUST

SERVES 6

Orzo is a small seed-shaped pasta. Any small pasta shapes, or even rice, can be substituted in this hearty soup. The melted cheese crust provides an unusual presentation and helps elevate this soup, if you like, from a starter to a satisfying entree.

5 qt (5 l) water
1 tablespoon salt
12 oz (375 g) orzo
2 tablespoons olive oil
1 small red (Spanish) onion, peeled and cut lengthwise into thin strips
1 tablespoon minced garlic
4 cups (32 fl oz/1 l) Chicken Stock (recipe on page 30)
4 tomatoes, peeled, seeded and diced (see page 299)
3 tablespoons minced fresh flat-leaf (Italian) parsley
salt and freshly ground pepper
3 cups (12 oz/375 g) grated Fontina cheese

Preheat an oven to 325°F (165°C).
❧ In a large pot over high heat, bring the water to a boil. Add the 1 tablespoon salt and the orzo and cook according to the package directions or until almost al dente, 5–10 minutes. Drain. Place in a large bowl.
❧ In a medium pot over medium heat, heat the olive oil. Add the onion and sauté, stirring frequently, until soft, about 5 minutes. Add the garlic and sauté for 2 minutes. Add the Chicken Stock and tomatoes, reduce the heat to medium-low and simmer for 8 minutes. Add the parsley, orzo and salt and pepper to taste. Stir to mix well.

❧ To serve, ladle the soup into individual ovenproof bowls. Top with an equal amount of the Fontina cheese. Place on a baking sheet and bake until the cheese is fully melted and the soup is steaming hot, about 10 minutes.

❧ Serve hot.

PENNETTE AND BEAN SOUP WITH A CHEESE CRUST

SERVES 6

A variation on pasta e fagioli, *Italy's traditional pasta-and-bean soup, this robust dish is ideal served as the first course of a winter dinner, preceding a hearty roast of meat or poultry. You could also offer it as a main dish in its own right. In that case, accompany it with a salad as well as more of the bread used for the topping, which guests may use in sopping up every last drop of delicious broth.*

8 oz (250 g) dried cannellini beans, soaked 3 hours to overnight in water

3 tablespoons olive oil

2 cups (8 oz/250 g) diced yellow onions

2 tablespoons minced garlic

4 oz (125 g) pancetta, finely chopped

2 tomatoes, peeled, seeded and diced (see page 299)

6 cups (48 fl oz/1.5 l) canned reduced-sodium beef stock

¼ cup (⅓ oz/10 g) minced fresh flat-leaf (Italian) parsley

2 tablespoons minced fresh oregano

4 qt (4 l) water

2 teaspoons salt

8 oz (250 g) dried pennette

salt and freshly ground pepper

6 slices country bread, toasted

3 cups (12 oz/375 g) grated Fontina cheese

Preheat an oven to 350°F (180°C).

❧ Drain the cannellini beans and place in a pot with water to cover. Cook, uncovered, over medium heat until almost tender, 30–35 minutes. Drain.

❧ In a heavy frying pan over low heat, heat the olive oil. Add the onions and sauté, stirring frequently, until tender and fragrant, about 15 minutes.

❧ Add the garlic and sauté for 2 minutes. Add the pancetta and sauté for 5 minutes.

❧ Add the tomatoes, beef stock, parsley, oregano and cooked beans and simmer, stirring occasionally, for 10 minutes.

❧ In a large pot over high heat, bring the 4 qt (4 l) water to a boil. Add the 2 teaspoons salt and the pennette and cook according to the package directions or until almost al dente, about 9 minutes. Drain. Add to the bean mixture. Add salt and pepper to taste.

❧ To serve, ladle into individual ovenproof bowls, leaving at least ½ inch (12 mm) of room at the top. Top with 1 piece of bread and the Fontina cheese. Place on a baking sheet and bake until the cheese is completely melted, about 10 minutes.

❧ Serve hot.

PENNE AND SQUASH SOUP WITH SAGE CROUTONS

SERVES 6

Smooth and creamy in texture, this quite substantial soup gains extra interest from cooked penne or other tube-shaped pasta stirred in just before serving.

Sage Croutons
1 tablespoon plus 1 teaspoon
    extra-virgin olive oil
2 lb (1 kg) butternut squash, halved
    lengthwise and seeded
4 qt (4 l) water
2 teaspoons salt
6 oz (185 g) dried penne
1 tablespoon unsalted butter
3 bacon slices, coarsely chopped
1 large yellow onion, peeled and
    coarsely chopped
6 cups (48 fl oz/1.5 l) Chicken Stock
    (recipe on page 30)
freshly ground nutmeg
salt and freshly ground pepper
¾ cup (3 oz/90 g) coarsely shredded
    Gruyère cheese
18 whole flat-leaf (Italian) parsley leaves

Prepare the Sage Croutons.

❧ Preheat an oven to 375°F (190°C).

❧ Coat a baking sheet with the 1 teaspoon olive oil. Place the squash on the baking sheet cut-side down. Bake the squash until soft, about 1 hour.

❧ With a large spoon, scoop the softened squash pulp away from the skin and discard the skin.

❧ In a large pot over high heat, bring the water to a boil. Add the 2 teaspoons salt and the penne and cook according to the package directions or until al dente, 10–12 minutes. Drain the penne and toss it immediately with the 1 tablespoon olive oil.

❧ In a large pot over medium heat, melt the butter. Add the bacon and onion and cook, uncovered, until the onion is soft, about 10 minutes. Add the squash and Chicken Stock and simmer, uncovered, until the squash falls apart, about 30 minutes. Cool slightly.

❧ Transfer to the work bowl of a food processor fitted with the metal blade or a blender and purée. Return to the pot. Add the penne, nutmeg and salt and pepper to taste. Stir to mix well.

❧ To serve, ladle into individual bowls and garnish with the Gruyère cheese, parsley and Sage Croutons.

❧ Serve hot.

Sage Croutons

MAKES 8 OZ (250 G)

Homemade croutons add zest to soups and salads. They are an excellent use of day-old bread; almost any kind of bread can be used for this recipe. Cool and place in an airtight container for storage.

2 tablespoons extra-virgin olive oil
1 tablespoon finely chopped fresh
    sage or 2 teaspoons dried sage
salt and freshly ground pepper
8 oz (250 g) country-style bread,
    crust removed and cut into
    ¾-inch (2-cm) cubes

Preheat an oven to 350°F (180°C).

❧ In a large bowl, combine the olive oil, sage and salt and pepper to taste. Add the bread cubes and toss to coat.

❧ Place the bread cubes on a baking sheet and bake, tossing occasionally, until crisp and golden, 10–15 minutes.

❧ Cool before storing.

Deep, heavy earthenware bowls are a good choice for serving a hearty pasta soup. To avoid marring your table, place the soup bowl on a charger plate and a sturdy mat, as in this tasteful arrangement.

HERBED TOMATO, GARLIC AND MACARONI SOUP

SERVES 6

Make this simple soup at the height of summer, when vine-ripened tomatoes are the most flavorful and fresh herbs are the most fragrant. If you're a real garlic lover, don't hesitate to double the quantity.

3 qt (3 l) water
2 teaspoons salt
4 oz (125 g) dried elbow pasta
2 tablespoons extra-virgin olive oil
1 small red (Spanish) onion, peeled
    and minced
¼ cup (1 oz/30 g) garlic cloves, peeled
    and minced
3 tomatoes, peeled and seeded (see
    page 299) or 3 cups (18 oz/560 g)
    chopped canned tomatoes
4 cups (32 fl oz/1 l) Chicken Stock
    (recipe on page 30)
1 tablespoon chopped fresh parsley
2 tablespoons chopped fresh chives
1½ teaspoons chopped fresh oregano
1½ teaspoons chopped fresh thyme
¼ teaspoon chopped fresh rosemary
1 tablespoon red wine vinegar
salt and freshly ground pepper

In a large pot over high heat, bring the water to a boil. Add the 2 teaspoons salt and the elbow pasta and cook according to the package directions or until al dente, 7–10 minutes. Drain the pasta and toss it immediately with 1 tablespoon of the olive oil.

In a large pot over medium-low heat, warm the remaining 1 tablespoon olive oil. Add the onion and garlic and sauté slowly, stirring, until the onion is soft, about 10 minutes.

❧ Add the tomatoes, Chicken Stock, parsley, chives, oregano, thyme and rosemary, and simmer for 20 minutes.

❧ Add the pasta, vinegar and salt and pepper to taste. Simmer until the pasta is heated through, about 2 minutes.

❧ To serve, ladle into individual bowls.

❧ Serve hot.

TORTELLINI AND ESCAROLE SOUP PARMESAN

SERVES 6

Each rendition of this favorite Italian soup will vary with the type of tortellini or other small filled pasta used. Look for good-quality, freshly made tortellini or imported dried tortellini, or other filled shapes, in Italian delicatessens and well-stocked food stores, choosing from those with cheese, poultry or meat fillings. Try substituting spinach or Swiss chard (silverbeet) for the escarole, if you like. Or try julienned sorrel, cutting the cooking time for the tender leaves to barely a minute; they will give the soup a refreshingly lemony edge of flavor. For an even more dramatic and sustaining presentation, stir into the pot along with the escarole three lightly beaten eggs to make what Italians call straciatelle, *"little rags."*

6 cups (48 fl oz/1.5 l) Chicken Stock
   (recipe on page 30)
2 cups (16 fl oz/500 ml) water
8 oz (250 g) tortellini
1 small head escarole
   (6–8 oz/185–250 g)
salt and freshly ground pepper
¾ cup (3 oz/90 g) grated Parmesan
   cheese

In a large pot over medium-high heat, bring the Chicken Stock and

water to a boil. Immediately reduce the heat to medium, add the tortellini, cover and simmer according to the package directions or until al dente, 10–12 minutes for dried, 4–5 minutes for fresh.

❧ Cut the core end from the escarole. Remove the leaves from the head, rinse and dry well. Pile the leaves on top of one another and cut the escarole into ¼-inch (6-mm) strips.

❧ When the tortellini are al dente, add the escarole and salt and pepper to taste. Simmer, uncovered, until the escarole is soft, about 2 minutes.

❧ To serve, ladle into individual bowls and garnish with the Parmesan cheese.

❧ Serve hot.

*Beautiful soup,
so rich and green,
waiting in a hot tureen!
Who for such dainties
would not stoop?
Soup of the evening,
beautiful soup!*

—LEWIS CARROLL

ORECCHIETTE, SAUSAGES AND BROCCOLI IN BROTH

SERVES 6

Serve this hearty pasta soup as an appetizer or entree, using orecchiette or other medium-sized pasta shapes. Select from the wide variety of fresh Italian-style sausages available today in well-stocked food stores, butcher shops and Italian delicatessens; choose mild or spicy, pork, chicken or turkey. For a more authentic touch, use broccoli rabe, a robust, pleasantly bitter cousin to broccoli.

8 cups (64 fl oz/2 l) Chicken Stock
   (recipe on page 30)
red pepper flakes
1 lb (500 g) spicy Italian sausages
1½ lb (750 g) broccoli, cut into
   florets
5 qt (5 l) water
1 tablespoon salt
12 oz (375 g) dried orecchiette
salt and freshly ground pepper

In a large pot over medium heat, bring the Chicken Stock and red pepper flakes to taste to a boil. Reduce the heat to low and simmer for 20 minutes.

❧ Using a fork, prick the skins of the sausages. In a medium frying pan over medium heat, cook the sausages until lightly browned on all sides and cooked through, 15–20 minutes. Transfer the sausages to paper towels to drain and cool. Cut into ⅜-inch (1-cm) rounds and add to the stock. Add the broccoli and simmer for 15 minutes.

❧ In a large pot over high heat, bring the water to a boil. Add the 1 tablespoon salt and the orecchiette and cook according to the package directions or until al dente, about 11 minutes. Drain.

❧ To the stock, add the orecchiette and salt and pepper to taste. Stir to mix well.

❧ To serve, ladle into individual warmed soup bowls.

❧ Serve hot.

PASTA, WHITE BEAN AND TOMATO SOUP

SERVES 6

A delightful variation on the signature soup of Tuscany known as pasta e fagioli, *this recipe includes more tomatoes and pasta than most of those bowls, and is made with white beans in place of the traditional borlotti beans. Warming the rosemary garnish in olive oil shortly before serving releases its distinctive fragrance. If you like, add a decorative sprig to each serving, too.*

1 cup (7 oz/220 g) dried small white
   (navy) beans
4 tablespoons (2 fl oz/60 ml)
   extra-virgin olive oil
1 onion, peeled and finely chopped
3 garlic cloves, peeled and minced
3 tomatoes, peeled and seeded (see
   page 299) or 3 cups (18 oz/560 g)
   chopped canned tomatoes
salt and freshly ground pepper
5 cups (40 fl oz/1.25 l) Chicken Stock
   (page 30) or water
1 tablespoon finely chopped fresh
   rosemary
5 oz (155 g) dried elbow pasta

Rinse the beans; remove and discard any stones or damaged beans. Place in a bowl, add water to cover and soak for about 3 hours.

❧ Drain the beans and place in a saucepan over high heat with water to cover by 2 inches (5 cm). Bring to a boil, reduce the heat to low and simmer gently, uncovered, until the skins begin to split and the beans are tender, 45–60 minutes. Drain and set aside.

❧ In a large pot over medium-low heat, warm 2 tablespoons of the olive oil. Add the onion and garlic and sauté slowly, stirring, until the onion is soft, about 10 minutes. Add the tomatoes and salt and pepper to taste and simmer for 20 minutes. Add the Chicken Stock or water and simmer, covered, for 20 minutes. Add the beans and simmer, covered, for 20 minutes.

❧ In a small saucepan over medium heat, warm the remaining 2 tablespoons olive oil. Add the rosemary and immediately remove the pan from the heat. Reserve at room temperature.

❧ To the pot, add the pasta and simmer until it is al dente, 12–15 minutes.

❧ To serve, ladle into individual bowls and drizzle with the rosemary mixture.

❧ Serve hot.

Vegetable Salads

The cornucopia, a cone-shaped basket brimming with fresh produce, has always symbolized the abundance and variety of the harvest. Add to that variety the myriad shapes of dried pasta and you can begin to imagine just how infinitely varied vegetable-and-pasta salads can be.

Vegetable salads, presented warm or chilled, are ideal served as a hearty meal opener. They also work well as a side dish, accompanying a simple piece of grilled meat, poultry or fish. Many are more deserving of entree status, especially on warm spring and summer evenings when a cool meal—and a cool kitchen—are welcomed.

Most of these salads can be made several hours ahead of serving, easing the meal preparation crunch, and most can be packed for a meal on-the-go, for picnics and lunch. However you serve them, enjoy this generous recipe harvest!

CATALONIAN RIGATONI SALAD

SERVES 6

Romesco, *a boldly flavored sauce from the Spanish province of Catalonia, inspired this dressing. If you're in a hurry, you could substitute bottled roasted red bell peppers (capsicums) for the fresh.*

5 qt (5 l) water
1 tablespoon salt
12 oz (375 g) dried rigatoni
5 tablespoons (3 fl oz/80 ml) extra-virgin olive oil
1 slice coarse-textured white bread, halved
¼ cup (1 oz/30 g) blanched almonds
1 tomato, peeled and seeded (see page 299), or 1 cup (6 oz/185 g) chopped canned tomatoes
2 garlic cloves, peeled and minced
2 teaspoons sweet paprika
¼ teaspoon red pepper flakes
3 tablespoons sherry vinegar
salt and freshly ground pepper
3 red bell peppers (capsicums), roasted, peeled, seeded, deribbed and diced (see page 298)
¼ cup (⅓ oz/10 g) coarsely chopped fresh parsley

In a large pot over high heat, bring the water to a boil. Add the 1 tablespoon salt and the rigatoni and cook according to the package directions or until al dente, 12–15 minutes. Drain the rigatoni and toss it immediately with 1 tablespoon of the olive oil. Cover and cool completely in the refrigerator, 1–24 hours.

❧ To make the dressing, in a frying pan over medium heat, heat 1 tablespoon of the olive oil. Add the bread and fry, turning occasionally, until golden on both sides, about 2 minutes.

❧ Using a slotted spoon, transfer the bread to the work bowl of a food processor fitted with the metal blade or to a blender.

❧ In the same frying pan over medium heat, toast the almonds until golden, about 2 minutes. Add the almonds, tomatoes, garlic, paprika and red pepper flakes to the food processor or blender and pulse several times.

❧ In a measuring cup, combine the vinegar and the remaining 3 tablespoons olive oil. With the motor running, pour the olive oil mixture in a steady stream into the work bowl. Add salt and pepper to taste. Cover and set aside for 1 hour before using.

❧ In a large bowl, combine the rigatoni, dressing, peppers and parsley. Toss to mix well.

❧ To serve, place in a serving bowl or divide among individual plates.

❧ Serve at room temperature.

ESCAROLE AND ORANGE WITH FUSILLI SALAD

SERVES 6

This vivid combination of colors and flavors will brighten even the dreariest of winter days. For variety, try substituting spinach or radicchio for the escarole and walnuts or hazelnuts (filberts) for the pine nuts.

5 qt (5 l) water
1 tablespoon salt
12 oz (375 g) dried fusilli
6 tablespoons (3 fl oz/90 ml)
    extra-virgin olive oil
4 seedless oranges
1 teaspoon hazelnut (filbert) or
    walnut oil
3 tablespoons balsamic vinegar
2 garlic cloves, peeled and minced
salt and freshly ground pepper
1 small head escarole (6 oz/185 g),
    torn into large bite-sized pieces
⅓ cup (2 oz/60 g) pine nuts, toasted
    (see page 297)
3 tablespoons finely chopped cilantro
    (fresh coriander)

In a large pot over high heat, bring the water to a boil. Add the 1 tablespoon salt and the fusilli and cook according to the package directions or until al dente, 10–12 minutes. Drain the fusilli and toss it immediately with 1 table-spoon of the olive oil. Cover and cool completely in the refrigerator, 1–24 hours.

❧ Using a knife, peel 3 of the oranges down to the flesh so that no white pith remains. Cut these oranges cross-wise into slices ¼-inch (6-mm) thick. Discard the peels.

❧ Using a zester or grater, shred the zest of the 1 remaining orange. Then, juice this orange.

❧ In a large bowl, whisk together the remaining 5 tablespoons (3 fl oz/80 ml) olive oil, hazelnut or walnut oil, grated orange zest, orange juice, vinegar, garlic and salt and pepper to taste. Add the fusilli, orange slices, escarole, pine nuts and cilantro. Toss to mix well.

❧ To serve, place in a serving bowl or divide among individual plates.

❧ Serve at room temperature.

GREENS AND RIGATONI SALAD

SERVES 6

A kitchen garden's mixture of spinach, arugula, watercress, basil and mint provide vibrant color and refreshing flavor to the dressing of this quick rigatoni and grilled squash salad. For the truly adventurous, add more herb flavor by substituting basil-infused oil for the dressing.

5 qt (5 l) plus 1 tablespoon water

1 tablespoon salt

12 oz (375 g) dried rigatoni

8 tablespoons (4 fl oz/125 ml) extra-virgin olive oil

2 cups (2 oz/60 g) packed stemmed spinach leaves

1 cup (1 oz/30 g) packed arugula

1 cup (1 oz/30 g) packed stemmed watercress

¼ cup (⅓ oz/10 g) packed fresh basil leaves

3 tablespoons chopped fresh mint leaves

6 tablespoons (3 fl oz/90 ml) fresh lemon juice

salt and freshly ground pepper

2 small yellow summer squashes, cut into slices ½-inch (12-mm) thick

2 small zucchini (courgettes), cut into slices ½-inch (12-mm) thick

Prepare a fire in an outdoor charcoal grill or preheat a broiler (griller).

❧ In a large pot over high heat, bring the water to a boil. Add the 1 tablespoon salt and the rigatoni and cook according to the package directions or until al dente, 12–15 minutes. Drain the rigatoni and toss it immediately with 1 tablespoon of the olive oil. Cover and cool, 1–24 hours.

❧ In the work bowl of a food processor or in a blender, combine 5 tablespoons (3 fl oz/80 ml) of the olive oil and the spinach. Process until smooth. Gradually add the arugula, watercress, basil and mint and process until a smooth paste is formed. Add the lemon juice, the 1 tablespoon water and salt and pepper to taste and process until very smooth.

❧ Coat the squash and zucchini with the remaining 2 tablespoons olive oil. Grill the squash and zucchini over a medium-hot fire or broil (grill), until golden brown, 3–4 minutes. Cool.

❧ To serve, in a bowl, combine the rigatoni and dressing and top with the squash and zucchini. Divide among individual plates.

❧ Serve at room temperature.

CHEESE TORTELLINI SALAD WITH PESTO DRESSING

SERVES 6

A colorful mixture of flavored tortellini adds dimension to this simple salad. You can find commercial versions made with green spinach and red tomato pasta along with plain egg pasta. Enliven the dish even more by including strips of roasted red bell pepper (capsicum), a sprinkle of peeled, seeded and diced fresh sun-ripened tomato or slivers of oil-packed sun-dried tomato.

5 qt (5 l) water
1 tablespoon salt
12 oz (375 g) cheese tortellini
5 tablespoons (3 fl oz/80 ml)
   extra-virgin olive oil
1 cup (1½ oz/45 g) packed fresh
   basil leaves
3 tablespoons pine nuts
3 garlic cloves, peeled and minced
½ cup (2 oz/60 g) grated Parmesan
   cheese
salt and freshly ground pepper

In a large pot over high heat, bring the water to a boil. Add the 1 tablespoon salt and the tortellini and cook according to the package directions or until al dente, 10–12 minutes for dried, 4–5 minutes for fresh.

❧ Drain the tortellini and toss it immediately with 1 tablespoon of the olive oil. Cover and cool completely in the refrigerator, 1–24 hours.

❧ To make the pesto dressing, in the work bowl of a food processor fitted with the metal blade or in a blender, combine the basil, pine nuts, garlic, the remaining 4 tablespoons (2 fl oz/60 ml) olive oil and one-half of the Parmesan cheese. Process at high speed for 1 minute. Scrape down the sides of the work bowl and continue to process until smooth. Add the remaining Parmesan cheese and pulse a few times to combine. Add salt and pepper to taste.

❧ In a large bowl, combine the tortellini and dressing. Toss to mix well.

❧ To serve, place in a serving bowl or divide among individual plates.

❧ Serve at room temperature.

RIGATONI SALAD WITH ARTICHOKE HEARTS

SERVES 6

When artichokes are in season, try making the salad with fresh artichokes. Strip away the leaves from the lower two thirds of the artichokes; pare away the tough green skin; and cut off the top third, all the while rubbing cut surfaces with lemon juice. Scoop out and discard the fibrous chokes and steam until tender. Cut into bite-sized wedges for use in this recipe. Frozen artichoke hearts will also work fine.

5 qt (5 l) water
1 tablespoon salt
12 oz (375 g) dried rigatoni
6 tablespoons (3 fl oz/90 ml)
   extra-virgin olive oil
3 tablespoons fresh lemon juice
3 garlic cloves, peeled and minced
1 tablespoon finely chopped fresh
   oregano
salt and freshly ground pepper
18 artichoke hearts bottled in olive
   oil, drained and cut into quarters
3 tablespoons finely chopped fresh
   parsley
3 oz (90 g) Parmesan cheese
1 lemon, cut into 6 wedges

In a large pot over high heat, bring the water to a boil. Add the 1 tablespoon salt and the rigatoni and cook according to the package directions or until al dente, 12–15 minutes. Drain the rigatoni and toss it immediately with 1 tablespoon of the olive oil. Cover and cool completely in the refrigerator, 1–24 hours.

❧ In a large bowl, whisk together the remaining 5 tablespoons (3 fl oz/80 ml) olive oil, lemon juice, garlic, oregano and salt and pepper to taste. Add the artichoke hearts, rigatoni and parsley. Toss to mix well.

❧ To serve, place in a serving bowl or divide among individual plates. Using a cheese grater or shredder, grate the Parmesan cheese over the salad. Garnish with the lemon wedges.

❧ Serve at room temperature.

A bowl of whole olives is a traditional Italian antipasto, served along with flavorful cheeses and cured meat to kick off a meal. Popular in a range of Mediterranean dishes, consider olives added into salads, baked into breads, mixed into pasta (recipe on page 12) or used in a sauce such as Tapenade (recipe on page 186). Served on their own, alongside the pasta or within the pasta itself, different curings and flavorings of olives create variety in your meal.

RIGATONI AND TOMATO SALAD WITH OLIVE TAPENADE DRESSING

SERVES 6

The classic southern French blend of black olives, capers, anchovies and garlic lends bite to the dressing for this summertime salad of rigatoni or other medium-sized pasta tubes. If yellow cherry tomatoes are unavailable, use all red ones. Try serving the salad as a first course before grilled seafood marinated in olive oil and lemon juice. Or, if you like, transform the salad into a meal in its own right by adding bite-sized chunks of tuna canned in olive oil. A julienne of fresh basil leaves makes a fragrant and lovely alternative garnish.

5 qt (5 l) water
1 tablespoon salt
12 oz (375 g) dried rigatoni
3 tablespoons extra-virgin olive oil
⅓ cup (2 oz/60 g) Niçoise or
    Kalamata olives, pitted
2 tablespoons capers, drained and
    chopped
2 garlic cloves, peeled and minced
3 anchovy fillets in olive oil, drained
    and mashed
4 tablespoons (2 fl oz/60 ml) fresh
    lemon juice
salt and freshly ground pepper
12 red cherry tomatoes, halved
12 yellow cherry tomatoes, halved
4 oz (125 g) dried tomatoes in olive oil,
    drained and cut into ¼-inch (6-mm)
    strips
whole flat-leaf (Italian) parsley leaves

In a large pot over high heat, bring the water to a boil. Add the 1 tablespoon salt and the rigatoni and cook according to the package directions or until al dente, 12–15 minutes.

🍂 Drain the rigatoni and toss it immediately with 1 tablespoon of the olive oil. Cover and cool completely in the refrigerator, 1–24 hours.

🍂 In the work bowl of a food processor with the metal blade or in a blender, pulse the olives, capers, garlic and anchovies several times to make a rough paste. Add the lemon juice and the remaining 2 tablespoons olive oil and pulse a few times to make a smoother paste. Add the salt and pepper to taste.

🍂 In a large bowl, combine the olive mixture, rigatoni, cherry tomatoes and dried tomatoes. Toss to mix well.

🍂 To serve, place in a serving bowl or divide among individual plates and garnish with the parsley.

🍂 Serve at room temperature.

ORZO AND VEGETABLE CONFETTI SALAD

SERVES 6

With its wide assortment of finely diced vegetables and chopped herbs, this salad does look like a celebration. Serve with grilled chicken.

2 qt (2 l) water

2 tablespoons salt

1½ cups (11 oz/345 g) orzo

5 tablespoons (3 fl oz/80 ml) extra-virgin olive oil

1 teaspoon grated lemon zest

⅓ cup (3 fl oz/80 ml) fresh lemon juice

salt and freshly ground pepper

12 radishes, diced

3 carrots, peeled and diced

8 green (spring) onions, green and white parts, thinly sliced

¼ cup (2 oz/10 g) capers, drained

¼ cup (⅓ oz/10 g) finely chopped fresh chives

2 tablespoons chopped fresh parsley

1 lemon, cut into 6 slices

In a large pot over high heat, bring the water to a boil. Add the 2 tablespoons salt and the orzo and cook until tender, 5–8 minutes.

❧ Drain the orzo and immediately toss it with 1 tablespoon of the olive oil. Cover and cool completely in the refrigerator, 1–24 hours.

❧ In a large bowl, whisk together the remaining 4 tablespoons olive oil, lemon zest, lemon juice and salt and pepper to taste. Add the radishes, carrots, green onions, capers, chives, parsley and orzo. Toss to mix well.

❧ To serve, place in a serving bowl or divide among individual plates and garnish with the lemon slices.

❧ Serve at room temperature.

ORZO-LENTIL SALAD

SERVES 6

This Mediterranean-inspired salad makes a good companion to grilled lamb chops.

6 cups (48 fl oz/1.5 l) water
1 tablespoon salt
1¼ cups (9 oz/280 g) orzo
6 tablespoons (3 fl oz/90 ml)
    extra-virgin olive oil
¾ cup (5 oz/155 g) brown lentils
¼ cup (2 fl oz/60 ml) red wine vinegar
3 garlic cloves, peeled and minced
salt and freshly ground pepper
½ cup (¾ oz/20 g) finely chopped
    fresh mint
½ cup (¾ oz/20 g) finely chopped
    fresh dill
1 small red (Spanish) onion, peeled
    and diced
10 oz (315 g) feta cheese, crumbled
¾ cup (4 oz/125 g) Kalamata olives,
    pitted and coarsely chopped

In a large saucepan over high heat, bring the water to a boil. Add the 1 tablespoon salt and the orzo and cook until tender, 5–8 minutes.

❧ Drain the orzo and toss it immediately with 1 tablespoon of the olive oil. Cover and cool completely in the refrigerator, 1–24 hours.

❧ Rinse the lentils; remove and discard any stones or damaged lentils. Drain and place in a saucepan over high heat with water to cover by 2 inches (60 cm). Bring to a boil, reduce the heat to low and simmer, uncovered, until tender, 15–20 minutes. Drain and cool.

❧ In a large bowl, whisk together the remaining 5 tablespoons (3 fl oz/80 ml) olive oil, vinegar, garlic and salt and pepper to taste. Add the orzo, lentils, mint, dill, onion, feta cheese and olives. Toss to mix well.

❧ Serve at room temperature.

125

FARFALLE SALAD WITH CAESAR DRESSING

SERVES 6

Simple to make and easy to transport, this pungent salad is a perfect addition to any Mediterranean buffet table. When packing food for a picnic, store the pasta and dressing separately and keep the dressing chilled. Mix the two together just prior to serving. Add grilled strips of chicken breasts to serve it as a lunch dish.

5 qt (5 l) water
2 teaspoons salt
12 oz (375 g) dried farfalle
1 tablespoon plus ¼ cup (2 fl oz/60 ml) extra-virgin olive oil
Caesar Dressing
¼ lb country-style bread, crust removed, cut into ¾-inch (2-cm) cubes
3 cloves garlic, peeled and minced
salt and freshly ground pepper
½ cup (2 oz/60 g) grated Parmesan cheese

Preheat an oven to 350°F (180°C).

❧ In a large pot over high heat, bring the water to a boil. Add the 2 teaspoons salt and the farfalle and cook according to the package directions or until al dente, 10–12 minutes.

❧ Drain the farfalle and toss it immediately with the 1 tablespoon olive oil. Cover and cool completely in the refrigerator, 1–24 hours.

❧ Prepare the Caesar Dressing.

❧ To make the croutons, toss the bread with the ¼ cup (2 fl oz/60 ml) olive oil, garlic and salt and pepper to taste. Place on a baking sheet and bake, tossing with a spatula occasionally, until golden and crisp, 10–15 minutes.

❧ To serve, place the farfalle in a serving bowl or divide among individual plates. Add the Caesar Dressing and salt and pepper to taste. Toss to mix well. Garnish with the croutons and Parmesan cheese.

❧ Serve at room temperature.

Caesar Dressing

MAKES ABOUT 1 CUP (8 FL OZ/250 ML)

The addition of cream to this version of the classic dressing makes it adhere better to the pasta. It is also good on lettuce greens or used as a vegetable dipping sauce.

2 garlic cloves, peeled and minced
2 teaspoons Dijon-style mustard
2 tablespoons fresh lemon juice
4 anchovy fillets in olive oil, drained and mashed
½ cup (4 fl oz/125 ml) bottled mayonnaise
¼ cup (2 fl oz/60 ml) extra-virgin olive oil
¼ cup (2 fl oz/60 ml) heavy (double) cream

In a large bowl, whisk together the garlic, mustard, lemon juice, anchovies and mayonnaise. In a slow, steady stream, whisk in the oil. Gradually stir in the cream.

You can put everything, and the more things the better, into a salad, as into a conversation; but everything depends on the skill of mixing.

—CHARLES DUDLEY WARNER

A variety of greens, whether grown in patio pots or purchased from the market, enliven salads, a natural accompaniment to a pasta meal. When growing your own greens, snip the new leaves regularly to enjoy fresh salads throughout the year.

ORECCHIETTE AND WINTER FRUIT SALAD

SERVES 6

Pears and pecans may be substituted for apples and walnuts in this version of the classic Waldorf salad, an old American favorite, traditionally made without pasta. Here, the orecchiette provides a heartiness that makes this salad a meal.

5 qt (5 l) water
1 tablespoon salt
12 oz (375 g) dried orecchiette
1 tablespoon olive oil
⅔ cup (5 fl oz/160 ml) bottled
   mayonnaise
1 tablespoon fresh lemon juice
salt and freshly ground pepper
1 celery stalk with leaves, cut into
   ¼-inch (6-mm) slices
2 ripe green apples, peeled, cored
   and diced
36 seedless red grapes, halved
¾ cup (3 oz/90 g) walnuts, toasted
   (see page 297)

In a large pot over high heat, bring the water to a boil. Add the 1 tablespoon salt and the orecchiette and cook according to the package directions or until al dente, 10–12 minutes.

❧ Drain the orecchiette and toss it immediately with the olive oil. Cover and cool completely in the refrigerator, 1–24 hours.

❧ In a large bowl, combine the mayonnaise, lemon juice and salt and pepper to taste. Whisk to mix well.

❧ Add the orecchiette, celery, apples, grapes and walnuts. Toss to mix well.

❧ To serve, place in a serving bowl or divide among individual plates.

❧ Serve cold.

CUMIN ORECCHIETTE AND CHICKPEA SALAD

SERVES 6

1 cup (7 oz/220 g) dried chickpeas
   (garbanzo beans)
5 qt (5 l) water
1 tablespoon salt
12 oz (375 g) dried orecchiette
6 tablespoons (3 fl oz/90 ml)
   extra-virgin olive oil
3 tablespoons red wine vinegar
2 tablespoons tomato paste
3 garlic cloves, peeled and minced
2 teaspoons ground cumin
salt and freshly ground pepper
¼ cup (⅓ oz/10 g) sliced fresh mint
fresh mint sprigs

Rinse the chickpeas; remove and discard any stones or damaged peas. In a large bowl, combine the chickpeas and water to cover. Soak for about 3 hours.

❧ Drain the chickpeas and place in a large saucepan over high heat with water to cover by 2 inches (5 cm). Bring to a boil, reduce the heat to low and simmer gently, uncovered, until the skins begin to split and the beans are tender, 45–60 minutes. Drain and set aside to cool.

❧ In a large pot over high heat, bring the 5 qt (5 l) water to a boil. Add the 1 tablespoon salt and the pasta and cook according to the package directions or until al dente, 12–15 minutes.

❧ Drain the orecchiette and toss it immediately with 1 tablespoon of the olive oil. Cover and cool completely in the refrigerator, 1–24 hours.

❧ In a large bowl, whisk together the remaining 5 tablespoons (3 fl oz/80 ml) olive oil, vinegar, tomato paste, garlic, cumin and salt and pepper to taste. Add the orecchiette and chopped mint. Toss to mix well.

❧ To serve, place in a serving bowl and garnish with the mint.

❧ Serve at room temperature.

ELBOW PASTA AND SPINACH SALAD

SERVES 6

Simple ingredients form lively contrasts of color, texture and flavor in this healthy salad. If you crave the addition of bacon, a classic component of spinach salads, try crisply frying thin slices of the Italian cured bacon known as pancetta. Add a few leaves of radicchio for still more color.

5 qt (5 l) water
1 tablespoon salt
12 oz (375 g) dried large elbow pasta
6 tablespoons (3 fl oz/90 ml)
　　extra-virgin olive oil
2 shallots, peeled and minced
3 tablespoons sherry vinegar
1 tablespoon Dijon-style mustard
salt and freshly ground pepper
8 oz (250 g) spinach, stemmed and cut
　　into ½-inch (12-mm) strips
¾ cup (3 oz/90 g) shelled walnuts,
　　toasted (see page 297)
3 oz (90 g) Gruyère cheese, sliced

In a large pot over high heat, bring the water to a boil. Add the 1 table-spoon salt and the elbow pasta and cook according to the package directions or until al dente, 7–10 minutes.

❧ Drain the pasta and toss it immediately with 1 tablespoon of the olive oil. Cover and cool completely in the refrigerator, 1–24 hours.

❧ In a large bowl, whisk together the shallots, vinegar, mustard, the remaining 5 tablespoons (3 fl oz/80 ml) olive oil and salt and pepper to taste. Add the elbow pasta, spinach and walnuts. Toss to mix well.

❧ To serve, place in a serving bowl. Top with the Gruyère cheese.

❧ Serve at room temperature.

Keep a variety of dried pastas in your pantry or cupboard. For best storage, remove the pasta from its packaging after purchase (retaining the cooking directions, if needed) and transfer it to glass jars with secure lids. Well sealed and away from direct sunlight, dried pasta will keep for many months.

SPRING ASPARAGUS AND SNAP PEA PENNE SALAD

SERVES 6

For a more substantial dish, add fresh fava beans to this bright-tasting salad. Shell them and blanch in boiling water for 20 seconds. Drain and, when they're cool enough to handle, peel their skins.

5 qt (5 l) water
1 tablespoon salt
12 oz (375 g) dried penne
5 tablespoons (3 fl oz/80 ml)
    extra-virgin olive oil
8 oz (250 g) asparagus, cut diagonally
    into 1½-inch (4-cm) pieces
8 oz (250 g) sugar snap peas
1 seedless orange
2 tablespoons red wine vinegar
salt and freshly ground pepper
3 tablespoons finely chopped fresh
    chives
1 orange, cut into 6 wedges

In a large pot over high heat, bring the water to a boil. Add the 1 tablespoon salt and the penne and cook according to the package directions or until al dente, 10–12 minutes.

❧ Drain the penne and toss it immediately with 1 tablespoon of the olive oil. Cover and cool, 1–24 hours.

❧ In another large pot of boiling salted water over high heat, cook the asparagus until tender, 4–5 minutes.

❧ Using a slotted spoon, remove the asparagus, drain and cool completely in the refrigerator. Add the sugar snap peas to the water, return to a boil and cook until tender, 1–2 minutes. Drain the peas and cool completely.

❧ Using a zester or grater, shred the zest of the orange. Juice the orange.

❧ In a large bowl, whisk together the remaining 4 tablespoons (2 fl oz/60 ml) olive oil, the orange zest, orange juice, vinegar and salt and pepper to taste. Add the penne, asparagus, sugar snap peas and chives. Toss to mix well.

❧ To serve, place in a serving bowl or divide among individual plates and garnish with the orange wedges.

❧ Serve at room temperature.

PENNE SALAD WITH PEPPERS AND TOMATOES

SERVES 6

A colorful confetti of summertime vegetables enlivens penne or other thin, tube-shaped pasta, served here as a side dish to grilled halibut. Yellow bell peppers provide a sweeter flavor than the green versions.

5 qt (5 l) water
1 tablespoon salt
12 oz (375 g) dried penne
6 tablespoons (3 fl oz/90 ml)
    extra-virgin olive oil
6 tablespoons (3 fl oz/90 ml) fresh
    lemon juice
3 garlic cloves, peeled and minced
1 jalapeño pepper, seeded and minced
1 teaspoon ground cumin
3 yellow bell peppers (capsicums),
    roasted, peeled, seeded, deribbed
    and diced (see page 298)
4 large ripe tomatoes, peeled, seeded
    and diced (see page 299)
1 large cucumber, peeled, seeded and
    diced
½ cup (¾ oz/20 g) finely chopped
    cilantro (fresh coriander)

In a large pot over high heat, bring the water to a boil. Add the 1 tablespoon salt and the penne and cook according to the package directions or until al dente, 10–15 minutes.

❧ Drain the penne and toss it immediately with 1 tablespoon of the olive oil. Cover and cool completely in the refrigerator, 1–24 hours.

❧ In a large bowl, whisk together the remaining 5 tablespoons (3 fl oz/80 ml) olive oil, lemon juice, garlic, jalapeño and cumin. Add the penne, peppers, tomatoes, cucumber and cilantro. Toss to mix well.

❧ To serve, place in a serving bowl or divide among individual plates.

❧ Serve at room temperature.

FARFALLE SALAD WITH SMOKED MOZZARELLA

SERVES 6

The classic combination of mozzarella, tomatoes and basil gains new distinction by using a smoked version of the cheese, widely available in Italian delicatessens and well-stocked food stores. Look for beautiful little basil leaves that you can use whole, as shown here, without overpowering the salad. For a satisfying-yet-light lunch, accompany the salad with crusty bread toasted with a topping of butter, Parmesan cheese and chopped herbs.

5 qt (5 l) water
1 tablespoon salt
12 oz (375 g) dried farfalle
5 tablespoons (3 fl oz/80 ml)
    extra-virgin olive oil
2 tablespoons balsamic vinegar
salt and freshly ground pepper
1¼ cups (5 oz/155 g) coarsely shredded
    smoked mozzarella cheese
18 cherry tomatoes, halved
1 cup (1 oz/30 g) packed fresh basil
    leaves

In a large pot over high heat, bring the water to a boil. Add the 1 tablespoon salt and the farfalle and cook according to the package directions or until al dente, 10–12 minutes.

❧ Drain the farfalle and toss it immediately with 1 tablespoon of the olive oil. Cover and cool completely in the refrigerator, 1–24 hours.

❧ In a large bowl, whisk together the remaining 4 tablespoons (2 fl oz/60 ml) olive oil, vinegar and salt and pepper to taste. Add the farfalle, mozzarella cheese, tomatoes and basil. Toss to mix well.

❧ To serve, place in a serving bowl or divide among individual plates.

❧ Serve at room temperature.

SUMMER VEGETABLE AND FARFALLE SALAD

SERVES 6

This salad makes a colorful addition to any barbecue table and goes very well with grilled swordfish.

5 qt (5 l) water
1 tablespoon salt
12 oz (375 g) dried farfalle
6 tablespoons (3 fl oz/90 ml) extra-virgin olive oil
6 tablespoons (3 fl oz/90 ml) red wine vinegar
salt and freshly ground pepper
2 carrots, peeled and cut into ½-inch (12-mm) dice
2 celery stalks with leaves, cut into ½-inch (12-mm) dice
1 small red (Spanish) onion, peeled and cut into ½-inch (12-mm) dice
3 small red bell peppers (capsicums), seeded, deribbed and cut into ½-inch (12-mm) dice (see page 298)
2 teaspoons finely chopped fresh thyme

In a large pot over high heat, bring the water to a boil. Add the 1 tablespoon salt and the farfalle and cook according to the package directions or until al dente, 10–12 minutes.

❧ Drain the farfalle and toss it immediately with 1 tablespoon of the olive oil. Cover and cool completely in the refrigerator, 1–24 hours.

❧ In a large bowl, whisk together the remaining 5 tablespoons (3 fl oz/80 ml) olive oil, vinegar and salt and pepper to taste. Add the farfalle, carrots, celery, onion, peppers and thyme. Toss to mix well.

❧ To serve, place in a serving bowl or divide among individual plates.

❧ Serve at room temperature.

BROKEN FETTUCCINE SALAD WITH RADICCHIO

SERVES 6

Breaking dried fettuccine into bite-sized lengths makes them easier to eat in a salad, especially when they are inter-mingled with similarly sized and shaped strips of radicchio. You can substitute linguine or other pasta noodles, if you like. Serve this salad as a first course, or add thin strips of grilled chicken breast to transform it into a light entree.

6 qt (6 l) water
1 tablespoon salt
1 lb (500 g) dried fettuccine, broken
    into 2-inch (5-cm) pieces
4 tablespoons (2 fl oz/60 ml)
    extra-virgin olive oil
1 small head radicchio (6–8 oz/
    185–250 g)
2 tablespoons red wine vinegar
4 oz (125 g) Gorgonzola cheese,
    cut into small pieces
¼ cup (2 fl oz/60 ml) heavy (double)
    cream
¼ cup (2 fl oz/60 ml) plain yogurt
salt and freshly ground pepper
½ cup (2½ oz/75 g) pecans, toasted
    (see page 297)

In a large pot over high heat, bring the water to a boil. Add the 1 table-spoon salt and the fettuccine and cook according to the package directions or until al dente, 7–10 minutes.

Drain the fettuccine and toss it immediately with 1 tablespoon of the olive oil. Cover and cool completely in the refrigerator, 1–24 hours.

Cut the core from the radicchio. Remove the leaves from the head, rinse and dry well. Pile the leaves on top of one another and cut the radicchio into ¼-inch (6-mm) strips. Set aside.

❧ To make the dressing, in the work bowl of a food processor fitted with the metal blade or a blender, combine the remaining 3 tablespoons olive oil, vinegar, Gorgonzola cheese, cream, yogurt and salt and pepper to taste. Pulse until smooth.

❧ In a large bowl, combine the fettuccine and dressing. Toss to mix well. Add the radicchio and pecans and toss again.

❧ To serve, place in a serving bowl or divide among individual plates.

❧ Serve at room temperature.

FUSILLI, COLORED BEAN AND TOMATO SALAD

SERVES 6

Prepare this recipe in summer when vine-ripened cherry tomatoes and fresh green and yellow beans are at their peak of flavor. The mixture pairs well with grilled fish or chicken. In place of the fusilli, try making the salad with bite-sized, slender tubes such as penne or rigatoni, both of which have similar sizes and shapes to the summer beans.

5 qt (5 l) water
1 tablespoon salt
12 oz (375 g) dried fusilli
1 tablespoon extra-virgin olive oil
8 oz (250 g) green beans, halved crosswise
8 oz (250 g) yellow beans, halved crosswise
¾ cup (6 fl oz/180 ml) bottled mayonnaise
1 teaspoon Dijon-style mustard
2 teaspoons fresh lemon juice
3 garlic cloves, peeled and minced
salt and freshly ground pepper
2 tablespoons warm water
12 red cherry tomatoes, halved

In a large pot over high heat, bring the water to a boil. Add the 1 tablespoon salt and the fusilli and cook according to the package directions or until al dente, 12–15 minutes.

❧ Drain the fusilli and toss it immediately with the olive oil. Cover and cool completely, 1–24 hours.

❧ In a large pot of boiling salted water over high heat, cook the green and yellow beans until tender, 4–6 minutes. Drain and cool completely.

❧ In a small bowl, whisk together the mayonnaise, mustard, lemon juice, garlic and salt and pepper to taste.

❧ Slowly whisk in enough of the warm water to thin the mixture and make it barely fluid.

❧ In a large bowl, combine the fusilli, mayonnaise mixture, green and yellow beans and tomatoes. Toss to mix well.

❧ To serve, place in a serving bowl or divide among individual plates.

❧ Serve at room temperature.

FARFALLE AND FRESH FIG SALAD

SERVES 6

Fruit and pasta make an unexpected combination of flavors and textures. Use your choice of fresh red, black or green figs. In place of the pistachios, you can substitute walnuts, pecans or pine nuts. For a more substantial dish, add thin julienne strips of prosciutto, which has a salty flavor that contrasts wonderfully with the figs.

5 qt (5 l) water
1 tablespoon salt
12 oz (375 g) dried farfalle
5 tablespoons (3 fl oz/80 ml)
    extra-virgin olive oil
1 tablespoon hazelnut (filbert) or
    walnut oil
1 tablespoon sherry vinegar
2 tablespoons white wine vinegar
salt and freshly ground pepper
1 lb (500 g) firm ripe figs, halved
    lengthwise
⅔ cup (3 oz/90 g) shelled unsalted
    pistachios

In a large pot over high heat, bring the water to a boil. Add the 1 tablespoon salt and the farfalle and cook according to the package directions or until al dente, 10–12 minutes.

❧ Drain the farfalle and toss it immediately with 1 tablespoon of the olive oil. Cover and cool completely in the refrigerator, 1–24 hours.

❧ In a large bowl, whisk together the remaining 4 tablespoons (2 fl oz/60 ml) olive oil, hazelnut or walnut oil, sherry vinegar, white wine vinegar and salt and pepper to taste. Add the farfalle, figs and pistachios. Toss to mix well.

❧ To serve, place in a serving bowl or divide among individual plates.

❧ Serve at room temperature.

SPICY FUSILLI WITH BROCCOLI AND CAULIFLOWER SALAD

SERVES 6

In Italy, broccoli and cauliflower are often served together, showing off their complementary flavors and contrasting colors. Serve with breaded veal scallopini.

5 qt (5 l) water
1 tablespoon salt
12 oz (375 g) dried fusilli
6 tablespoons (3 fl oz/90 ml)
    extra-virgin olive oil
5 cups (10 oz/300 g) broccoli florets
5 cups (10 oz/300 g) cauliflower florets
6 tablespoons fresh lemon juice
6 anchovy fillets in olive oil, drained
    and mashed
3 garlic cloves, peeled and minced
¼ teaspoon red pepper flakes
fresh chives

In a large pot over high heat, bring the water to a boil. Add the 1 tablespoon salt and the fusilli and cook according to the package directions or until al dente, 12–15 minutes.

❧ Drain the fusilli and toss it immediately with 1 tablespoon of the olive oil. Cover and cool completely in the refrigerator, 1–24 hours.

❧ In a large pot of boiling salted water over high heat, cook the broccoli and cauliflower until tender, 2–4 minutes. Drain and cool completely in the refrigerator.

❧ In a large bowl, whisk the remaining 5 tablespoons (3 fl oz/80 ml) olive oil, lemon juice, anchovies, garlic and red pepper flakes. Add the fusilli, broccoli and cauliflower. Toss to mix well.

❧ To serve, divide among individual plates. Garnish with the chives.

❧ Serve at room temperature.

Seafood Salads

Food historians note that pasta traveled around the world with the ancient sailors. It makes sense then, the plethora of pasta-and-seafood combinations. Which came first, the pasta shells or the logical and pleasing combination of shells and seafood?

While the answer to that question remains forever lost in the past, the inspiration behind it lives on in the many delightful matches to be found among pasta salads featuring fish and shellfish.

Regard the recipes that follow and you'll catch glimpse after glimpse of sensible-but-inspired salad pairings. Assemblages range from such rustic fare using steamed clams and grilled fish to more elegant combinations including lobster and caviar. Widely cast though this recipe net may be, pasta's ability to please pulls everything together.

MOROCCAN ORECCHIETTE WITH GRILLED FISH SALAD

SERVES 6

In Morocco, the simple, robust sauce for this salad is called chermoula, *and tradition holds that, if you gather 30 cooks in one room, you will have 30 different recipes for making it. The combination of seasonings also works well with boneless skinless chicken breasts, although you would have to almost double the overall grilling time. Make sure to squeeze lemon over the salad just before eating. The burst of citrus juice really makes the flavors come alive.*

5 qt (5 l) water
1 tablespoon salt
12 oz (375 g) dried orecchiette
5 tablespoons (3 fl oz/80 ml) extra-virgin olive oil
2 teaspoons cumin
1 teaspoon sweet paprika
½ teaspoon ground turmeric
¼ teaspoon cayenne pepper
3 garlic cloves, peeled and minced
½ small yellow onion, peeled and minced
⅓ cup (½ oz/15 g) finely chopped cilantro (fresh coriander)
¼ cup (⅓ oz/10 g) finely chopped fresh parsley
⅓ cup (3 fl oz/80 ml) fresh lemon juice
salt and freshly ground pepper
1 lb (500 g) fresh tuna or swordfish fillet
1 lemon, cut into 6 wedges

Prepare a fire in an outdoor charcoal grill or preheat a broiler (griller).

❧ In a large pot over high heat, bring the water to a boil. Add the 1 tablespoon salt and the orecchiette and cook according to the package directions or until al dente, 12–15 minutes.

❧ Drain the orecchiette and toss it immediately with 1 tablespoon of the olive oil. Cover and cool completely in the refrigerator, 1–24 hours.

❧ To make the sauce, in the work bowl of a food processor with the metal blade or in a blender, combine the cumin, paprika, turmeric, cayenne, garlic, onion, cilantro, parsley, lemon juice, 3 tablespoons of the olive oil and salt and pepper to taste. Purée until smooth.

❧ Coat the tuna or swordfish with the remaining 1 tablespoon olive oil. Grill the fish over a medium-hot fire or broil (grill), turning occasionally, until opaque throughout when pierced with a knife, 6–8 minutes. Set aside until the fish is cool enough to handle. Place on a cutting surface and cut into 1-inch (2.5-cm) cubes.

❧ In a large bowl, combine the sauce, orecchiette and fish. Toss to mix well.

❧ To serve, place in a serving bowl or divide among individual plates and garnish with the lemon wedges.

❧ Serve at room temperature.

DILLED PENNE AND SWORDFISH SALAD

SERVES 6

Yogurt, dill and cucumbers is a classic Mediterranean flavor combination, nicely complemented by grilled swordfish in this refreshing pasta salad. The fish can be broiled in the oven if an outdoor grill is not available.

5 qt (5 l) water
1 tablespoon salt
12 oz (375 g) dried penne
4 tablespoons (2 fl oz/60 ml)
    extra-virgin olive oil
1 lb (500 g) swordfish, skinned
⅓ cup (3 oz/90 g) plain yogurt
4 tablespoons (2 fl oz/60 ml) fresh
    lime juice
1 large cucumber, halved lengthwise,
    seeded and sliced crosswise
6 tablespoons (¾ oz/20 g) finely
    chopped fresh dill
salt and freshly ground pepper

Prepare a fire in an outdoor charcoal grill or preheat a broiler (griller).
❧ In a large pot over high heat, bring the water to a boil. Add the 1 table-spoon salt and the penne and cook according to the package directions or until al dente, 10–12 minutes.
❧ Drain the penne and toss it imme-diately with 1 tablespoon of the olive oil. Cover and cool completely in the refrigerator, 1–24 hours.
❧ Coat the swordfish with 1 table-spoon of the olive oil. Grill over a medium-hot fire or broil (grill), turning occasionally, until opaque throughout when pierced with a knife, 6–8 minutes. Set aside to cool.
❧ When the fish is cool, place on a work surface and cut into 1-inch (2.5-cm) cubes.

❧ In a large bowl, whisk together the yogurt, remaining 2 tablespoons olive oil and lime juice. Add the penne, swordfish, cucumber, 3 tablespoons of the dill and salt and pepper to taste. Toss to mix well.

❧ To serve, divide among individual plates. Garnish with the remaining 3 tablespoons dill.

❧ Serve at room temperature.

GRILLED SALMON AND SHELLS SALAD

SERVES 6

Caperberries are the edible flower buds of the same plant that produces the more familiar capers, which may be substituted. Soak wooden or bamboo skewers in water to cover for 30 minutes to prevent burning.

5 qt (5 l) water
1 tablespoon salt
10 oz (315 g) dried large pasta shells
7 tablespoons (4 fl oz/100 ml)
    extra-virgin olive oil
1¼ lb (625 g) salmon fillet, skinned
⅓ cup (3 fl oz/80 ml) fresh lemon juice
1 tablespoon finely chopped fresh
    oregano
2 teaspoons finely chopped fresh thyme
½ teaspoon finely chopped fresh
    rosemary
¾ cup (6 oz/185 g) caperberries,
    drained
salt and freshly ground pepper

Prepare a fire in an outdoor charcoal grill or preheat a broiler (griller).

❧ In a large pot over high heat, bring the water to a boil. Add the 1 tablespoon salt and the pasta shells and cook according to the package directions or until al dente), 12–15 minutes.

❧ Drain the pasta and toss it immediately with 1 tablespoon of the olive oil. Cover and cool, 1–24 hours.

❧ On a cutting surface, cut the salmon into ¾-inch (2-cm) cubes. Thread onto 6 skewers, distributing the cubes evenly. Brush with 1 tablespoon of the olive oil. Grill over a medium-hot fire or broil (grill), turning occasionally, until opaque throughout when pierced with a knife, 5–6 minutes.

❧ When the fish is cool, remove the salmon from the skewers.

❧ In a large bowl, whisk together the remaining 5 tablespoons (3 fl oz/80 ml) olive oil, lemon juice, oregano, thyme and rosemary. Add the pasta shells, salmon, caperberries and salt and pepper to taste. Toss to mix well.

❧ To serve, place in a serving bowl or divide among individual plates.

❧ Serve at room temperature.

Fish Stock

MAKES 5 CUPS (40 FL OZ/1.25 L)

The best bones for fish stock are those from mild-tasting fish including snapper, grouper, cod, perch, sole, trout and pike. Avoid bones from stronger-flavored fish such as tuna and mackerel. If fish bones are not available or time is short and you must substitute the fish stock in recipes, use bottled clam juice or frozen or canned fish stock, sometimes called fumet.

2 lb (1 kg) fish bones
4 cups (32 fl oz/4 l) water
1 cup (8 fl oz/250 ml) dry white wine
1 small onion, peeled and chopped
1 small carrot, peeled and chopped
12 fresh parsley stems
1 teaspoon minced fresh thyme or ½
 teaspoon crumbled dried thyme
1 bay leaf

Remove the gills, fat, tail and any traces of blood from the fish bones. Carefully wash the bones.

❧ In a large pot over high heat, combine the fish bones, water, wine, onion, carrot, parsley stems, thyme and bay leaf. Bring to a boil.

❧ Reduce the heat to low and simmer, uncovered, for 40 minutes. Using a wooden spoon, crush the bones.

❧ Line a colander with cheesecloth (muslin) and strain the stock through it into a large bowl.

❧ Cool, cover and refrigerate until a layer of fat solidifies on top. Remove and discard the hardened fat.

❧ If not using immediately, store in a tightly covered container in the refrigerator for up to 3 days or in the freezer for up to 2 months.

SHELLS, SCALLOPS AND SAFFRON SALAD

SERVES 6

You can use either bay or sea scallops in this lively seafood salad; the latter, though, should be cut in halves horizontally before cooking. For the most colorful effect, use a combination of three different bell peppers.

5 qt (5 l) water
1 tablespoon salt
12 oz (375 g) dried large pasta shells
5 tablespoons (3 fl oz/80 ml)
 extra-virgin olive oil
1 lb (500 g) scallops
1 cup (5 oz/155 g) shelled fresh peas
 or frozen peas
¼ cup (2 fl oz/60 ml) Champagne
 vinegar
¼ cup (2 fl oz/60 ml) Fish Stock
2 tablespoons tomato paste
1½ teaspoons saffron threads
3 bell peppers (capsicums), roasted,
 peeled, seeded, deribbed and cut into
 ½-inch (12-mm) strips (see page 298)

In a large pot over high heat, bring the water to a boil. Add the 1 tablespoon salt and the pasta shells and cook according to the package directions or until al dente, 12–15 minutes.

❧ Drain the pasta and toss it immediately with 1 tablespoon of the olive oil. Cover and cool completely in the refrigerator, 1–24 hours.

❧ In a medium frying pan over medium-high heat, warm 1 tablespoon of the olive oil. Add the scallops in batches and sauté, turning once, until opaque throughout, about 1 minute on each side. Set aside to cool.

❧ In a medium saucepan of boiling salted water over high heat, blanch the peas for 1 minute. Drain and cool.

❧ In a large bowl, whisk together the remaining 3 tablespoons olive oil, vinegar, Fish Stock, tomato paste and saffron. Add the peppers, pasta shells and scallops. Toss to mix well.

❧ To serve, place in a serving bowl or divide among individual plates.

❧ Serve at room temperature.

Fresh shelling peas, such as the English peas shown here, are a culinary treat during their brief season. To shell fresh peas, pop open the pod using your thumb.

CREAMY SHELL SALAD WITH LOBSTER

SERVES 6

Luxurious lobster coated with rose-colored dressing makes this pasta salad an ideal choice for a special luncheon. Serve with white wine.

5 qt (5 l) plus 7 cups (56 fl oz/1.75 l)
    water
1 tablespoon salt
12 oz (375 g) dried pasta shells
2 tablespoons extra-virgin olive oil
1 live lobster, about 1½ lb (750 g)
½ cup (4 fl oz/125 ml) heavy (double)
    cream
2 tablespoons tomato paste
3 tablespoons red wine vinegar
cayenne pepper
8 red cherry tomatoes, halved
salt and freshly ground pepper
fresh parsley sprigs

In a large pot over high heat, bring
the 5 qt (5 l) water to a boil. Add the
1 tablespoon salt and the pasta shells
and cook according to the package
directions or until al dente, 12–15
minutes.

❧ Drain the pasta and toss it immediately with 1 tablespoon of the olive
oil. Cover and cool completely in the
refrigerator, 1–24 hours.

❧ In another large pot over high heat,
bring the 7 cups (56 fl oz/1.75 l) water
to a boil. Add the lobster, immersing
completely, and cook until dark red,
about 10 minutes. Using tongs, remove
the lobster from the pot and set aside
to cool. Discard the cooking liquid.

❧ When the lobster is cool, crack
the claws and remove the meat. Using
kitchen shears, cut down the inside
of the tail and remove the meat. Dice
the meat into ½-inch (12-mm) pieces.

❧ In a large bowl, whisk the cream just until it begins to thicken, about 1 minute. Add the remaining 1 table-spoon olive oil, tomato paste, vinegar and cayenne to taste. Whisk until mixed thoroughly. Add the pasta shells, lobster, tomatoes and salt and pepper to taste. Toss to mix well.

❧ To serve, place in a serving bowl or divide among individual plates and garnish with the parsley sprigs.

❧ Serve at room temperature.

SALSA VERDE SHELLS AND SHRIMP SALAD

SERVES 6

This rich pasta and seafood salad gets its bright color and enticing aroma from a mixture of fresh herbs, capers, garlic and lemon juice.

5 qt (5 l) water
1 tablespoon salt
12 oz (375 g) dried large pasta shells
6 tablespoons (3 fl oz/90 ml)
     extra-virgin olive oil
½ cup (4 fl oz/125 ml) Fish Stock
     (recipe on page 145)
1 lb (500 g) large shrimp (prawns),
     shelled and deveined (see page 299)
¾ cup (1 oz/30 g) finely chopped
     fresh parsley
⅓ cup (½ oz/15 g) finely chopped
     fresh chives
¾ teaspoon finely chopped fresh thyme
¾ teaspoon finely chopped fresh
     oregano
¼ cup (2 oz/60 g) capers, drained and
     chopped
3 garlic cloves, peeled and minced
6 tablespoons (3 fl oz/90 ml) fresh
     lemon juice
salt and freshly ground pepper
1 lemon, cut into 6 slices

In a large pot over high heat, bring the water to a boil. Add the 1 table-spoon salt and the pasta shells and cook according to the package directions or until al dente, 12–15 minutes.

❧ Drain the pasta and toss it imme-diately with 1 tablespoon of the olive oil. Cover and cool completely in the refrigerator, 1–24 hours.

❧ In a large frying pan over high heat, bring the Fish Stock to a boil. Add the shrimp, reduce the heat to low, cover and simmer for 1 minute. Stir lightly, cover again, and cook until the shrimp are pink, curled and firm to the touch, about 2 minutes.

❧ Using a slotted spoon, remove the shrimp from the pan and set aside to cool. Boil the cooking liquid over high heat to reduce it to 2 tablespoons, about 2 minutes.

❧ In a large bowl, whisk together the remaining 5 tablespoons (3 fl oz/80 ml) olive oil, parsley, chives, thyme, oregano, capers, garlic, lemon juice and reduced cooking liquid. Add the pasta shells, shrimp and salt and pepper to taste. Toss to mix well.

❧ To serve, place in a serving bowl or divide among individual plates and garnish with the lemon slices.

❧ Serve at room temperature.

Green (spring) onions, also called scallions or bunching onions, are available year-round. They are young onions, harvested before their bulb is fully formed. Eat them raw or use them in recipes whenever a mild onion taste is desired.

FUSILLI, SMOKED SALMON AND CAVIAR SALAD

SERVES 6

Depending upon the occasion and availability, use domestic sturgeon or salmon roe or, if budget permits, imported beluga, sevruga or osetra caviar. Serve accompanied with Champagne or iced vodka.

5 qt (5 l) water
1 tablespoon salt
12 oz (375 g) dried fusilli
4 tablespoons (2 fl oz/60 ml)
    extra-virgin olive oil
¼ cup (2 oz/60 g) crème fraîche
5 tablespoons (3 fl oz/80 ml)
    Champagne vinegar
½ lb (250 g) smoked salmon, cut into
    thin strips
½ cup (¾ oz/20 g) finely chopped
    fresh chives
6 green (spring) onions, green and
    white parts, thinly sliced
salt and freshly ground pepper
1 oz (30 g) caviar
8 whole fresh chives

In a large pot over high heat, bring the water to a boil. Add the 1 tablespoon salt and the fusilli and cook according to the package directions or until al dente, 12–15 minutes.

❧ Drain the fusilli and toss it immediately with 1 tablespoon of the olive oil. Cover and cool completely in the refrigerator, 1–24 hours.

❧ In a large bowl, whisk together the remaining 3 tablespoons olive oil, crème fraîche and vinegar. Add the fusilli, salmon, chives, green onions and salt and pepper to taste. Toss to mix well.

❧ To serve, place in a serving bowl and top with the caviar and whole chives.

❧ Serve at room temperature.

SHELLS SALAD WITH CLAMS, LEMON AND GARLIC

SERVES 6

Fresh lemon highlights this simple salad. It can also be made with orange juice and garnished with orange wedges.

5 qt (5 l) water
1 tablespoon salt
12 oz (375 g) dried large pasta shells
6 tablespoons (3 fl oz/90 ml)
    extra-virgin olive oil
4 lb (2 kg) clams, scrubbed well
½ cup (4 fl oz/125 ml) Fish Stock
    (recipe on page 145)
⅓ cup (3 fl oz/80 ml) fresh lemon juice
3 garlic cloves, peeled and minced
½ cup (¾ oz/20 g) finely chopped
    fresh parsley
salt and freshly ground pepper
1 lemon, cut into 6 slices

In a large pot over high heat, bring the water to a boil. Add the 1 table-spoon salt and the pasta shells and cook according to the package directions or until al dente, 12–15 minutes.

❧ Drain the pasta and toss it imme-diately with 1 tablespoon of the olive oil. Cover and cool completely in the refrigerator, 1–24 hours.

❧ Discard any clams that do not close to the touch. In a large frying pan, bring the Fish Stock to a boil. Add the clams, reduce the heat to medium, cover and cook, shaking the pan periodically, until the clams open, 3–5 minutes. Using a slotted spoon, lift out the clams and set aside to cool. Discard any unopened clams. Boil the cooking liquid over high heat to reduce it to 2 tablespoons, 3–4 minutes. Remove from the heat.

❧ In a large bowl, whisk together the remaining 5 tablespoons (3 fl oz/80 ml) olive oil, lemon juice, garlic and reduced cooking liquid. Add the pasta shells, clams, parsley and salt and pepper to taste. Toss to mix well.

❧ To serve, place in a serving bowl or divide among individual plates and garnish with the lemon slices.

❧ Serve at room temperature.

FUSILLI AND SQUID SALAD WITH FENNEL

SERVES 6

Light and bright, this seafood salad makes an entree for six or appetizer for more. If you wish, substitute orange juice for the lemon juice.

5 qt (5 l) water
1 tablespoon salt
12 oz (375 g) dried fusilli
6 tablespoons (3 fl oz/90 ml) extra-virgin olive oil
1 lb (500 g) squid
½ cup (4 fl oz/125 ml) Fish Stock (recipe on page 145)
5 tablespoons (3 fl oz/80 ml) fresh lemon juice
2 garlic cloves, peeled and minced
1 large fennel bulb, cut lengthwise into paper-thin slices
2 celery stalks, cut diagonally into pieces ½-inch (12-mm) thick
salt and freshly ground pepper
¼ cup (½ oz/10 g) finely chopped fresh fennel leaves

In a large pot over high heat, bring the water to a boil. Add the 1 tablespoon salt and the fusilli and cook according to the package directions or until al dente, 10–12 minutes.

❧ Drain the fusilli and toss it immediately with 1 tablespoon of the olive oil. Cover and cool completely in the refrigerator, 1–24 hours.

❧ To clean the squid, separate the head from the body by tugging gently. Pull any remaining insides and the transparent quill bone from the body and discard. Remove the tentacles by cutting just below the eyes of the head. Remove and discard the beak by turning the head inside out and pressing the center. Remove and discard the skin from the body by scraping the body with a knife. Cut the body into ½-inch (12-mm) rings, place in a colander, add the tentacles and rinse with water.

❧ In a medium frying pan over medium-high heat, bring the Fish Stock to a boil.

❧ Add the squid, cover and cook until it turns opaque, about 30 seconds. Using a slotted spoon, remove the squid from the pan and set aside to cool. Boil the cooking liquid, uncovered, over high heat to reduce to 2 tablespoons, 2–3 minutes. Remove from the heat.

❧ In a large bowl, whisk together the remaining 5 tablespoons (3 fl oz/80 ml) olive oil, lemon juice and garlic. Add the fusilli, squid, fennel bulb slices, celery and salt and pepper to taste. Toss to mix well.

❧ To serve, place in a serving bowl and garnish with the fennel leaves.

❧ Serve at room temperature.

RIGATONI AND MUSSELS SALAD

SERVES 6

The flavors of mussels, thyme and cream marry well in this pasta salad inspired by foods popular in the south of France. In place of the lemon juice, you might wish to try adding the anise-flavored spirit known as Pernod, a classic flavoring for the sweet, succulent shellfish. Provide extra bowls for the shells and extra napkins for the guests, who will be shelling the mussels at table. For a truly spectacular presentation, look for fresh green-lipped mussels.

5 qt (5 l) water

1 tablespoon salt

12 oz (375 g) dried rigatoni

4 tablespoons (2 fl oz/60 ml)
    extra-virgin olive oil

½ cup (4 fl oz/125 ml) Fish Stock
    (recipe on page 145)

12 fresh thyme sprigs

6 shallots, peeled and minced

2 lb (1 kg) mussels, debearded and
    scrubbed well

¼ cup (2 fl oz/60 ml) heavy (double)
    cream

¼ cup (2 fl oz/60 ml) fresh lemon
    juice

2 teaspoons finely chopped fresh
    thyme

salt and freshly ground pepper

1 lemon, cut into 6 wedges

In a large pot over high heat, bring the water to a boil. Add the 1 tablespoon salt and the rigatoni and cook according to the package directions or until al dente, 12–15 minutes.

❧ Drain the rigatoni and toss it immediately with 1 tablespoon of the olive oil. Cover and cool completely in the refrigerator, 1–24 hours.

❧ In a large frying pan over high heat, bring the Fish Stock, 6 of the thyme sprigs and the shallots to a boil. Discard any mussels that do not close to the touch. Add the mussels, reduce the heat to medium, cover and cook, shaking the pan periodically, until the mussels open, 2–4 minutes.

❧ Using a slotted spoon, lift out the mussels and set aside to cool. Discard any unopened mussels. Boil the cooking liquid over high heat to reduce it to 2 tablespoons, 3–4 minutes. Remove from the heat. Remove and discard the thyme sprigs.

❧ In a large bowl, whisk together the remaining 3 tablespoons olive oil, cream, lemon juice, reduced cooking liquid, chopped thyme and salt and pepper to taste. Add the rigatoni and mussels. Toss to mix well.

❧ To serve, place in a serving bowl and garnish with the remaining thyme sprigs and lemon wedges.

❧ Serve at room temperature.

An appetizing array of fresh raw vegetables strikes a great balance with a rich pasta entree. Serve cucumbers, carrots, celery and green (spring) onions in a festive manner by placing them upright in flower vases as your table's centerpiece.

SCALLOP AND CHEESE TORTELLINI SALAD

SERVES 6

Use either bay or larger sea scallops, cutting the latter in half horizontally.

5 qt (5 l) water
1 tablespoon salt
12 oz (375 g) cheese tortellini
5 tablespoons (3 fl oz/80 ml)
    extra-virgin olive oil
1 lb (500 g) scallops
3 tablespoons red wine vinegar
½ cup (3½ oz/105 g) green olives,
    pitted and coarsely chopped
½ cup (3½ oz/105 g) black olives,
    pitted and coarsely chopped
2 tablespoons finely chopped fresh
    parsley
salt and freshly ground pepper

In a large pot over high heat, bring the water to a boil. Add the 1 tablespoon salt and the tortellini and cook according to the package directions or until al dente, 10–12 minutes for dried, 4–5 minutes for fresh.

❧ Drain the tortellini and toss them immediately with 1 tablespoon of the olive oil. Cover and cool completely in the refrigerator, 1–24 hours.

❧ In a medium frying pan over medium-high heat, heat 1 tablespoon of the olive oil. Add the scallops and sauté, turning once, until opaque throughout when pierced with a knife, about 1 minute on each side. Set aside to cool.

❧ In a large bowl, whisk together the remaining 3 tablespoons olive oil and vinegar. Add the tortellini, scallops, green and black olives, parsley and salt and pepper to taste. Toss to mix well.

❧ To serve, divide among plates.

❧ Serve at room temperature.

AVOCADO, SHELLS AND SHRIMP SALAD

SERVES 6

Avocado halves filled with shrimp are a favorite seafood appetizer. Here, the concept becomes a salad by tossing seafood and pasta shells with a rich avocado purée. For the best flavor, seek out the dark-skinned Hass variety of avocado.

5 qt (5 l) water
1 tablespoon salt
12 oz (375 g) dried pasta shells
3 tablespoons extra-virgin olive oil
½ cup (4 fl oz/125 ml) Fish Stock
    (recipe on page 145)
1 lb (500 g) large shrimp (prawns),
    peeled and deveined (see page 299)
1 avocado, halved, peeled and seeded
cayenne pepper
3 tablespoons white wine vinegar
¼ cup (2 fl oz/60 ml) heavy (double)
    cream
5 green (spring) onions, green and
    white parts, thinly sliced
salt and freshly ground pepper

In a large pot over high heat, bring the water to a boil. Add the 1 tablespoon salt and the pasta shells and cook according to the package directions or until al dente, 12–15 minutes.

❧ Drain the pasta and toss it immediately with 1 tablespoon of the olive oil. Cover and cool completely in the refrigerator, 1–24 hours.

❧ In a medium frying pan over high heat, bring the Fish Stock to a boil. Add the shrimp, reduce the heat to low, cover and simmer for 1 minute. Stir lightly, re-cover and cook until the shrimp are pink, curled and firm to the touch, about 2 minutes.

❧ Using a slotted spoon, remove the shrimp and set aside to cool. Boil the cooking liquid over high heat to reduce it to 2 tablespoons, 1–2 minutes.

❧ In the work bowl of a food processor with the metal blade or a blender, combine the avocado, cayenne to taste, reduced cooking liquid and vinegar and purée until smooth. With the motor running, add the remaining 2 tablespoons olive oil in a steady stream until it has been completely incorporated. Add the cream and pulse a few times to mix well.

❧ In a large bowl, combine the avocado mixture, fusilli, shrimp, green onions and salt and pepper to taste. Toss to mix well.

❧ To serve, divide among plates.

❧ Serve at room temperature.

Meat Salads

Add meat—whether beef, lamb chicken or pork—to any salad and you instantly transform it from first course to entree. Include pasta in that salad combination and it becomes a complete, balanced meal, with its fair share of vitamins, proteins and complex carbohydrates.

Maybe that's why meat and pasta salads have become so popular for both lunch and dinner meals. Or perhaps the answer lies in the simple, robust satisfaction offered by such recipes as those that follow.

As demonstrated here, a recipe doesn't even need much meat to gain that advantage, making them a logical choice for a healthful diet. Not that all pasta salads featuring meat tend toward heartiness. You'll find that those featuring chicken and ham are exceptionally light on palate and stomach alike.

PEAS AND HAM PASTA SALAD

SERVES 6

Rich, colorful and with a distinctive edge of smoky sweetness, this salad is a traditional outdoor dining favorite, and makes a great addition to any summertime buffet. If you find whole, edible sugar snap peas in the market, by all means include some of them in the salad as shown in the photograph at right. If fresh peas are not in season, substitute a good-quality brand of frozen petite peas, which will work exceptionally well. For a variation on the recipe, thin slices of a sweet-tasting smoke-cured sausage such as turkey kielbasa, smoked turkey or chicken may replace the ham. A sprinkling of diced raw or roasted and peeled red bell pepper (capsicum) will add its own delightful texture and sweet flavor to the combination.

5 qt (5 l) water
1 tablespoon salt
12 oz (375 g) dried large elbow pasta
4 tablespoons (2 fl oz/60 ml) extra-virgin olive oil
1 cup (5 oz/155 g) fresh shelled peas or frozen peas
¼ cup (2 fl oz/60 ml) heavy (double) cream
3 tablespoons red wine vinegar
½ cup (2 oz/60 g) finely grated Parmesan cheese
6 oz (185 g) smoked ham (Virginia, Smithfield, Black Forest or Westphalian), cut into thin strips
salt and freshly ground pepper
fresh parsley sprigs

In a large pot over high heat, bring the water to a boil. Add the 1 tablespoon salt and the elbow pasta and cook according to the package directions or until al dente, 7–10 minutes.

✣ Drain the pasta and toss it immediately with 1 tablespoon of the olive oil. Cover and cool completely in the refrigerator, 1–24 hours.

✣ In a medium saucepan of boiling salted water over high heat, blanch the peas for 1 minute. Drain immediately and set aside to cool.

✣ In a large bowl, whisk together the remaining 3 tablespoons olive oil, cream, vinegar and Parmesan cheese. Add the elbow pasta, peas, ham and salt and pepper to taste. Toss to mix well.

✣ To serve, place in a serving bowl or divide among individual plates and garnish with the parsley sprigs.

✣ Serve at room temperature.

Prosciutto, Penne and Squash Salad

Serves 6

This colorful combination presents a rich array of satisfying tastes and textures. Other varieties of squash, such as pumpkin, hubbard or turban, may be substituted for the butternut; and crisply cooked bacon or Italian pancetta may replace the prosciutto. If you like, substitute finely shredded orange zest for the grated zest called for in the recipe.

5 qt (5 l) water
1 tablespoon salt
12 oz (375 g) dried penne
7 tablespoons (4 fl oz/100 ml) extra-virgin olive oil
1½ lb (750 g) butternut squash, peeled, seeded and cut into ½-inch (12-mm) cubes
⅓ cup (3 fl oz/80 ml) fresh orange juice
3 tablespoons balsamic vinegar
2 tablespoons red wine vinegar
1 teaspoon grated orange zest
¼ teaspoon freshly grated nutmeg
4 oz (125 g) thinly sliced prosciutto, cut into thin strips
¼ cup (1 oz/30 g) grated Parmesan cheese
salt and freshly ground pepper

Preheat an oven to 400°F (200°C).

❧ In a large pot over high heat, bring the water to a boil. Add the 1 tablespoon salt and the penne and cook according to the package directions or until al dente, 10–12 minutes.

❧ Drain the penne and toss it immediately with 1 tablespoon of the olive oil. Cover and cool completely in the refrigerator, 1–24 hours.

❧ Coat the squash cubes with 2 tablespoons of the olive oil. Spread them in a single layer on a baking sheet. Bake, turning occasionally, until golden, about 20 minutes. Set aside to cool.

ॐ In a large bowl, whisk together the remaining 4 tablespoons (2 fl oz/60 ml) olive oil, orange juice, balsamic vinegar, red wine vinegar, orange zest and nutmeg. Add the penne, squash, prosciutto, Parmesan cheese and salt and pepper to taste. Toss to mix well.

ॐ To serve, divide among plates.

ॐ Serve at room temperature.

WARM LINGUINE SALAD WITH BACON AND GOAT CHEESE

SERVES 6

The simple, vivid colors of this salad make a beautiful presentation for a special repast. If you like, the bacon may be omitted to make a vegetarian version of the salad; in that case, consider garnishing each portion with a scattering of toasted pine nuts, to lend it another earthy flavor and a hint of crunchy texture. Breaking the linguine pieces before cooking makes it easier to eat them; but they may also be left long, as shown here, for a more dramatic effect.

5 qt (5 l) water
1 tablespoon salt
12 oz (375 g) dried linguine, broken into 3-inch (7.5-cm) pieces
6 tablespoons (3 fl oz/90 ml) extra-virgin olive oil
3 oz (90 g) bacon, cut into 1-inch (2.5-cm) squares
2 garlic cloves, peeled and minced
3 tablespoons balsamic vinegar
2 cups (2 oz/60 g) packed arugula
salt and freshly ground pepper
1 cup (4 oz/125 g) fine dried bread crumbs
12 oz (375 g) fresh goat cheese, cut into 6 pieces

Preheat an oven to 400°F (200°C).

ॐ In a large pot over high heat, bring the water to a boil. Add the 1 tablespoon salt and the linguine and cook according to the package directions or until al dente, 5–8 minutes.

ॐ Drain the linguine and toss it immediately with 1 tablespoon of the olive oil.

ॐ In a large frying pan over medium heat, fry the bacon, uncovered, stirring occasionally, until golden and crisp, about 5 minutes. Reduce the heat to low, add the garlic and continue to cook uncovered for 1 minute. Add 3 table-

spoons of the olive oil, vinegar, linguine, arugula and salt and pepper to taste. Warm over low heat until the pasta is heated through, about 1 minute.

ॐ Place the bread crumbs in a shallow bowl. Coat the goat cheese pieces with the remaining 2 tablespoons olive oil and then roll them in the bread crumbs. Place on a baking sheet. Bake until warm and slightly bubbling around the edges, about 4 minutes.

ॐ To serve, place the pasta mixture in a serving bowl or divide among individual plates. Top with the goat cheese.

ॐ Serve warm.

ORECCHIETTE AND SALAMI SALAD

SERVES 6

Zesty, cool and colorful, this pasta salad is an ideal entree for a hot summer evening. Try other medium-sized pasta shapes such as farfalle or elbows instead of the orecchiette, if you like.

5 qt (5 l) water
1 tablespoon salt
12 oz (375 g) dried orecchiette
6 tablespoons (3 fl oz/90 ml) extra-virgin olive oil
1 cup (6 oz/185 g) fresh or frozen corn kernels (about 2 ears of corn)
3 tablespoons red wine vinegar
2 garlic cloves, peeled and minced
3 anchovy fillets in olive oil, drained and mashed
3 tablespoons capers, drained
5 oz (155 g) salami, thinly sliced and cut into thin strips
1 each red, yellow and green bell pepper (capsicum), seeded, deribbed and diced (see page 298)
1 small red (Spanish) onion, peeled and diced
salt and freshly ground pepper

In a large pot over high heat, bring the water to a boil. Add the 1 table-spoon salt and the orecchiette and cook according to the package directions or until al dente, 12–15 minutes.

❧ Drain the orecchiette and toss it immediately with 1 tablespoon of the olive oil. Cover and cool completely in the refrigerator, 1–24 hours.

❧ In a medium saucepan of boiling salted water over high heat, blanch the corn for 1 minute. Drain immediately and set aside to cool.

❧ In a large bowl, whisk together the remaining 5 tablespoons (3 fl oz/80 ml) olive oil, vinegar, garlic, anchovies and capers. Add the orecchiette, corn, salami, peppers, red onion and salt and pepper to taste. Toss to mix well.

❧ To serve, place in a serving bowl or divide among individual plates.

❧ Serve at room temperature.

MINTED FUSILLI AND LAMB SALAD

SERVES 6

The lamb and eggplant (aubergine) may be grilled and combined with the pasta up to 8 hours ahead. Add the dressing at the last minute so it stays bright green.

5 qt (5 l) water
1 tablespoon salt
12 oz (375 g) dried fusilli
7 tablespoons (4 fl oz/100 ml) extra-virgin olive oil
3 slender (Asian) eggplants (aubergines), halved lengthwise
1½ lb (750 g) boneless leg of lamb, butterflied and trimmed of fat
3 tablespoons red wine vinegar
2 garlic cloves, peeled and minced
¼ cup (⅓ oz/10 g) finely chopped fresh mint
4 plum (Roma) tomatoes, sliced
salt and freshly ground pepper
fresh mint sprigs

Prepare a fire in an outdoor charcoal grill or preheat a broiler (griller).

❧ In a large pot over high heat, bring the water to a boil. Add the 1 table-spoon salt and the fusilli and cook according to the package directions or until al dente, 10–12 minutes.

❧ Drain the fusilli and toss it imme-diately with 1 tablespoon of the olive oil. Cover and cool completely in the refrigerator, 1–24 hours.

❧ Brush the lamb with 1 tablespoon of the olive oil. Grill the lamb over a medium-hot fire or broil (grill), turning once, 8–10 minutes on each side. Test by cutting a small slit in the thickest part. The meat should be slightly pink on the inside and well browned on the outside. Place on a work surface and cut the meat across the grain into thin strips.

❧ Brush the eggplant with 2 table-spoons of the olive oil. Grill or broil, turning once, until golden, 3–5 minutes on each side. Cool and cut into slices.

❧ In a large bowl, whisk together the remaining 3 tablespoons olive oil, vinegar, garlic and mint. Add the fusilli, lamb, eggplant, tomatoes and salt and pepper to taste. Toss to mix well.

❧ To serve, place in a serving bowl or divide among individual plates and garnish with the mint sprigs.

❧ Serve at room temperature.

Because pasta salads are popular with most people, generally contain inexpensive ingredients and usually can be made hours in advance, they are mainstays of the party buffet. Make your meal a success by serving salads featuring small to medium pasta shapes, which are easier to eat than noodles, and arranging your table with sturdy plates. Have a plentiful assortment of beverages and lots of crusty bread on hand, to go with your hearty pasta meal. To further convey a sense of abundance, use large bowls of fresh fruit as your centerpiece.

HERBED FARFALLE AND BEEF SALAD

SERVES 6

The combination of fresh herbs and lemon juice makes this salad featuring beef steak a particularly refreshing starter or entree. It will serve 6 as a first course, followed by a light entree such as a vegetable soup, hearty bread and a cheese and fresh fruit plate. As a main course, serve it for 4 with a side dish of steamed mixed vegetables. Other medium-sized pasta shapes may be used in place of the farfalle. Great served warm or cold, easily made ahead and effort-free to double, this recipe is an excellent candidate for a party buffet.

5 qt (5 l) water

1 tablespoon salt

12 oz (375 g) dried farfalle

7 tablespoons (4 fl oz/100 ml)
    extra-virgin olive oil

12 oz (375 g) New York strip, sirloin
    or filet mignon beef steak

salt and freshly ground pepper

5 tablespoons (3 fl oz/80 ml) fresh
    lemon juice

3 garlic cloves, peeled and minced

1 teaspoon ground cumin

¼ cup (⅓ oz/10 g) packed fresh
    flat-leaf (Italian) parsley leaves

1 cup (1 oz/30 g) packed cilantro
    (fresh coriander) sprigs

½ cup (½ oz/15 g) packed fresh basil
    leaves, torn

¼ cup (⅓ oz/10 g) packed fresh mint
    leaves

1 cup (1 oz/30 g) packed arugula

In a large pot over high heat, bring the water to a boil. Add the 1 tablespoon salt and the farfalle and cook according to the package directions or until al dente, 10–12 minutes.

❧ Drain the farfalle and toss it immediately with 1 tablespoon of the olive oil. Cover and cool completely in the refrigerator, 1–24 hours.

❧ In a medium frying pan over medium heat, heat 1 tablespoon of the olive oil. Add the steak and cook until browned on one side, 4 minutes. Turn over the steak, add salt and pepper to taste and continue to cook to the desired doneness or until there is resistance to the touch, 5–6 minutes longer. Place on a work surface and cut into slices.

❧ In a large bowl, whisk together the remaining 5 tablespoons (3 fl oz/80 ml) olive oil, lemon juice, garlic and cumin. Add the farfalle, steak slices, parsley, cilantro, basil, mint and arugula. Toss to mix well.

❧ To serve, place in a serving bowls.

❧ Serve at room temperature.

FUSILLI AND MORTADELLA SALAD

SERVES 6

Use other medium-sized pasta shapes in place of the fusilli and substitute such cured meats as salami, prosciutto, coppacola or smoked turkey or chicken for the mortadella, if desired.

5 qt (5 l) water
1 tablespoon salt
12 oz (375 g) dried fusilli
4 tablespoons (2 fl oz/60 ml)
　　extra-virgin olive oil
¼ cup (2 fl oz/60 ml) heavy (double)
　　cream
¼ cup (2 fl oz/60 ml) fresh lemon juice
3 garlic cloves, peeled and minced
6 oz (185 g) thinly sliced mortadella,
　　cut into thin strips
1 cup (1 oz/30 g) packed fresh flat-leaf
　　(Italian) parsley leaves
½ cup (2 oz/60 g) grated Parmesan
　　cheese
salt and freshly ground pepper

In a large pot over high heat, bring the water to a boil. Add the 1 tablespoon salt and the fusilli and cook according to the package directions or until al dente, 10–12 minutes.

❧ Drain the fusilli and toss it immediately with 1 tablespoon of the olive oil. Cover and cool completely in the refrigerator, 1–24 hours.

❧ In a large bowl, whisk together the remaining 3 tablespoons olive oil, cream, lemon juice and garlic. Add the fusilli, mortadella, parsley, Parmesan cheese and salt and pepper to taste. Toss to mix well.

❧ To serve, place in a serving dish or divide among individual plates.

❧ Serve at room temperature.

To prepare a pasta recipe as the Italians do, grate hard cheeses such as Parmesan or Asiago fresh as you use them in a recipe. To present a pasta meal in true Italian style, place a block of the cheese on the dining table for guests to grate themselves.

Spicy Penne and Hot Pepper Chicken Salad

SERVES 6

In Italy, this salad is known as pollo forte, *"strong chicken"—a reference to the powerful, pleasing aroma and taste resulting from its combination of balsamic vinegar, garlic, red onion and hot chili pepper.*

5 qt (5 l) water

1 tablespoon salt

12 oz (375 g) dried penne

7 tablespoons (4 fl oz/100 ml) extra-virgin olive oil

1 lb (500 g) skinned and boned chicken breast meat (about 1 large whole breast)

salt and freshly ground pepper

3 tablespoons red wine vinegar

3 tablespoons balsamic vinegar

2 garlic cloves, peeled and minced

½ each red, yellow and green bell pepper (capsicum), seeded, deribbed and thinly sliced (see page 298)

1 large jalapeño pepper, seeded and minced

½ small red (Spanish) onion, peeled and thinly sliced

24 fresh large basil leaves

12 red cherry tomatoes

In a large pot over high heat, bring the water to a boil. Add the 1 tablespoon salt and the penne and cook according to the package directions or until al dente, 10–12 minutes.

❧ Drain the penne and toss it immediately with 1 tablespoon of the olive oil. Cover and cool completely in the refrigerator, 1–24 hours.

❧ In a medium frying pan over medium heat, heat 1 tablespoon of the olive oil. Add the chicken and cook until golden on one side, about 4 minutes. Turn over the chicken, salt and pepper to taste and continue to cook until opaque throughout when pierced with a knife, 6–8 minutes longer.

❧ Place on a cutting surface and cut the chicken on the diagonal into thin strips. Set aside to cool.

❧ In a large bowl, whisk together the remaining 5 tablespoons (3 fl oz/80 ml) olive oil, the red wine vinegar, balsamic vinegar and garlic. Add the penne, chicken, peppers, jalapeño and red onion. Toss to mix well.

❧ To serve, place in a bowl. Garnish with the basil and cherry tomatoes.

❧ Serve at room temperature.

CHICKEN AND MUSHROOM FUSILLI SALAD WITH HERBS

SERVES 6

Fresh herbs enliven the simple dressing for this springtime salad. Use other medium-sized pasta shapes instead of the fusilli, if you like. For added flavor, use an herb-flavored oil rather than plain olive oil in the dressing.

5 qt (5 l) water
1 tablespoon salt
12 oz (375 g) dried fusilli
7 tablespoons (4 fl oz/100 ml) extra-virgin olive oil
1 large whole chicken breast, skinned and boned (about 1 lb/500 g meat)
salt and freshly ground pepper
1 cup (8 fl oz/250 ml) Chicken Stock (recipe on page 30)
3 tablespoons red wine vinegar
1½ tablespoons balsamic vinegar
1 tablespoon finely chopped fresh sage
1½ teaspoons finely chopped fresh thyme
½ teaspoon finely chopped fresh rosemary
8 oz (250 g) fresh mushrooms, thinly sliced

In a large pot over high heat, bring the water to a boil. Add the 1 tablespoon salt and the fusilli and cook according to the package directions or until al dente, 10–12 minutes.

❧ Drain the fusilli and toss it immediately with 1 tablespoon of the olive oil. Cover and cool completely in the refrigerator, 1–24 hours.

❧ In a medium frying pan over medium heat, warm 1 tablespoon of the olive oil. Add the chicken and cook until golden on one side, about 4 minutes. Turn over the chicken, add salt and pepper to taste and continue to cook until opaque throughout when pierced with a knife, 6–8 minutes longer. Add the Chicken Stock and stir over high heat, scraping the bottom of the pan to loosen the cooked bits, and boil to reduce the liquid to about ¼ cup (2 fl oz/60 ml), about 5 minutes.

❧ Using a slotted spoon, remove the chicken, reserving the cooking liquid. Place the chicken on a work surface and cut on the diagonal into thin strips. Set aside to cool.

❧ In a large bowl, whisk together the remaining 5 tablespoons (3 fl oz/80 ml) olive oil, the red wine vinegar, balsamic vinegar, sage, thyme, rosemary and ¼ cup (2 fl oz/60 ml) of the reduced cooking liquid. Add the fusilli and mushrooms. Toss to mix well.

❧ To serve, place in a serving bowl or divide among individual plates and top with the chicken strips.

❧ Serve at room temperature.

*Focaccia is probably Italy's oldest bread.
A flat-bread and most likely the foundation of
the original pizza, focaccia is traditionally cooked
on a stone slab in a wood-fired oven. Today, plain
and flavored versions are available from bakeries,
delicatessens and most major food markets.
Serve it as a snack or pair it with soups,
salads, pasta or risotto dishes.*

GARLIC LOVER'S PENNE AND CHICKEN SALAD

SERVES 6

*If you're a devotee of garlic, this salad is a
real treat. Cooked for almost 30 minutes,
the garlic here loses its strong, assertive
flavor and develops a sweet, nutty taste
that perfectly complements the chicken and
pasta and herbs.*

5 qt (5 l) water
1 tablespoon salt
12 oz (375 g) dried penne
7 tablespoons (4 fl oz/100 ml)
    extra-virgin olive oil
1 lb (500 g) skinned and boned
    chicken breast meat (about 1 large
    whole breast)
salt and freshly ground pepper
24 garlic cloves, peeled
2½ cups (20 fl oz/625 ml) Chicken
    Stock (recipe on page 30)
3 tablespoons red wine vinegar
2 teaspoons finely chopped fresh
    rosemary
2 tablespoons finely chopped fresh
    parsley
fresh rosemary sprigs

In a large pot over high heat, bring the
water to a boil. Add the 1 tablespoon
salt and the penne and cook according
to the package directions or until al
dente, 10–12 minutes.

❧ Drain the penne and toss it immediately with 1 tablespoon of the olive
oil. Cover and cool completely in the
refrigerator, 1–24 hours.

❧ In a medium frying pan over medium heat, warm 1 tablespoon of the
olive oil. Add the chicken and cook
until browned on one side, about 4
minutes. Turn over the chicken, season
with salt and pepper to taste and continue to cook until opaque throughout
when pierced with a knife, 6–8 minutes
longer.

❧ Using a spatula, remove the chicken,
reserving the frying pan. Place the
chicken on a work surface and cut on
the diagonal into thin strips. Let cool.

❧ To the reserved frying pan over
medium heat, add the garlic and cook,
uncovered, stirring occasionally, until
golden brown, 3–4 minutes. Add the
Chicken Stock and continue to cook
until the stock has reduced to 2 tablespoons and the garlic is soft, 20–25
minutes. Using a slotted spoon, remove
the garlic from the pan and cool, reserving the reduced cooking liquid.

❧ In a large bowl, whisk together the
remaining 5 tablespoons (3 fl oz/80 ml)
olive oil, reduced cooking liquid,
vinegar, chopped rosemary and parsley.
Add the penne, chicken and garlic
cloves. Toss to mix well.

❧ To serve, place in a serving bowl and
garnish with the rosemary sprigs.

❧ Serve at room temperature.

Sauced Entrees

It's the way almost all of us first learned to love dried pasta: boiled until al dente, and then simply tossed with a flavorful sauce made quickly on the stovetop. Whatever ingredients that sauce featured is really beside the point; the pasta made its impression, and we kept coming back for more.

You'll encounter outstanding examples of all such sauces on the pages that follow. There are old Italian favorites, including carbonara (recipe on page 192) and Bolognese Sauce (recipe on page 195); new recipes of utter simplicity, featuring just olive oil, herbs and vegetables and pasta extravaganzas that show off poultry and seafood along with the sauce. Love meatballs? They're here, in all their traditional glory (recipe on page 196).

Along with their use of dried pasta, all of these dishes have in common an ease in preparation that belies their delicious results. Each has the uncanny ability to make you fall in love with pasta all over again.

BUCATINI TOPPED WITH GARLICKY SHRIMP

SERVES 6

Try substituting fresh scallops or bite-sized chunks of swordfish fillet for the shrimp in this flavorful main dish. Exchange the parsley with cilantro (fresh coriander) or arugula for a different flavor. Bucatini are long, thin tubes of pasta similar in appearance to spaghetti, which may be substituted. You can also use other dried strands such as linguine. Serve the pasta with crusty bread for soaking up any garlicky sauce left on the plate.

1 lb (500 g) shrimp (prawns), peeled and deveined (see page 299)
6 tablespoons (3 oz/90 g) unsalted butter
2 tablespoons minced shallots
1 tablespoon minced garlic
1 cup (8 fl oz/250 ml) dry white wine
¼ cup (2 fl oz/60 ml) fresh lemon juice
2 tablespoons minced fresh flat-leaf (Italian) parsley
salt and freshly ground pepper
6 qt (6 l) water
1 tablespoon salt
1 lb (500 g) dried bucatini
salt and freshly ground pepper
fresh flat-leaf (Italian) parsley sprigs
1 lemon, cut into 6 wedges

In a medium pot of boiling water, cook the shrimp, stirring once, until the shrimp turn pink and curl, about 4 minutes. Drain and set aside to cool.

In a large frying pan over medium heat, melt 2 tablespoons of the butter until foamy. Add the shallots and garlic, reduce the heat to low and sauté, stirring frequently, for 2 minutes. Add the wine and lemon juice. Increase the heat to medium and simmer until the liquid is reduced by half, about 10 minutes. Add the minced parsley. Stir to mix well.

Reduce the heat to low. Add the remaining 4 tablespoons (2 oz/60 g) butter, 1 tablespoon at a time, stirring, until all of the butter has melted. Add the shrimp and salt and pepper to taste. Stir to mix well. Keep warm.

In a large pot over high heat, bring the water to a boil. Add the 1 tablespoon salt and the bucatini and cook according to the package directions or until al dente, about 12 minutes. Drain.

In a large warmed bowl, combine the bucatini and shrimp mixture. Toss to mix well.

To serve, divide among individual warmed plates. Garnish with a parsley sprig and lemon wedge.

Serve hot.

SARDINES AND CELERY OVER LINGUINE

SERVES 6

If fresh sardines are available, sauté them in a frying pan and use them in place of the canned sardines. Other noodles or strands can be substituted for the linguine.

3 tablespoons Clarified Butter
   (recipe on page 45)
1 lb (500 g) celery (about 8 stalks),
   cut into thin diagonal slices
3 tablespoons fresh lemon juice
salt and freshly ground pepper
6 qt (6 l) water
1 tablespoon salt
1 lb (500 g) dried linguine
3 tablespoons extra-virgin olive oil
2 tablespoons grated lemon zest
   (see page 295)
36 canned brisling sardines, drained
1½ cups (6 oz/185 g) freshly grated
   Parmesan cheese

Make the Clarified Butter.

❧ In a medium saucepan over medium heat, combine the Clarified Butter and celery and sauté, stirring frequently, until just tender, 6–7 minutes. Add the lemon juice and salt and pepper to taste. Stir to mix well. Keep warm.

❧ In a large pot over high heat, bring the water to a boil. Add the 1 tablespoon salt and the linguine and cook according to the package directions or until al dente, about 9 minutes. Drain well and toss it immediately with the olive oil.

❧ In a large warmed bowl, combine the linguine, celery mixture and lemon zest. Toss to mix well.

❧ To serve, divide the linguine mixture among individual warmed plates. Top with the sardines and Parmesan cheese.

❧ Serve hot.

PENNE WITH SHRIMP AND PEPPERS

SERVES 6

Fresh shrimp (prawns) and multicolored bell peppers (capsicums) are a familiar combination; what surprises here is the addition of fresh ginger. Often used in the cuisines of Asia, Chinese cooks were using ginger as far back as the sixth century B.C. Ginger has a long tradition elsewhere, too. It was brought to the Mediterranean about 1 A.D. and into Europe by the Crusaders. It lends a piquant flavor to sweet and savory recipes. The fresh root is more mild than the candied version.

6 tablespoons (3 oz/90 g) Ginger
 Butter (recipe on page 294)
 at room temperature
2 red bell peppers (capsicums)
2 golden or orange bell peppers
 (capsicums)
1 green bell pepper (capsicum)
1¼ lb (625 g) shrimp (prawns), peeled
 and deveined (see page 299)
salt
cayenne pepper
6 qt (6 l) water
1 tablespoon salt
1 lb (500 g) dried penne

Make the Ginger Butter.

❧ Halve, seed and derib the red, golden or orange and green peppers (see page 298). Cut each half into lengthwise strips ¼ inch (6 mm) wide. In a medium frying pan over medium heat, melt half of the Ginger Butter. Reduce the heat to low, add the peppers and sauté, stirring frequently, until tender, about 10 minutes.

❧ Increase the heat to medium and add the shrimp. Cook, stirring occasionally, until the shrimp turn pink and curl, about 4 minutes. Add salt and cayenne to taste. Stir to mix well. Remove from the heat and keep warm.

❧ In a large pot over high heat, bring the water to a boil. Add the 1 tablespoon salt and the penne and cook according to the package directions or until al dente, about 11 minutes.

❧ Drain and toss it immediately with the remaining Ginger Butter.

❧ To serve, in a warmed serving bowl, combine the penne and shrimp mixture and toss to mix well.

❧ Serve hot.

*Old Tray licked all the
oysters up,
Puss never stood at crimps,
But munched the cod,
and little Kit
Quite feasted on the shrimps.*

—THOMAS HOOD

RIGATONI WITH ARTICHOKES AND ANCHOVIES

SERVES 6

This sauce can be made up to 3 days in advance and refrigerated until ready to use.

2 tablespoons unsalted butter
¼ cup (2 fl oz/60 ml) extra-virgin olive oil
2 cups (10 oz/315 g) chopped yellow onions
2 teaspoons minced garlic
3 anchovy fillets packed in oil, drained and diced
1 cup (8 fl oz/250 ml) dry white wine
1½ lb (750 g) plum (Roma) tomatoes, peeled, seeded and diced (see page 299) or canned tomatoes
28 oz (880 g) frozen artichoke hearts, thawed and cut into quarters
salt and freshly ground pepper
6 qt (6 l) water
1 tablespoon salt
1 lb (500 g) dried rigatoni
¾ cup (3 oz/90 g) freshly grated Parmesan cheese

In a heavy, medium frying pan over medium heat, melt the butter and olive oil. Reduce the heat to medium-low, add the onions and sauté, stirring frequently, until the onions are translucent, about 8 minutes.

❧ Add the garlic and anchovies and sauté for 2 minutes. Add the wine, increase the heat to medium-high and simmer until the wine is reduced by half, about 5 minutes.

❧ Stir in the tomatoes, reduce the heat and simmer for 5 minutes. Add the artichoke hearts and salt and pepper to taste. Stir to mix well. Keep warm.

❧ In a large pot over high heat, bring the water to a boil. Add the 1 tablespoon salt and the rigatoni and cook according to the package directions or until al dente, 11–12 minutes. Drain.

❧ To serve, divide the rigatoni among individual bowls. Top with the anchovy mixture and Parmesan cheese.

❧ Serve hot.

PASTA WITH TUNA SAUCE

SERVES 6

If casareccia are not available, any medium-sized dried pasta shape or noodle will work with this traditional sauce.

⅓ cup (3 fl oz/80 ml) extra-virgin olive oil
4 garlic cloves, peeled and minced
4 anchovy fillets packed in olive oil, drained
¼ cup (⅓ oz/10 g) minced fresh flat-leaf (Italian) parsley
6½ oz (185 g) canned tuna packed in oil
¼ cup (2 fl oz/60 ml) dry white wine
¼ cup (2 fl oz/60 ml) Chicken Stock (recipe on page 30)
red pepper flakes
¼ cup (2 fl oz/60 ml) fresh lemon juice
6 qt (6 l) water
1 tablespoon salt
1 lb (500 g) dried casareccia
1 lemon, cut into 6 wedges

In a small saucepan over low heat, heat the olive oil. Add the garlic and anchovy fillets and simmer slowly until the anchovies begin to fall apart. Add the parsley, tuna and its oil, white wine, Chicken Stock and red pepper flakes to taste. Simmer, stirring to break up the anchovies and tuna, for 5 minutes. Add the lemon juice and stir to mix well. Keep warm.

❧ In a large pot over high heat, bring the water to a boil. Add the 1 tablespoon salt and the casareccia and cook according to the package directions or until al dente, 9–10 minutes. Drain.

❧ In a large warmed bowl, combine the casareccia and anchovy mixture. Toss to mix well.

❧ To serve, divide among individual plates. Garnish with a lemon wedge.

❧ Serve hot.

LINGUINE WITH CLAMS AND MUSSELS

SERVES 6

Flattened linguine noodles are traditionally served with simple, garlicky clam sauces. This dish is all the better for the addition of mussels. While you can make the recipe with just one, it is the combination of seafood flavors that really gives this dish its style. You'll probably want to pair this recipe with a hearty loaf of bread as the sauce is fabulous for dipping.

¼ cup (2 oz/60 g) unsalted butter
2 shallots, peeled and minced
6 garlic cloves, peeled and minced
¾ teaspoon red pepper flakes
1 cup (8 fl oz/250 ml) dry white wine
3 tablespoons fresh lemon juice
3 tablespoons minced fresh flat-leaf
  (Italian) parsley
4 lb (2 kg) cherrystone clams, scrubbed
3 lb (1.5 kg) mussels, scrubbed and
  debearded
6 qt (6 l) water
1 tablespoon salt
1 lb (500 g) dried linguine

In a large, heavy pot over medium heat, melt the butter until foamy. Reduce the heat to medium-low, add the shallots and garlic and sauté, stirring frequently, until translucent, about 5 minutes.

❧ Add the red pepper flakes and wine, increase the heat to medium and simmer until the liquid is evaporated by one-third, about 7 minutes.

❧ Stir in the lemon juice and parsley. Add the clams and mussels, discarding any that do not close to the touch. Cover the pan tightly and simmer until the shellfish just open, 3–5 minutes. Using a slotted spoon, remove and discard any shellfish that do not open. Remove from the heat and keep warm.

❧ In a large pot over high heat, bring the water to a boil. Add the salt and the linguine and cook according to the package directions or until al dente, about 10 minutes. Drain.

❧ In a large warmed platter, combine the linguine, clams, mussels and cooking liquid. Toss to mix well.

❧ To serve, divide among individual soup plates.

❧ Serve hot.

A most delicious shellfish, mussels are bivalves with a blue-black shell and tan to orange flesh. Sold live, they are found naturally in both the Atlantic and Pacific oceans and are produced successfully by aquaculture as well. Atlantic mussels are available year-round. Pacific ones are usually quarantined in summer. Be sure to scrub the shells well using a stiff-bristled brush before using them in recipes. Discard any mussels that open before cooking and any that stay closed after cooking.

ZITI WITH SALMON AND ASPARAGUS

SERVES 6

Salmon and asparagus, the classic spring mealtime companions, make a wonderful, simple pasta topping. Any other medium-sized dried pasta tubes such as penne, tubetti or other shapes of the same size will also work well in this recipe.

3 tablespoons Clarified Butter
    (recipe on page 45)
1½ lb (750 g) skinned salmon fillet
¼ cup (2 fl oz/60 ml) fresh lemon juice
1 lb (500 g) asparagus, cut into 1-inch
    (2.5-cm) pieces
12 green (spring) onions, green and
    white parts, cut into 1-inch
    (2.5-cm) pieces
2 tablespoons grated lemon zest
    (see page 295)
salt and freshly ground pepper
6 qt (6 l) water
1 tablespoon salt
1 lb (500 g) dried ziti
1 tablespoon extra-virgin olive oil
2 cups (8 oz/250 g) dried bread crumbs
    (see page 294)

Make the Clarified Butter.

❧ On a cutting board, slice the salmon crosswise into ¼-inch (6-mm) strips. Place the salmon in a small glass, porcelain or stainless steel bowl, add half of the lemon juice and toss gently. Marinate for 30 minutes.

❧ In a small pot of boiling water, cook the asparagus until tender-crisp, about 6 minutes. Drain.

❧ In a medium frying pan over medium heat, melt the Clarified Butter. Add the green onions and sauté, stirring frequently, until tender, about 4 minutes. Add the asparagus and sauté another 2 minutes.

❧ Increase the heat to high, add the salmon and stir gently until the salmon just begins to turn opaque. Add the remaining lemon juice, lemon zest and salt and pepper to taste. Remove from the heat and keep warm.

❧ In a large pot over high heat, bring the water to a boil. Add the 1 tablespoon salt and the ziti and cook according to the package directions or until al dente, 8–10 minutes.

❧ Drain the ziti and toss it immediately with the olive oil.

❧ In a large warmed bowl, combine the ziti, salmon mixture and half of the bread crumbs. Toss to mix well.

❧ To serve, divide among individual warmed plates. Top with the remaining bread crumbs.

❧ Serve hot.

PASTA SEEDS WITH TUNA, CAPERS AND ROASTED GARLIC BUTTER

SERVES 6

You can't grow pasta from these seeds! Instead, these small pasta shapes resemble melon seeds, melone *in Italian. If fresh tuna is not available, substitute another firm-fleshed fish such as salmon, swordfish or sea bass.*

6 tablespoons (3 oz/90 g) Roasted
　Garlic Butter (recipe on page 294)
2 lb (1 kg) tuna steaks
salt and freshly ground pepper
6 qt (6 l) water
1 tablespoon salt
1 lb (500 g) dried melone
2 tablespoons capers, drained
1 tablespoon grated lemon zest
　(see page 295)
1 lemon, cut into 6 wedges

Make the Roasted Garlic Butter.

❧ To season the fish, cut the tuna into 1-inch (2.5-cm) pieces and place in a bowl. Add the salt and pepper to taste and toss gently.

❧ In a medium frying pan over high heat, melt 2 tablespoons of the Roasted Garlic Butter. Add the tuna and cook, stirring frequently, until the fish is opaque on all sides but still pink in the center, about 7 minutes.

❧ Remove the fish from the heat but keep warm. In a large pot over high heat, bring the water to a boil. Add the 1 tablespoon salt and the melone and cook according to the package directions or until al dente, about 8 minutes.

❧ Drain the melone and toss it immediately with 2 tablespoons of the Roasted Garlic Butter until the butter is melted.

❧ To serve, divide among individual plates. Top with the tuna, capers, lemon zest and remaining Roasted Garlic Butter. Garnish with the lemon wedges.

❧ Serve hot.

SPAGHETTI WITH OLIVE OIL, GARLIC AND RED PEPPER

SERVES 6

A classic and absolutely simple recipe, this spicy dish will fill your kitchen with the aromas of an authentic Italian trattoria. Any other thin strands of dried pasta, from angel hair to spaghettini, bucatini to linguine, may be substituted for the spaghetti. Although it is not absolutely necessary, you might want to have a wedge of imported Italian Parmesan cheese close at hand for guests to grate over their individual portions to taste. When available, pass around whole cherry tomatoes, which look beautiful on the serving plates and provide refreshing bursts of sun-ripened sweetness between bites of the pasta.

⅓ cup (3 fl oz/80 ml) extra-virgin olive oil
6 garlic cloves, peeled and minced
6 qt (6 l) water
1 tablespoon salt
1 lb (500 g) dried spaghetti
red pepper flakes
salt

In a small saucepan over low heat, heat the olive oil. Add the garlic and sauté, stirring frequently, until tender, about 5 minutes.

❧ In a large pot over high heat, bring the water to a boil. Add the 1 tablespoon salt and the spaghetti and cook according to the package directions or until al dente, about 7 minutes. Drain.

❧ In a large warmed bowl, combine the spaghetti, olive oil and garlic mixture and red pepper flakes and salt to taste. Toss to mix well.

❧ To serve, divide among individual warmed plates.

❧ Serve hot.

FUSILLI LUNGHI WITH SHRIMP AND TOMATOES

SERVES 6

Found in Italian restaurants the world over, this classic seafood dish is easily made at home. If you like, substitute scallops or chunks of firm-fleshed fish such as swordfish or sea bass for the shrimp (prawns). If none of these are available, you can make this dish with bay shrimp. These smaller shrimp are often sold cooked and frozen. Simply thaw and then warm them at the last minute before combining with the sauce and pasta.

1 lb (500 g) shrimp (prawns), shelled and deveined (see page 299)

6 tablespoons (3 fl oz/90 ml) extra-virgin olive oil

2 tablespoons minced garlic

½ cup (4 fl oz/125 ml) dry white wine

1½ lb (750 g) plum (Roma) tomatoes, peeled, seeded and diced (see page 299)

2 tablespoons fresh lemon juice

6 qt (6 l) water

1 tablespoon salt

1 lb (500 g) fusilli lunghi

1 tablespoon minced fresh chives

1 tablespoon minced fresh flat-leaf (Italian) parsley

salt

fresh chives

In a medium pot of boiling water, cook the shrimp, stirring once, until they turn pink and curl, about 4 minutes. Drain and set aside.

❧ In a large frying pan over medium heat, heat 2 tablespoons of the olive oil. Add the garlic, reduce the heat to low and sauté for 2 minutes. Add the wine, increase the heat to medium and simmer until the liquid is reduced to 2 tablespoons, about 10 minutes. Add the tomatoes and lemon juice, reduce the heat to low and simmer for 5 minutes. Remove from the heat but keep warm.

❧ In a large pot over high heat, bring the water to a boil. Add the 1 tablespoon salt and the fusilli lunghi and cook according to the package directions or until al dente, about 12 minutes. Drain.

❧ Meanwhile, five minutes before the fusilli is done, return the sauce to low heat.

❧ Add the shrimp, minced chives, parsley, the remaining olive oil and salt to taste. Stir to mix well.

❧ In a large warmed bowl, combine the fusilli and shrimp mixture. Toss to mix well.

❧ To serve, divide among individual bowls. Garnish with the chives.

❧ Serve hot.

DOUBLE TWISTS WITH GREEN BEANS AND GOAT CHEESE

SERVES 6

Two strands of pasta twisted together form gemelli in Italian. The tiny green beans, haricots verts, can be found throughout the summer and autumn.

12 oz (375 g) baby haricots verts or
    Blue Lake green beans
2 red bell peppers (capsicums), seeded
    and deribbed (see page 298)
4 tablespoons (2 oz/60 g) unsalted
    butter
1 teaspoon herbes de Provence
6 qt (6 l) water
1 tablespoon salt
1 lb (500 g) dried gemelli
2 tablespoons extra-virgin olive oil
salt and freshly ground pepper
6 oz (185 g) fresh mild goat cheese,
    crumbled
1 cup (4 oz/125 g) shelled walnuts,
    toasted (see page 297)

In a medium pot of boiling salted water over high heat, cook the green beans until just tender, about 2 minutes for haricots verts and about 6 minutes for Blue Lake green beans. Drain the beans, refresh in cold water for 5 minutes and drain again.

❧ Cut the bell peppers into strips ¼ inch (6 mm) wide and 2 inches (5 cm) long. In a large frying pan over medium heat, melt the butter until foamy. Reduce the heat, add the peppers and sauté until tender, about 8 minutes.

❧ Add the herbes de Provence and the beans and sauté until heated through, 3–4 minutes. Remove from the heat and keep warm.

❧ In a large pot over high heat, bring the water to a boil. Add the 1 tablespoon salt and the gemelli and cook according to the package directions or until al dente, about 9 minutes. Drain and immediately toss it with the olive oil.

❧ In a large warmed bowl, combine the gemelli, bell pepper and green bean mixture and salt and pepper to taste. Toss to mix well. Add the goat cheese and toss again. Add the walnuts and toss once more.

❧ To serve, divide among individual warmed plates.

❧ Serve hot.

LARGE SHELLS WITH TOMATOES AND CHEESE

SERVES 6

The heat of the mildly spiced tomato sauce will slightly melt the strips of mozzarella, leaving them pleasantly chewy. Large pasta shells may be found under their Italian name, conchiglie.

¼ cup (2 fl oz/60 ml) extra-virgin
    olive oil
1 lb (500 g) yellow onions, diced
6 garlic cloves, peeled and minced
1½ lb (750 g) plum (Roma) tomatoes,
    peeled, seeded and diced (see
    page 299) or canned tomatoes
1 tablespoon minced fresh oregano
salt and freshly ground pepper
red pepper flakes
6 qt (6 l) water
1 tablespoon salt
1 lb (500 g) dried conchiglie
8 oz (250 g) whole-milk mozzarella
    cheese, cut into thin strips
fresh oregano sprigs

In a medium frying pan over medium heat, heat the olive oil. Reduce the heat to low, add the onions, cover and cook, stirring frequently, until completely tender, about 15 minutes. Add the garlic and sauté another 2 minutes. Add the tomatoes, minced oregano and salt, pepper and red pepper flakes to taste and simmer for 5 minutes. Keep warm.

❧ In a large pot over high heat, bring the water to a boil. Add the 1 tablespoon salt and the conchiglie and cook according to the package directions or until al dente, about 11 minutes. Drain.

❧ In a large warmed bowl, combine the conchiglie, onion mixture and mozzarella cheese. Toss to mix well.

❧ To serve, divide among individual warmed bowls. Garnish with an oregano sprig.

❧ Serve hot.

SPAGHETTI WITH SWISS CHARD AND LEMON

SERVES 6

Like many simple recipes, this one can be varied in many ways. Substitute other favorite greens such as spinach for the Swiss chard (silverbeet). Add more garlic, if you like, and more or less of the red pepper flakes to your taste.

1½ lb (750 g) Swiss chard (silverbeet), stemmed
4 tablespoons (2 fl oz/60 ml) extra-virgin olive oil
1 tablespoon minced garlic
6 qt (6 l) water
1 tablespoon salt
1 lb (500 g) spaghetti
2 tablespoons grated lemon zest (see page 295)
red pepper flakes
salt

Cut the chard leaves into crosswise slices ¾ inch (2 cm) thick. In a medium saucepan over medium-low heat, heat 2 tablespoons of the olive oil. Add the garlic and sauté for 1 minute. Add the chard, cover the pan and cook until the chard is wilted, about 3 minutes. Stir to mix well. Keep warm.

In a large pot over high heat, bring the water to a boil. Add the 1 tablespoon salt and the spaghetti and cook according to the package directions or until al dente, about 9 minutes. Drain.

On a large warmed platter, combine the spaghetti, chard, lemon zest, the remaining 2 tablespoons olive oil and red pepper flakes and salt to taste. Toss to mix well.

To serve, divide among individual warmed plates.

Serve hot.

FUSILLI WITH GRILLED VEGETABLES

SERVES 6

This recipe presents a lot of options. Use other favorite fresh vegetables, including small green (spring) onions, slender (Asian) eggplant (aubergine) or an assortment of summer squashes.

¼ cup (2 oz/60 g) Roasted Garlic
    Butter (recipe on page 294)
1 red (Spanish) onion, peeled
4 small zucchini (courgettes)
2 ears fresh corn, husks and silk
    removed
2 red bell peppers (capsicums), seeded
    and deribbed (see page 298)
2 green bell peppers (capsicums), seeded
    and deribbed (see page 298)
6 qt (6 l) water
1 tablespoon salt
1 lb (500 g) dried fusilli
salt and freshly ground pepper

Make the Roasted Garlic Butter.
❧ Prepare a fire in an outdoor charcoal grill, heat a stove-top grill to medium-hot or preheat a broiler (griller).
❧ Grill or broil (grill) the onion, zucchini, corn and red and green peppers over medium coals or on the stovetop, turning frequently, until they are evenly marked and tender: the onion about 20 minutes, the zucchini and corn 8–15 minutes and the peppers until their skins are blackened. Cool.
❧ Cut the onion in half crosswise and each half into strips ¼ inch (6 mm) thick. Cut each zucchini into strips 1½ by ¼ inch (4 cm by 6 mm) thick. Cut the corn from the cob. Peel the peppers and slice them into ¼-inch (6-mm) thick strips.

❧ In a large pot over high heat, bring the water to a boil. Add the 1 table-spoon salt and the fusilli and cook according to the package directions or until al dente, about 9 minutes. Drain.

❧ In a large warmed bowl, combine the vegetables, fusilli, Roasted Garlic Butter and salt and pepper to taste.
❧ To serve, divide among plates.
❧ Serve hot.

LINGUINE TAPENADE WITH BASIL AND TOMATOES

SERVES 6

While designed as an entree in itself, this will serve 8–10 as a side dish.

Tapenade
6 qt (6 l) water
1 tablespoon salt
1 lb (500 g) dried linguine
2 cups (12 oz/375 g) cherry tomatoes, stemmed and cut into quarters
3 tablespoons minced fresh basil
fresh basil leaves

Prepare the Tapenade.

❧ In a large pot over high heat, bring the water to a boil. Add the salt and the linguine and cook according to the package directions or until al dente, about 8 minutes. Drain.

❧ In a large warmed bowl, combine the hot linguine and Tapenade. Toss to mix well. Add half of the cherry tomatoes and all of the minced basil. Toss to mix well again.

❧ To serve, divide among individual warmed plates. Top with the remaining tomatoes. Garnish with a basil leaf.

❧ Serve hot.

Tapenade

MAKES ABOUT 2 CUPS (16 FL OZ/500 ML)

The classic Provençal black olive spread known as tapenade is easy to make at home and will keep for several days covered in the refrigerator. You can substitute one of the excellent commercial brands.

1½ cups (7½ oz/225 g) Kalamata olives, pitted
4 garlic cloves, peeled
6 anchovy fillets, packed in oil, drained
1 tablespoon Dijon-style mustard
½ cup (4 fl oz/125 ml) extra-virgin olive oil

In the work bowl of a food processor with the metal blade or in a blender, combine the olives, garlic, anchovies and mustard. Pulse until the mixture is a dense purée.

❧ With the motor running, slowly add the olive oil in a steady stream.

❧ Use immediately or store in a tightly covered container in the refrigerator for up to 3 days.

Make dried pasta noodles, including spaghetti, linguine and fettuccine, mainstays of your pantry. Always keep plenty on hand and you can prepare a delicious meal in minutes. With pasta in your house you'll always be prepared for an emergency meal or to serve unexpected guests. If you need to increase the amount of pasta in a recipe in order to serve more people, be sure to increase the amount of water you use to cook it as well. To cook evenly and without sticking, noodles need plenty of water in which to float while boiling.

MEZZE LASAGNE WITH TOMATOES AND OLIVES

SERVES 6

The ideal pasta for this dish is mezze lasagne—ripple-edged ribbons about twice as wide as fettuccine, which have a wide surface to carry the robust sauce. If it is unavailable, substitute the widest pasta noodles available.

2 lb (1 kg) ripe yellow tomatoes, peeled, seeded and diced (see page 299)
1 shallot, peeled and minced
3 garlic cloves, peeled and minced
1½ cups (7½ oz/225 g) Kalamata olives, pitted and sliced
¼ cup (¼ oz/7 g) firmly packed fresh basil leaves, minced
salt and freshly ground pepper
6 qt (6 l) water
1 tablespoon salt
1 lb (500 g) dried mezze lasagne
fresh basil sprigs

In a medium saucepan over medium heat, combine the tomatoes, shallot, garlic, olives, minced basil and salt and pepper to taste. Simmer until the ingredients are heated through, about 10 minutes.

❧ In a large pot over high heat, bring the water to a boil. Add the 1 table-spoon salt and the mezze lasagne and cook according to the package directions or until al dente, about 12 minutes. Drain.

❧ In a large warmed bowl, combine the mezze lasagne and tomato mixture. Toss to mix well.

❧ To serve, divide among individual plates. Garnish with a basil sprig.

❧ Serve hot.

FARFALLINE WITH ZUCCHINI AND MINT

SERVES 6

Make this dish with small young zucchini (courgettes), which have no trace of the bitterness sometimes found in larger ones. After grating the zucchini, place them in a strainer until ready to use, so their excess liquid can drain away.

¼ cup (2 oz/60 g) unsalted butter
1 lb (500 g) zucchini (courgettes), grated
6 qt (6 l) water
1 tablespoon salt
1 lb (500 g) farfalline
1 tablespoon extra-virgin olive oil
¼ cup (¼ oz/7 g) fresh mint leaves, thinly sliced
salt and freshly ground pepper

In a medium frying pan over medium heat, melt the butter until foamy. Add the zucchini and sauté, stirring frequently, until it is heated through and begins to soften, 3–4 minutes. Remove from the heat; keep warm.
∽ In a large pot over high heat, bring the water to a boil. Add the 1 tablespoon salt and the farfalline and cook according to the package directions or until al dente, 10–12 minutes.
∽ Drain the farfalline and toss it immediately with the olive oil.
∽ In a large warmed bowl, combine the farfalline, zucchini and butter, half of the mint leaves and salt and pepper to taste. Toss to mix well.
∽ To serve, divide among individual warmed plates. Top with the remaining mint leaves.
∽ Serve hot.

PASTA WITH ONIONS, SHALLOTS AND LEEKS

SERVES 6

Lengthy cooking releases the natural sugars present in the onions.

⅓ cup (3 fl oz/90 ml) Clarified Butter (recipe on page 45)
1¼ lb (625 g) yellow onions, diced
½ cup (2½ oz/75 g) minced shallots
1 lb (500 g) leeks, thinly sliced (see page 297)
2 cups (8 oz/250 g) dried bread crumbs (see page 294)
salt and freshly ground pepper
6 qt (6 l) water
1 tablespoon salt
1 lb (500 g) dried cavatelli
¾ cup (3 oz/90 g) freshly grated aged Asiago cheese

Make the Clarified Butter.

☙ In a heavy frying pan over low heat, combine the Clarified Butter and onions. Cover and cook until the onions are completely tender, about 15 minutes.

☙ Remove the lid and stir the onions. Continue to cook over very low heat, stirring occasionally, until the onions begin to color and turn slightly sweet, 30 minutes. Add the shallots and sauté for 5 minutes.

☙ Add the leeks and sauté, stirring frequently, until the leeks are tender, 15–20 minutes. Keep warm.

☙ In a small bowl combine the bread crumbs and salt and pepper to taste.

☙ In a large pot over high heat, bring the water to a boil. Add the 1 tablespoon salt and the cavatelli and cook according to the package directions or until al dente, about 12 minutes. Drain.

☙ To serve, combine the cavatelli, onions, cheese and bread crumbs.

☙ Serve hot.

FARFALLE WITH CHICKEN LIVERS, SAUSAGE AND SAGE

SERVES 6

For the best results, take care not to overcook the chicken livers, which should remain juicy and slightly pink at the center. Use just the barest pinches of the ground nutmeg and ground cloves, which will nonetheless add a rich aromatic dimension. If you prefer something a little spicier, substitute spicy Italian sausages. For an even more flavorful version of this dish, make your own farfalle using fresh Basil Pasta (recipe on page 12). If you cannot find fresh sage, substitute half the amount of dried, but not powdered, sage leaves.

3 mild Italian sausages
5 tablespoons (3 fl oz/80 ml) extra-virgin olive oil
1 shallot, minced
2 tablespoons minced garlic
1 lb (500 g) fresh chicken livers, trimmed of fat and veins and cut into ½-inch (12-mm) slices
ground nutmeg
ground cloves
2 tablespoons minced fresh sage
6 qt (6 l) water
1 tablespoon salt
1 lb (500 g) dried farfalle
fresh sage sprigs

Prick the skins of the sausages all over with a fork.

❧ In a medium frying pan over medium heat, cook the sausages until evenly browned on the outside and cooked through, 15–20 minutes.

❧ Transfer to paper towels to drain and cool. Cut the sausages crosswise into slices ⅜ inch (1 cm) thick and then cut the slices in half. Discard any fat remaining in the frying pan.

❧ In the same frying pan over medium heat, heat 2 tablespoons of the olive oil. Add the shallot and sauté, stirring frequently, until tender and translucent, about 5 minutes. Stir in the garlic and sauté until tender, about 2 minutes.

❧ Add the chicken livers and sauté for 2 minutes. Add the nutmeg and cloves to taste and sauté until the chicken livers are cooked through, about 2 minutes longer. Add the sausages and minced sage. Toss to mix well. Remove from the heat and keep warm.

❧ In a large pot over high heat, bring the water to a boil. Add the salt and the farfalle and cook according to the package directions or until al dente, about 12 minutes. Drain and immediately toss it with the remaining 3 tablespoons olive oil.

❧ In a large warmed bowl, combine the sausage mixture and farfalle. Toss to mix well.

❧ To serve, divide among individual warmed plates. Garnish with the sage.

❧ Serve hot.

Eggs are a nutritious food rich in protein, vitamins and minerals; only their yolks contain cholesterol. An essential ingredient in fresh pasta, eggs are also an interesting element in some sauces. The recipes in this book were created using large eggs. White and brown eggs are identical nutritionally, indistinguishable in taste and interchangeable in recipes.

The egg is to cuisine what the article is to speech.

—ANONYMOUS

PASTA COILS CARBONARA

SERVES 6

In Italian, carbonara means an old-fashioned charcoal maker, referring to the humble working people who first devised this simple but rich and satisfying dish. This traditional, cream-free Roman version of carbonara works well with substantial pasta shapes such as these plump coils called cavatappi, as well as with the more usual spaghetti or linguine.

2 tablespoons pure olive oil
4 oz (125 g) pancetta, cut into strips
4 eggs, lightly beaten
1½ cups (6 oz/185 g) freshly grated
    Parmesan cheese
3 tablespoons minced fresh flat-leaf
    (Italian) parsley
salt
6 qt (6 l) water
1 tablespoon salt
1 lb (500 g) dried cavatappi
freshly ground pepper

In a small frying pan over medium-low heat, heat the olive oil. Add the pancetta and sauté, stirring frequently, until golden and nearly crisp, 9–10 minutes. Set aside to cool.

❧ In a large warmed bowl, combine the eggs, Parmesan cheese, parsley and salt to taste. Add the pancetta, and any pan drippings, and stir to mix well.

❧ In a large pot over high heat, bring the water to a boil. Add the 1 table-spoon salt and the cavatappi and cook according to the package directions or until al dente, about 12 minutes. Drain and add to the egg mixture. Toss to mix well.

❧ To serve, divide among individual warmed plates. Top with pepper to taste.

❧ Serve hot.

SPINACH SPAGHETTI WITH BOLOGNESE SAUCE

SERVES 6

Dried spinach spaghetti, available in most major food stores, provides excellent contrasts of color and taste to this flavorful red meat sauce. If you can't find it, substitute regular spaghetti or other dried strands.

Bolognese Sauce
6 qt (6 l) water
1 tablespoon salt
1 lb (500 g) dried spinach spaghetti
¾ cup (3 oz/90 g) freshly grated
    Parmesan cheese

Prepare the Bolognese Sauce.
❧ In a large pot over high heat, bring the water to a boil. Add the salt and the spaghetti and cook according to the package directions or until al dente, about 9 minutes. Drain.
❧ If it is not hot, heat the Bolognese Sauce in a medium saucepan over medium heat.
❧ In a large warmed bowl, combine the spaghetti and Bolognese Sauce. Toss to mix well.
❧ To serve, divide among individual warmed plates. Top with an equal amount of the Parmesan cheese.
❧ Serve hot.

Bolognese Sauce

MAKES ABOUT 4 CUPS (32 FL OZ/1 L)

The cooking of Bologna is best described as full-bodied. There are no subtle flavors nor fine textures here. This hearty sauce can top just about any pasta as well as Classic Risotto (recipe on page 20) and Classic Polenta (recipe on page 199).

3 tablespoons pure olive oil
1 yellow onion, peeled and diced
1 celery stalk, finely chopped
1 small carrot, peeled and finely
    chopped
1 lb (500 g) lean ground (minced) beef
¾ cup (6 fl oz/180 ml) milk
¾ cup (6 fl oz/180 ml) dry white wine
3 lb (1.5 kg) plum (Roma) tomatoes,
    peeled, seeded and diced (see page
    299), or 28 oz (875 g) canned
    tomatoes
6 oz (185 g) canned tomato sauce
ground nutmeg
salt
red pepper flakes

In a large, heavy frying pan over medium-low heat, heat the olive oil. Add the onion and sauté, stirring frequently, until it is translucent, about 8 minutes.
❧ Add the celery and carrots and sauté, stirring frequently, for 10 minutes.
❧ Add the ground beef, breaking it up with a fork. Sauté, stirring frequently, until the beef just loses its pink color.
❧ Stir in the milk and simmer until it has evaporated, about 8 minutes.
❧ Add the wine and simmer until it has evaporated, about 8 minutes longer.
❧ Add the tomatoes, the tomato sauce and nutmeg, salt and red pepper flakes to taste. Increase the heat to medium, stirring, bring the sauce to a simmer then reduce the heat to very low. Simmer, stirring occasionally, for at least 2½ hours.
❧ If not using immediately, store in a tightly covered container in the refrigerator for up to 1 week.
❧ Reheat before using.

A table set with rustic painted Italian earthenware dramatically enhances the European mood of a meal featuring traditional pasta with meat sauce.

ANGEL HAIR PASTA WITH ROASTED GARLIC MEATBALLS

SERVES 6

A rich garlic-infused poultry broth bathes the thin strands of angel hair pasta and small meatballs in this light yet satisfying dish. If you wish, substitute ground turkey for the beef and pork in the meatballs.

3 garlic bulbs, cloves separated
8 cups (64 fl oz/2 l) Chicken Stock
    (recipe on page 30)
6 fresh thyme sprigs
1 teaspoon black peppercorns
2 tablespoons pure olive oil
2 large shallots, minced
12 oz (375 g) ground (minced) beef
12 oz (375 g) ground (minced) pork
⅓ cup (3 fl oz/80 ml) Roasted Garlic
    Purée (see page 296)
2 teaspoons minced fresh thyme leaves
1 egg, lightly beaten
salt and freshly ground pepper
1 cup (4 oz/125 g) dried bread crumbs
    (see page 294)
¾ cup (3 oz/90 g) freshly grated
    Parmesan cheese
½ cup (2½ oz/75 g) all-purpose (plain)
    flour
6 qt (6 l) water
1 tablespoon salt
1 lb (500 g) dried angel hair pasta

Preheat an oven to 325°F (165°C).

🕊 In a small ovenproof pan with a tight-fitting lid, combine the garlic cloves, 2 cups (16 fl oz/500 ml) of the Chicken Stock, the thyme sprigs and the peppercorns. Bake until the garlic is soft, 45–90 minutes. Cool.

🕊 In a medium saucepan over medium heat, heat the olive oil. Add the shallots and sauté, stirring frequently, until tender and fragrant, about 7 minutes. Set aside to cool.

🕊 In a medium bowl, combine the shallots, beef, pork, Roasted Garlic Purée, minced thyme, egg and salt and pepper to taste. Stir to mix well. Add the bread crumbs and Parmesan cheese and mix well.

🕊 Place the flour in a bowl. Shape the meat mixture into 36 meatballs. Coat each meatball thoroughly with flour.

🕊 In a small frying pan over medium heat, fry the meatballs in batches, turning frequently, until uniformly browned. Drain on paper towels.

🕊 Strain the garlic-infused stock into a medium saucepan over medium heat. Add the remaining Chicken Stock and bring to a boil. Reduce the heat to low, add the meatballs and simmer for 7 minutes.

🕊 In a large pot over high heat, bring the water to a boil. Add the 1 tablespoon salt and the pasta and cook according to the package directions or until al dente, about 4 minutes. Drain.

🕊 To serve, in a large bowl combine the pasta, stock and meatballs.

🕊 Serve hot.

It is not really an exaggeration to say that peace and happiness begin, geographically, where garlic is used in cooking.

—X. MARCEL BOULESTIN

RUOTE WITH SAUSAGE AND ZUCCHINI

SERVES 6

Round, wagon wheel–shaped ruote nicely match the size and shape of the sausage and zucchini (courgette) slices. For a milder version of the dish, use sweet Italian sausage, omit the red pepper flakes and add the black pepper sparingly. You might also try this technique with any number of the interesting new sausages on the market, including ones made from turkey or even chicken and apple.

1 lb (500 g) hot Italian sausage
1 cup (8 fl oz/250 ml) plus 4 qt (4 l)
    water
1 cup (8 fl oz/250 ml) dry white wine
1 tablespoon unsalted butter
2 tablespoons extra-virgin olive oil
1 lb (500 g) zucchini (courgettes), cut
    into slices ¼ inch (6 mm) thick
2 teaspoons salt
8 oz (250 g) dried ruote
salt and freshly ground pepper
red pepper flakes

In a heavy medium frying pan over high heat, arrange the sausages in a single layer. Add the 1 cup (8 fl oz/250 ml) water and wine and bring to a boil. Reduce the heat and simmer the sausages, turning once, until almost cooked through, about 15 minutes.

❧ Using tongs, remove the sausages from the liquid and set on paper towels to drain and cool. Increase the heat under the liquid to reduce to about 1 tablespoon. Cut the sausages into slices ¼ inch (6 mm) thick.

❧ In the same frying pan over high heat, melt the butter. Add 1 tablespoon of the olive oil, the zucchini and sausages and cook, stirring frequently until the zucchini is tender-crisp and the sausage slices are no longer pink, 7–10 minutes. Remove from the heat and keep warm.

❧ In a large pot over high heat, bring the 4 qt (4 l) water to a boil. Add the 2 teaspoons salt and the ruote and cook according to the package directions or until al dente, about 12 minutes.

❧ Drain the ruote and toss it immediately with the remaining 1 tablespoon olive oil.

❧ In a large warmed bowl, combine the ruote, zucchini and sausages and salt, pepper and red pepper flakes to taste. Toss to mix well.

❧ To serve, divide among individual warmed plates.

❧ Serve hot.

CLASSIC POLENTA

SERVES 6

Italy's popular cornmeal mush (not pictured) provides another ideal backdrop for pasta sauces, turning this warm cereal into an interesting entree. The sausage and zucchini ragout on this page, Bolognese Sauce (recipe on page 195) and Pesto Sauce (recipe on page 36) all make good choices. The grain is sold as cornmeal and polenta.

2 tablespoon olive oil
2 shallots, minced
2 green (spring) onions, green and
    white parts, finely chopped
2 garlic cloves, minced
6 cups (48 fl oz/1.5 l) Chicken Stock
    (recipe on page 30) or Vegetable
    Stock (recipe on page 238) or water
¼ teaspoon salt
2 cups (10 oz/210 g) coarse yellow
    cornmeal
2 tablespoons Parmesan cheese

In a large saucepan over medium heat, warm the olive oil. Add the shallots and sauté, stirring, until softened and just beginning to caramelize, 5-7 minutes. Add the onions and garlic and cook for 1 minute longer, being careful not to brown the garlic.

❧ Add the stock or water and bring to a boil. Using a measuring cup with a spout, pour in the cornmeal in a very slow, thin, steady stream, stirring constantly. Reduce the heat to medium-low and continue cooking, stirring occasionally, until the mixture is very thick, smooth and creamy, about 25 minutes. Add the Parmesan cheese and stir until it melts.

❧ To serve, transfer to individual bowls. Top with the sauce of your choice.

❧ Serve hot.

Lasagne

A pasta dish as old as ancient Rome itself, where it was known originally as *laganum*, today lasagne is regarded as a specialty of the region around Bologna. The basic recipe has not changed for centuries, consisting of layering cooked broad pasta ribbons of the same name with cheeses, other ingredients and sauces, then baking the casserole in the oven.

Within the recipes that follow, you'll find a definitive example of the traditional Bolognese delight (recipe on page 207), but you'll also discover clear evidence of how dramatically this historic dish continues to evolve with the imaginative inclusion of herbs, vegetables and seafood in the sauce.

No matter how innovative a lasagne recipe might be, however, it owes a debt of gratitude to history, as what Italian lexicographer Alfredo Panzini calls "a survivor of the culinary glory of ancient times."

TOMATO, ANCHOVY AND ARTICHOKE HEART LASAGNE

SERVES 6

This meat-free variation on layered and baked lasagne features easily found frozen artichoke hearts, highlighted by the sweet flavor of tomatoes and the pungency of garlic and anchovies. If you have the time, make the dish with zesty fresh Lemon Pasta, aromatic Basil Pasta or pungent Black Pepper Pasta (recipes on page 12). If you are likely to be so pressed for time that you wonder if you can even cook the dried lasagne noodles, look in well-stocked markets and specialty foods stores for "instant" lasagne noodles, which may be layered dry with the other ingredients and soften during baking. Serve this lasagne with sesame-crusted Italian breadsticks, whose crispness will nicely complement its tender textures.

2 tablespoons unsalted butter
¼ cup (2 fl oz/60 ml) extra-virgin olive oil
1¼ lb (625 g) yellow onions, chopped
1 tablespoon minced garlic
5 anchovy fillets, drained and diced
2 tomatoes, peeled, seeded and diced (see page 299)
salt and freshly ground pepper
6 qt (6 l) water
1 tablespoon salt
15 dried lasagne noodles
6 frozen artichoke hearts, thawed and cut into thin strips
4 cups (1 lb/500 g) grated Fontina cheese
fresh flat-leaf (Italian) parsley sprigs

Preheat an oven to 350°F (180°C). Coat the inside of a 9-by-13-inch (23-by-33-cm) baking dish with olive oil.

❧ In a medium frying pan over medium-low heat, heat the butter and olive oil until the butter is melted. Add the onions, reduce the heat to low and sauté, stirring frequently, until the onions are tender and fragrant, about 15 minutes.

❧ Add the garlic and anchovies and sauté for 2 minutes. Add the tomatoes and simmer for 10 minutes. Add salt and pepper to taste. Stir to mix well.

❧ In a large pot over high heat, bring the water to a boil. Add the 1 tablespoon salt and the lasagne noodles and cook according to the package directions or until al dente, about 12 minutes. Drain, rinse in cool water and drain again.

❧ Cover the bottom of the baking dish with 3 lasagne noodles, touching but not overlapping. Make 5 layers of the tomato mixture, artichoke strips, Fontina cheese and noodles, ending with the cheese.

❧ Bake until the top of the lasagne is golden brown and the sauce is bubbling, 30–35 minutes.

❧ To serve, cool for 10 minutes and divide among individual warmed plates. Garnish with a parsley sprig.

❧ Serve warm.

CARAMELIZED ONION AND PANCETTA LASAGNE

SERVES 6

With its hearty ingredients, this lasagne works best when made with dried noodles. If possible, make this casserole a few hours before baking and serving to give the flavors time to marry.

Béchamel Sauce (recipe on page 96)
Caramelized Onions
6 qt (6 l) water
1 tablespoon salt
15 dried lasagne noodles
1 tablespoon olive oil
8 oz (250 g) pancetta, minced
12 oz (375 g) fresh mozzarella cheese, thinly sliced
fresh flat-leaf (Italian) parsley sprigs

Make the Béchamel Sauce.
❧ Prepare the Caramelized Onions.
❧ Preheat an oven to 350°F (180°C). Coat the inside of a 9-by-13-inch (23-by-33-cm) baking dish with olive oil.

❧ In a large pot over high heat, bring the water to a boil. Add the 1 tablespoon salt and the lasagne noodles and cook according to the package directions or until al dente, about 12 minutes. Drain, rinse in cool water and drain again. Immediately toss with the olive oil.
❧ Spread ¼ cup (2 fl oz/60 ml) of the Béchamel Sauce in the bottom of the baking dish. Cover with 3 lasagne noodles, touching but not overlapping. Make 5 layers of the Caramelized Onions, pancetta, mozzarella cheese and noodles, ending with the cheese. Top with the remaining Béchamel Sauce.
❧ Cover the baking dish tightly with aluminum foil and bake for 30 minutes. Remove the foil and bake until the top is just beginning to brown, about 10 minutes longer.
❧ To serve, cool for 10 minutes and divide among individual warmed plates. Garnish with a parsley sprig.
❧ Serve warm.

Caramelized Onions

MAKES 4 CUPS (14 OZ/420 G)

Slow cooking turns these onions sweet. Slice the pieces close in size for even cooking. This recipe can be reduced or expanded easily.

½ cup (4 fl oz/125 ml) Clarified Butter (recipe on page 45) or pure olive oil
5 lb (2.5 kg) yellow onions, peeled, halved and very thinly sliced

In a large, heavy frying pan over medium heat, heat the butter or olive oil. Add the onions, cover and cook, stirring occasionally, until the onions are completely limp, 10–15 minutes.
❧ Remove the lid, reduce the heat to medium-low and cook, stirring frequently, until the onions are golden brown and sweet, 35–45 minutes. Do not let them burn.
❧ Remove from the heat, cool, cover and refrigerate for up to 10 days or freeze for up to 2 months.

While onions are not particularly high in nutrients, they add remarkable taste and texture to dishes. Both white and yellow onions are categorized as globe onions and are fairly interchangeable in recipes. Choose onions that are firm with a mild aroma. Store them away from light, which can make them taste bitter, and away from potatoes, which give off gases that hasten onions' spoiling.

*There is in every cook's opinion
No savoury dish without
an onion.*

—JONATHAN SWIFT

FRESH LASAGNE WITH BASIL AND BÉCHAMEL SAUCE

SERVES 6

Try this aromatic dish in summer or early fall, when fresh basil is most abundant. Larga lasagne noodles are shorter and wider than the more standard dried lasagne noodles. They are sold in boxes of about 24 noodles. You can use fresh Egg Pasta (recipe on page 12) as well, cutting the noodles and cooking them until tender before putting together the casserole. For a satisfying vegetarian meal, accompany it with crusty bread and a platter of sun-ripened sliced tomatoes topped with fresh basil leaves.

Béchamel Sauce (recipe on page 96)
4 cups (4 oz/125 g) packed fresh
    basil leaves
8 garlic cloves, peeled and chopped
¾ cup (4 oz/125 g) pine nuts, lightly
    toasted (see page 297)
salt
⅔ cup (5 fl oz/160 ml) extra-virgin
    olive oil
6 qt (6 l) water
1 tablespoon salt
24 dried larga lasagne noodles
1½ cups (6 oz/185 g) grated pecorino
    romano cheese
fresh basil sprigs

Make the Béchamel Sauce.

❧ Preheat an oven to 375°F (190°C). Coat the inside of a 9-by-13-inch (23-by-33-cm) baking dish with olive oil.

❧ In a food processor with the metal blade or a blender, mince the basil and garlic. Add ½ cup (2½ oz/75 g) of the pine nuts and salt to taste and pulse several times. With the motor running, add the ⅔ cup (5 fl oz/160 ml) olive oil in a steady stream.

❧ In a large pot over high heat, bring the water to a boil. Add the 1 table-spoon salt and the lasagne noodles and cook until al dente, about 12 minutes. Drain, rinse in cool water and drain again. Immediately toss with the remaining 1 tablespoon olive oil.

❧ In a medium bowl, combine the basil mixture, 1 cup (4 oz/125 g) of the pecorino romano cheese and the Béchamel Sauce. Stir to mix well.

❧ Spread ¼ cup (3 fl oz/90 ml) into the baking dish. Cover with 3 lasagne noodles, touching but not overlapping. Make 6 layers of the basil and Béchamel mixture and noodles, ending with the basil and Béchamel mixture. Top with the remaining pecorino romano cheese and pine nuts.

❧ Bake until the top is just beginning to brown, 12–15 minutes.

❧ To serve, cool for 10 minutes and divide among individual warmed plates. Garnish with a basil sprig.

❧ Serve warm.

Store basil and other fresh herbs upright in glasses or small vases, as you do cut flowers. Keep the stems trimmed and change the water regularly and they'll keep for about a week. Enjoy their color and scent on a kitchen counter or as a table decoration while you use them up in recipes.

BOLOGNESE LASAGNE

SERVES 8

Although many different kinds of Italian lasagne may be found in trattorias and homes throughout the nation, this version from the northern city that lends the dish its name is undoubtedly a classic. Some cooks elaborate Bolognese lasagne by adding layers of sliced cooked meatballs or Italian sausage, and stir the grated cheese into Béchamel Sauce (recipe on page 96).

4 cups (32 fl oz/1 l) Bolognese Sauce
    (recipe on page 195)
6 qt (6 l) water
1 tablespoon salt
18 dried lasagne noodles
1½ cups (6 oz/185 g) grated pecorino
    romano cheese
¼ cup (⅓ oz/10 g) minced fresh
    flat-leaf (Italian) parsley

Make the Bolognese Sauce.

❧ Preheat an oven to 350°F (180°C). Coat the inside of a 9-by-13-inch (23-by-33-cm) baking dish with olive oil.

❧ In a large pot over high heat, bring the water to a boil. Add the 1 table-spoon salt and the lasagne noodles and cook according to the package directions or until al dente, about 12 minutes. Drain, rinse in cool water and drain again.

❧ Cover the bottom of the baking dish with 3 lasagne noodles, touching but not overlapping. Make 6 layers of the Bolognese Sauce, pecorino romano cheese and noodles, ending with the cheese. Top with the parsley.

❧ Bake until the top of the lasagne is golden brown and the sauce is bubbling, 35–45 minutes.

❧ To serve, cool for 10 minutes and divide among individual warmed plates.

❧ Serve warm.

When you speak of Bolognese cooking, make the bow it deserves.

—PELLEGRINO ARTUSI

LASAGNE PINWHEELS WITH PANCETTA AND LEEK SAUCE

SERVES 6

Following the instructions in this recipe, you can use a variety of smooth filling mixtures to form pretty pinwheels of many different colors. Possible fillings include the sweet potato filling from the Sweet Potato Crespelle with Walnut Sauce (recipe on page 92), eggs and feta cheese from Cheese Crespelle with Sweet Tomato Sauce (recipe on page 96), greens and goat cheese from Manicotti with Greens and Spicy Tomato Sauce (recipe on page 225) or ricotta and spinach from Ricotta Filled Shells with Bolognese Sauce (recipe on page 210). Try making the lasagne noodles from fresh pasta.

1½ cups (12 fl oz/375 ml) Pancetta
    and Leek Sauce
6 tablespoons (3 fl oz/90 ml)
    extra-virgin olive oil
1 small yellow onion, peeled and diced
6 garlic cloves, peeled and minced
3 cups (21 oz/655 g) canned cannellini
    beans, drained
1 cup (4 oz/125 g) freshly grated
    Parmesan cheese
salt and freshly ground pepper
6 qt (6 l) water
1 tablespoon salt
18 dried lasagne noodles
6 tablespoons (½ oz/15 g) minced fresh
    flat-leaf (Italian) parsley
fresh flat-leaf (Italian) parsley sprigs

Make the Pancetta and Leek Sauce.

❧ Preheat an oven to 350°F (180°C). Coat the inside of a 9-by-13-inch (23-by-33-cm) baking dish with olive oil.

❧ To make the filling, in a medium frying pan over medium heat, heat 2 tablespoons of the olive oil. Add the onion and sauté, stirring frequently, until the onion is tender and fragrant, about 15 minutes.

❧ Add the garlic and sauté for 2 minutes. Add the beans and mash into a smooth purée. Add another 3 tablespoons of the olive oil, the Parmesan cheese and salt and pepper to taste. Stir to mix well. Cool to room temperature.

❧ In a large pot over high heat, bring the water to a boil. Add the 1 tablespoon salt and the lasagne noodles and cook according to the package directions or until al dente, about 12 minutes. Drain, rinse in cool water and drain again. Spread them out on a work surface.

❧ Spread an equal amount of the filling over each noodle and sprinkle with 1 teaspoon of the parsley. Roll each noodle lengthwise, then cut in half. Set them, cut side down, in the baking dish. Using a pastry brush, coat the top and outside of each with some of the remaining 1 tablespoon olive oil.

❧ Bake until heated through, about 15 minutes.

❧ To serve, divide an equal amount of the Pancetta and Leek Sauce among individual warmed plates. Top with 6 lasagne pinwheels. Garnish with a parsley sprig.

❧ Serve hot.

Pancetta and Leek Sauce

MAKES ABOUT 1½ CUPS (12 FL OZ/375 ML)

Perhaps more appreciated in European than in American kitchens, the leek is a mild-tasting member of the onion family. The white part of a leek is sweeter and milder in flavor, and is often used on its own; the darker green parts are more pronounced and assertive, and are frequently included as a flavoring for long-simmered dishes. Because leeks grow in sandy soil, they often contain a great deal of grit packed between their leaves at the point at which green and white parts meet. Be sure to wash the leeks thoroughly before using them in any recipe (see page 297).

2 tablespoons extra-virgin olive oil
1 lb (500 g) leeks, white parts and
    2 inches (5 cm) green parts, cut
    into thin rounds
4 oz (125 g) pancetta, finely chopped
1 cup (8 fl oz/250 ml) Chicken Stock
    (recipe on page 30)
2 tablespoons fresh lemon juice
salt and freshly ground pepper

Preheat an oven to 375°F (190°C).

❧ In an ovenproof frying pan, combine the olive oil, leeks and pancetta. Bake until the leeks are fragrant and tender, about 30 minutes.

❧ Place the frying pan on the stove top over medium heat. Add the Chicken Stock and the lemon juice, reduce the heat to low and simmer for 15 minutes. Add salt and pepper to taste. Reheat before serving.

Baked Entrees

The next group of recipes comprise a wonderfully wide variety of intricately designed, hearty baked dishes. The simplest of these involve tossing cooked pasta noodles with other ingredients in a casserole dish and popping it in the oven before serving it for a quick family meal. To others, add beaten eggs, and the dish literally is elevated to the status of a flan or soufflé.

With a little more effort in assembly, you can bake richly filled pasta shapes, making a fancy casserole that will impress the most discerning gourmet.

Finally, on the following pages there are examples of the most elegant of all pastas dishes, those *en papillote*: baked and served inside parchment paper parcels (or aluminum foil packets), well worthy of the most sophisticated dinner party. Whatever pasta you bake and however you serve it, you will find these dishes fall well beyond the ordinary.

RICOTTA FILLED SHELLS WITH BOLOGNESE SAUCE

SERVES 6

A blend of ricotta and spinach is one of the classic fillings for baked shells, and contrasts wonderfully with the flavor of a traditional tomato-based Italian pasta sauce. For a vegetarian version of this dish, omit the prosciutto and use Spicy Tomato Sauce (recipe on page 225) in place of the Bolognese Sauce. You can also make a lower-fat version of this dish by substituting ricotta made from skim milk, although it will not have the richness or fluffiness of the whole-milk variety. For a tangier filling, replace about half of the ricotta with a fresh, mild, creamy goat cheese.

4 cups (32 fl oz/1 l) Bolognese Sauce (recipe on page 195)

3 tablespoons butter

1 shallot, peeled and minced

6 garlic cloves, peeled and minced

1 lb (500 g) spinach, stemmed and coarsely chopped

1 cup (8 oz/250 g) whole-milk ricotta cheese

4 oz (125 g) prosciutto, diced

¾ cup (3 oz/90 g) plus 2 tablespoons grated Parmesan cheese

salt and freshly ground pepper

6 qt (6 l) water

1 tablespoon salt

18 dried jumbo pasta shells

Make the Bolognese Sauce.

❧ Preheat an oven to 325°F (165°C).

❧ To make the filling, in a large frying pan over medium-low heat, melt the butter until it foams. Add the shallot and sauté, stirring frequently, until soft, about 5 minutes. Add the garlic and sauté for 2 minutes. Add the spinach and cook, stirring frequently, until it is wilted, about 8 minutes. Cool to room temperature. Add the ricotta cheese, prosciutto, the ¾ cup (3 oz/90 g) Parmesan cheese and salt and pepper to taste. Stir to mix well.

❧ In a large pot over high heat, bring the water to a boil. Add the 1 tablespoon salt and the shells and cook according to the package directions or until almost al dente, about 8 minutes. Drain, rinse in cool water and drain again.

❧ Fill each shell with 2 tablespoons of the filling and place in a 9-by-13-inch (23-by-33-cm) baking dish. Top with half of the Bolognese Sauce.

❧ Bake until heated through but not brown, about 15 minutes.

❧ Meanwhile, heat the remaining Bolognese Sauce.

❧ To serve, divide the remaining Bolognese Sauce among individual warmed plates. Top with the shells and the 2 tablespoons Parmesan cheese.

❧ Serve hot.

ANGEL HAIR PASTA FLAN

SERVES 6

Delicate pasta strands combine with a custard sauce to make a baked pasta of surprising finesse. The goat cheese will cause the surface of the custard to darken more than you might expect before it sets. If the surface seems to be darkening too fast, loosely shield the baking dish with a sheet of aluminum foil.

4 qt (4 l) water

1 tablespoon salt

8 oz (250 g) dried angel hair pasta

1 red bell pepper (capsicum), roasted, peeled, seeded, deribbed and diced (see page 298)

½ cup (2½ oz/75 g) Kalamata olives, pitted and sliced

8 oz (250 g) fresh mild white goat cheese at room temperature

2 cups (16 fl oz/500 ml) milk

8 eggs, lightly beaten

2 cups (16 fl oz/500 ml) heavy (double) cream

1 cup (4 oz/125 g) grated Parmesan cheese

freshly ground pepper

fresh flat-leaf (Italian) parsley sprigs

Preheat an oven to 325°F (165°C). Butter the sides and bottom of a 3-qt (3-l) baking dish.

❧ In a large pot over high heat, bring the water to a boil. Add the salt and angel hair pasta and cook according to the package directions or until almost al dente, about 4 minutes. Drain, rinse in cool water and drain again.

❧ Place in a large bowl. Add the pepper and olives and stir to mix well.

❧ In a food processor with the metal blade or a blender, blend the goat cheese and milk until smooth. Stir in the eggs, cream and Parmesan cheese.

❧ Transfer the pasta to the baking dish and add the cheese and egg mixture. Add the pepper to taste.

❧ Bake until the center is set and a knife inserted in the center comes out clean, 40–50 minutes.

❧ To serve, cool for 5 minutes and divide among individual warmed plates. Garnish with a parsley sprig.

❧ Serve warm.

MACARONI AND CHEESE WITH BACON

SERVES 6

Based on the traditional recipe, this rich, cheese-filled comfort food makes a perfect one-dish meal with just a sliced tomato. Tubetti are a common macaroni that are a bit smaller than elbow pasta, which may be substituted.

4 oz (125 g) bacon, cut into strips ½ inch (12 mm) wide

6 qt (6 l) water

1 tablespoon salt

1 lb (500 g) dried tubetti

2 cups (16 fl oz/500 ml) milk

1 cup (8 fl oz/250 ml) heavy (double) cream

3 eggs, lightly beaten

2 teaspoons mustard powder

hot pepper sauce

freshly ground pepper

2 cups (8 oz/250 g) grated Fontina cheese

2 cups (8 oz/250 g) grated Gruyère cheese

2 cups (8 oz/250 g) grated Cheddar cheese

2 tablespoons minced fresh flat-leaf (Italian) parsley

fresh flat-leaf (Italian) parsley sprigs

Preheat an oven to 375°F (190°C).

❧ In a heavy frying pan over medium heat, sauté the bacon until it is just crisp. Drain on paper towels.

❧ In a large pot over high heat, bring the water to a boil. Add the salt and tubetti and cook according to the package directions or until almost al dente, about 7 minutes. Drain.

❧ In a large bowl, stir together the milk and cream. In a medium bowl, combine the eggs, mustard and hot pepper sauce and pepper to taste. Stir to mix well.

❧ Pour the egg mixture into the milk mixture. Add half of the Fontina, Gruyère and Cheddar cheeses and then the tubetti and stir to mix well. Add the remaining half of each cheese and the bacon.

❧ Transfer the mixture to a heavy 3-qt (3-l) baking dish. Cover with aluminum foil and bake for 15 minutes. Remove the foil and bake until the center is set, about 15 minutes. Do not overbake.

❧ To serve, cool for 5 minutes and divide among individual warmed plates. Sprinkle with the minced parsley and garnish with a parsley sprig.

❧ Serve warm.

FARFALLINE WITH OLIVES AND SUN-DRIED TOMATOES

SERVES 6

Because the Preserved Lemons must age for 7 days, you must plan ahead to make this recipe. If time is limited, you can substitute ¼ cup (2 fl oz/60 ml) fresh lemon juice and an additional teaspoon of salt, but the taste will be less complex.

¼ cup (1½ oz/45 g) Preserved Lemons
12 sun-dried tomatoes in olive oil,
    drained
5 qt (5 l) water
1 tablespoon salt
12 oz (375 g) dried farfalline
½ cup (4 fl oz/125 ml) extra-virgin
    olive oil
¼ cup (2½ oz/75 g) thinly sliced garlic
1 cup (5 oz/155 g) Kalamata or other
    black olives, pitted
2 tablespoons capers, drained
1 tablespoon grated lemon zest
2 tablespoons minced fresh flat-leaf
    (Italian) parsley
8 oz (250 g) mozzarella cheese, cut
    into small pieces
¾ cup (3 oz/90 g) chopped walnuts

Make and age the Preserved Lemons.
❧ Preheat an oven to 325°F (165°C).
❧ In a food mill or blender, purée 9 of the sun-dried tomatoes to make ⅔ cup (5 oz/155 g) of purée. Halve the remaining tomatoes.
❧ In a large pot over high heat, bring the water to a boil. Add the salt and the farfalline and cook according to the package directions or until al dente, about 6 minutes. Drain and place in a large bowl.
❧ In a small, heavy saucepan over low heat, heat the olive oil. Add the garlic and sauté, stirring frequently, until tender but not brown, about 5 minutes. Remove from the heat and cool.
❧ Add the Preserved Lemons, purée, olives, capers, zest, parsley and cheese.
❧ Add the lemon mixture to the pasta. Stir to mix well.
❧ Place in a 2-qt (2-l) baking dish and top with the walnuts. Bake until the cheese is melted, about 20 minutes.
❧ To serve, cool for 5 minutes and divide among individual plates. Garnish with the remaining tomato halves.
❧ Serve warm.

Preserved Lemons

MAKES 1 PT (2 CUPS/12 OZ/370 G)

Preserved lemons have an enticing flavor that lends brightness to a variety of dishes. Middle Eastern in origin, they warrant space in any pantry. Although they must age for a week, preparation time is minimal.

4 lemons
¼ cup (2 oz/60 g) kosher salt
1 tablespoon sugar
½ cup (4 fl oz/125 ml) fresh lemon
    juice

Wash and thoroughly dry the lemons.
❧ Using a sharp knife, cut each lemon crosswise into 6 slices. Remove and discard the seeds. In a small bowl, combine the lemons, salt and sugar.
❧ Pack the lemons into an impeccably clean dry pint jar. Pour in the lemon juice. Cover the jar with plastic wrap and place its lid on tightly.
❧ Set the jar of lemons in a cool dark place for at least 7 days. Every other day, turn it upside down so that all of the lemon slices are evenly bathed in the juice. Preserved lemons will keep in the refrigerator for up to 2 months.

Extra-virgin olive oil comes from the first pressing of the olives, processed without the use of heat or chemicals. Its distinctive flavor and smooth texture is preferred for the recipes in this book, especially the salads. Less expensive pure olive oil, processed from later pressings, is fine for cooking. An array of oils from Italy, France, Greece, California and elsewhere fill market shelves. In addition, olive oils are available flavored with citrus and infused with herbs. Each type has a distinctive flavor and appeal; try various ones to find a favorite.

CAPONATA FILLED SHELLS WITH BÉCHAMEL SAUCE

SERVES 6

Caponata, Italy's resounding answer to the ratatouille of southern France, has a tangy flavor that results from the presence of olives, capers and vinegar, all popular ingredients in the dish's native island of Sicily. Every town there boasts its own variation. Some traditional versions of caponata, which is also known as caponatina, may include seafood such as lobster claws, anchovies, crayfish tails or chunks of octopus; other vegetables, including artichokes and asparagus; and hard-boiled eggs. The shells may be stuffed with the caponata and assembled in the baking dish well ahead of time and refrigerated; if you do so, allow an extra 5 to 10 minutes of baking time.

Béchamel Sauce (recipe on page 96)
¼ cup (2 fl oz/60 ml) extra-virgin
    olive oil
1 yellow onion, peeled and finely diced
2 tablespoons minced garlic
1 large eggplant (aubergine), peeled
    and cubed
2 tomatoes, peeled, seeded and diced
    (see page 299)
½ cup (2½ oz/75 g) black olives, pitted
    and halved
½ cup (2½ oz/75 g) green olives, pitted
    and halved
2 tablespoons capers, drained
1 tablespoon red wine vinegar
¼ cup (⅓ oz/10 g) minced fresh
    flat-leaf (Italian) parsley
salt and freshly ground pepper
6 qt (6 l) water
1 tablespoon salt
18 dried jumbo pasta shells
fresh flat-leaf (Italian) parsley leaves

Make the Béchamel Sauce.

❧ Preheat an oven to 350°F (180°C). Coat the inside of a 9-by-13-inch (23-by-33-cm) baking dish with olive oil.

❧ To make the filling, in a large frying pan over low heat, heat the olive oil. Add the onion and sauté, stirring frequently, until tender and fragrant, about 15 minutes.

❧ Add the garlic and sauté for 2 minutes. Add the eggplant and sauté until the eggplant is very soft, about 20 minutes. Add the tomatoes, olives, capers, vinegar and minced parsley and simmer for 15 minutes. Add salt and pepper to taste.

❧ In a large pot over high heat, bring the water to a boil. Add the 1 tablespoon salt and the shells and cook according to the package directions or until almost al dente, about 8 minutes. Drain, rinse in cool water and drain again.

❧ Fill each pasta shell with about 2 tablespoons of filling and place in the baking dish. Top with half of the Béchamel Sauce.

❧ Bake until heated through but not brown, about 15 minutes. Meanwhile, heat the remaining Béchamel Sauce.

❧ To serve, divide the remaining Béchamel Sauce among individual warmed plates. Top with the shells. Garnish with a few parsley leaves.

❧ Serve hot.

He who has not eaten a caponatina of eggplant has never reached the antechamber of the terrestrial paradise.
—GAETANO FALZONE

Beautiful eggplants add a rich texture to pasta dishes. They range in color from deep purple to white. The tastiest eggplants are small, young and tender. Larger, older eggplants become tough on the outside and taste bitter when cooked.

LAMB FILLED SHELLS WITH SPICED RED SAUCE

SERVES 6

You can make these shells several hours in advance and bake them just before serving.

Spiced Red Sauce
1¼ lb (625 g) ground (minced) lamb
3 garlic cloves, peeled and minced
8 oz (250 g) spinach, stemmed and
    coarsely chopped
2 teaspoons grated lemon zest
3½ oz (105 g) feta cheese, cut into
    ¼-inch (6-mm) cubes
6 qt (6 l) water
1 tablespoon salt
18 dried jumbo pasta shells
3 tablespoons pine nuts, toasted
    (see page 297)

Preheat an oven to 325°F (165°C).
❧ Prepare the Spiced Red Sauce.
❧ In a large frying pan over medium heat, cook the lamb, breaking it up with a fork, until it is no longer pink. Drain off any excess fat and return the frying pan to the heat. Add the garlic and spinach, cover and cook until the spinach is wilted, 3–4 minutes. Cool to room temperature. Add the lemon zest and feta cheese and toss to mix well.
❧ In a large pot over high heat, bring the water to a boil. Add the 1 tablespoon salt and the shells and cook according to the package directions or until almost al dente, about 8 minutes. Drain, rinse in cool water and drain again.
❧ Fill each pasta shell and place in a baking dish. Top with half the Spiced Red Sauce and the pine nuts.
❧ Bake until heated through but not brown, about 15 minutes. Meanwhile, heat the remaining Spiced Red Sauce.
❧ To serve, divide among individual warmed plates. Top with the remaining Spiced Red Sauce.
❧ Serve hot.

Spiced Red Sauce

MAKES ABOUT 1½ CUPS (12 FL OZ/375 ML)

Ready in minutes and made from pantry items, this sauce is an excellent light topping to meaty pasta dishes like the lamb-filled shells on this page. The amount of sauce is just enough to add a contrasting flavor but not enough to overwhelm the other ingredients. For a quick yet delicious meal, use this topping on purchased beef or chicken-filled ravioli.

1 cup (8 fl oz/250 ml) canned
    tomato sauce
½ cup (4 fl oz/125 ml) Chicken Stock
    (recipe on page 30)
3 tablespoons fresh lemon juice
salt and freshly ground pepper

In a heavy saucepan over medium-low heat, combine the tomato sauce, Chicken Stock, lemon juice and salt and pepper to taste. Bring to a boil. Remove from the heat. Stir to mix well.

Whether made at home or store-bought, crusty Italian bread makes an ideal accompaniment to a pasta meal. Offer the bread in an attractive basket and place a small bowl of herb-infused olive oil alongside. Encourage guests to dip the bread in the oil rather than spreading it with butter.

Radiatori Bolognese with Italian Meatballs

SERVES 8

Think of this as a baked version of spaghetti and meatballs, in which radiatori replace the usual slender pasta strands. The version shown here makes use of multicolored radiatori, made from plain egg, green spinach and red tomato pasta. Note that you will need bread crumbs for the crust and the meatballs.

4 cups (32 fl oz/1 l) Bolognese Sauce
    (recipe on page 195)
Italian Meatballs
6 qt (6 l) water
1 tablespoon salt
1 lb (500 g) dried radiatori
4 oz (125 g) mozzarella cheese, cut into
    small pieces
2 cups (8 oz/250 g) dried bread crumbs
    (see page 294)
fresh flat-leaf (Italian) parsley sprigs

Preheat an oven to 350°F (180°C).
❧ Make the Bolognese Sauce.
❧ Prepare the Italian Meatballs.
❧ In a large pot over high heat, bring the water to a boil. Add the 1 tablespoon salt and the radiatori and cook according to the package directions or until almost al dente, about 7 minutes. Drain and place in a large bowl.
❧ Add two-thirds of the Bolognese Sauce. Carefully fold in the Italian Meatballs and mozzarella cheese.
❧ Transfer the mixture into a 3-qt (3-l) baking dish. Add the remaining Bolognese Sauce and stir to mix well. Top with the bread crumbs.
❧ Bake until bubbly, 25–30 minutes.
❧ To serve, cool for 5 minutes and divide among individual warmed plates. Garnish with a parsley sprig.
❧ Serve warm.

Italian Meatballs

MAKES 40 MEATBALLS

These bite-sized meatballs are made with a combination of beef and pork. If you like, replace a little of both meats with some mild or spicy Italian pork sausage. Or, for a healthier version, make the meatballs with ground turkey or chicken, including if you like some fresh sausage made with either type of poultry.

12 oz (375 g) ground (minced) beef
8 oz (250 g) ground (minced) pork
½ cup (2 oz/60 g) dried bread crumbs
    (see page 294)
½ cup (2 oz/60 g) grated pecorino
    romano cheese
¼ cup (½ oz/10 g) minced fresh
    flat-leaf (Italian) parsley
2 garlic cloves, peeled and minced
3 eggs, lightly beaten
salt and freshly ground pepper
½ cup (2½ oz/75 g) unbleached
    all-purpose (plain) flour
2 tablespoons olive oil

In a medium bowl, combine the beef, pork, bread crumbs, pecorino romano cheese, parsley, garlic, eggs and salt and pepper to taste. Stir to mix well.
❧ Place the flour in a small bowl. In a small frying pan over medium heat, heat the olive oil. Shape the meat mixture into 40 teaspoon-sized meatballs.
❧ Drop each meatball into the bowl of flour and, shaking the bowl, lightly coat each meatball. Fry the meatballs in batches, turning frequently, until uniformly browned, 6–7 minutes. Drain on paper towels.

'Tis not the meat, but 'tis the appetite makes eating a delight.
—SIR JOHN SUCKLING

Shallots are a mild member of the onion family with papery reddish skin and white flesh. Carrying a hint of garlic flavor, they are essential to French beurre blanc and its variations. You can substitute shallots for garlic or onions in most recipes. Store shallots hanging in a basket in a cool, dark place and they will keep for about a month.

MANICOTTI WITH MUSHROOMS AND GOAT CHEESE SAUCE

SERVES 6

Though this recipe calls for a mixture of cremini, button and shiitake mushrooms, feel free to use any combination that you like and can find, or use all button mushrooms.

Goat Cheese Sauce
¼ cup (2 oz/60 g) unsalted butter
2 shallots, peeled and minced
1 tablespoon minced garlic
24 green (spring) onions, green and white parts, cut into small rounds
4 cups (12 oz/360 g) cremini mushrooms
4 cups (12 oz/360 g) button mushrooms
4 cups (12 oz/360 g) shiitake mushrooms, stemmed
6 qt (6 l) water
1 tablespoon salt
12 dried manicotti
fresh chives

Preheat an oven to 350°F (180°C). Coat the inside of a 9-by-13-inch (23-by-33-cm) baking dish with olive oil.

❧ Prepare the Goat Cheese Sauce.

❧ To make the filling, in a large frying pan over medium-low heat, melt the butter until it foams. Add the shallots and sauté until tender, about 5 minutes. Add the garlic and green onions and sauté for 2 minutes. Add the mushrooms, cover and sauté until they are limp, 10–12 minutes.

❧ Remove the lid, increase the heat to medium-high and cook until all the liquid has evaporated, 10–15 minutes. Cool to room temperature.

❧ In a large pot over high heat, bring the water to a boil. Add the 1 tablespoon salt and the manicotti and cook according to the package directions or until al dente, about 12 minutes. Drain, rinse in cool water and drain again.

❧ Fill the manicotti with the filling and place in the baking dish. Top with the Goat Cheese Sauce.

❧ Bake until the sauce is bubbly, about 20 minutes.

❧ To serve, cool for 5 minutes and divide among individual warmed plates. Garnish with the chives.

❧ Serve warm.

Goat Cheese Sauce

MAKES ABOUT 2 CUPS (16 FL OZ/500 ML)

Young, fresh goat cheese is mild and creamy. As it ages, its flavor gets more pronounced. Try this sauce on elbow pasta, for a new twist on the children's favorite, macaroni and cheese.

2 cups (16 fl oz/500 ml) heavy (double) cream
5 oz (155 g) fresh mild goat cheese, crumbled
1 tablespoon minced fresh chives
salt and freshly ground pepper

In a medium saucepan over medium heat, simmer the cream until it is reduced by one-third, about 15 minutes.

❧ Remove from the heat, add the goat cheese and stir until the sauce is smooth. Add the chives and salt and pepper to taste.

MANICOTTI WITH GREENS AND SPICY TOMATO SAUCE

SERVES 6

Large tubes of dried pasta used for filling are called manicotti. Similar tubes made from fresh pasta rectangles are called cannelloni. The greens mixture can be made from all Swiss chard (silverbeet) or all spinach.

Spicy Tomato Sauce
3 tablespoons unsalted butter
1 small yellow onion, peeled and diced
1 tablespoon minced garlic
1½ lb (750 g) Swiss chard (silverbeet), stemmed and chopped
1 lb (500 g) spinach, stemmed and chopped
4 oz (125 g) mild white goat cheese
1 cup (4 oz/125 g) grated pecorino romano cheese
1 egg, lightly beaten
6 qt (6 l) water
1 tablespoon salt
12 dried manicotti
1 tablespoon chopped flat-leaf (Italian) parsley

Preheat an oven to 325°F (165°C). Coat the inside of a 9-by-13-inch (23-by-33-cm) baking dish with olive oil.

❧ Prepare the Spicy Tomato Sauce.

❧ To make the filling, in a large frying pan over medium-low heat, melt the butter until it foams. Add the onion and sauté, stirring frequently, until the onion is tender and fragrant, about 15 minutes.

❧ Add the garlic and sauté for 2 minutes. Add the chard and spinach, cover and cook until the greens wilt, about 8 minutes. Cool to room temperature.

❧ Add the goat and pecorino romano cheeses and egg. Stir to mix well.

❧ In a large pot over high heat, bring the water to a boil. Add the 1 tablespoon salt and the manicotti and cook according to the package directions or until al dente, about 12 minutes. Drain, rinse in cool water and drain again.

❧ Fill the manicotti with the filling and place in the baking dish. Top with the Spicy Tomato Sauce.

❧ Bake until the sauce is bubbly, about 25 minutes.

❧ To serve, garnish with an equal amount of the parsley.

❧ Serve hot.

Spicy Tomato Sauce

MAKES ABOUT 3 CUPS (24 FL OZ/750 ML)

Great over pasta, Classic Risotto (recipe on page 20) or Classic Polenta (recipe on page 199), this spicy hot version of a simple marinara sauce is often preferred by an adult palate. When cooking this dish for children, consider skipping the red pepper flakes.

3 tablespoons olive oil
1 small yellow onion, peeled and finely diced
1 tablespoon minced garlic
1½ lb (750 g) tomatoes, peeled, seeded and chopped (see page 299)
red pepper flakes
salt

In a medium frying pan over medium heat, heat the olive oil. Add the onion and sauté, stirring frequently, until the onion is tender and fragrant, about 15 minutes.

❧ Add the garlic and sauté for 2 minutes. Reduce the heat to medium-low, add the tomatoes and red pepper flakes and salt to taste and simmer for 15 minutes.

❧ Using a food mill or a blender, purée the sauce.

A tomato's peel is a veil which obscures the wonders of its flesh.
—MARCELLA HAZAN

SPAGHETTINI AND SCALLOPS IN PARCHMENT

SERVES 6

Baking pasta in parchment provides a beautiful presentation, making this an ideal dish for entertaining. The packages can be filled, sealed and refrigerated several hours ahead, so that all you need do is pop them into the oven shortly before you plan to serve them. For the showiest service, snip the packets open with scissors at the table in front of each guest. Take care, however, to keep your hands clear of the steam that will rise as you open them.

4 tablespoons (2 oz/60 g) Ginger
    Butter (recipe on page 294)
5 qt (5 l) water
1 tablespoon salt
12 oz (375 g) dried spaghettini
2 tablespoons extra-virgin olive oil
18 sea scallops (about 1¼ lb/625 g)
1 green and 3 red bell peppers
    (capsicums), roasted, peeled, seeded,
    deribbed and cut into thin strips
    (see page 298)
2 tablespoons fresh lime juice
salt and freshly ground pepper
1 lime, cut into 6 slices

Make the Ginger Butter.

❧ Preheat an oven to 375°F (190°C). Cut parchment paper into six 12-by-18-inch (30-by-45-cm) rectangles.

❧ In a large pot over high heat, bring the water to a boil. Add the 1 table-spoon salt and the spaghettini and cook according to the package directions or until al dente, about 8 minutes. Drain, rinse in cool water, drain again and place in a medium bowl. Immediately toss with 1 tablespoon of the olive oil.

❧ In a medium frying pan over medium-low heat, melt 1 tablespoon of the Ginger Butter. Add the scallops in batches and sauté for about 2 minutes on each side.

❧ Place the parchment rectangles on a work surface, fold in half crosswise to score and fold open. In the center of one side of each rectangle, place an equal amount of the spaghettini, peppers, scallops, the remaining Ginger Butter, lime juice and salt and pepper to taste. Top with a lime slice.

❧ To seal the packets closed, brush the outside edge of the parchment with some of the remaining olive oil. Bring the shorter sides together and press to bond the edges. Make a ½-inch (12-mm) hem around each packet to shape semicircles of parchment.

❧ Set the packets on a baking sheet and bake until the puffy packets turn golden, about 8 minutes.

❧ To serve, using scissors, carefully cut open each package.

❧ Serve hot.

LEMONY LINGUINE AND CRAB IN PARCHMENT

SERVES 6

The popularity of pasta has led to a plethora of flavored pastas available in many markets. The spinach in the pasta itself gives this dish extra dimension, but plain pasta works well, too. If you have the time, using fresh pasta (recipes on page 12) gives these easily assembled parchment parcels a special highlight. Slice the fennel bulb very thinly so its taste doesn't overwhelm the sauce.

12 oz (375 g) dried spinach linguine
6 qt (6 l) water
1 tablespoon salt
2 tablespoons extra-virgin olive oil
1 small fennel bulb, thinly sliced
    crosswise
3 celery stalks, thinly sliced diagonally
9 oz (280 g) cooked crabmeat
2 tablespoons unsalted butter
2 tablespoons fresh lemon juice
salt and freshly ground pepper
1 lemon, cut into 6 slices
fresh fennel fronds

Preheat an oven to 375°F (190°C).

❧ Cut parchment paper into six 12-by-18-inch (30-by-45-cm) rectangles.

❧ In a large pot over high heat, bring the water to a boil. Add the 1 tablespoon salt and the linguine and cook according to the package directions or until almost al dente, about 10 minutes. Drain, rinse in cool water, drain again and immediately toss with 1 tablespoon of the olive oil.

❧ Place the parchment rectangles on a work surface, fold in half crosswise to score and fold open. In the center of one side of each rectangle, place an equal amount of the linguine, fennel, celery, crabmeat, butter, lemon juice and salt and pepper to taste. Top with a lemon slice.

❧ To seal the packets closed, brush the outside edge of the parchment with some of the remaining olive oil. Bring the shorter sides together and press to bond the edges. Make a ½-inch (12-mm) hem around each packet to shape semicircles of parchment.

❧ Set the packets on a baking sheet and bake until the puffy packets turn golden, about 6 minutes.

❧ To serve, using scissors, carefully cut open each package. Garnish with a fennel frond.

❧ Serve hot.

ORZO WITH WINTER SQUASH AND LEEKS

SERVES 6

Any winter squash, including sugar pumpkin, Delicata or butternut, will work well in this comforting dish. Use a slightly larger pasta, such as farfalline or small shells, if you cannot locate orzo. Serve with a simple green salad.

1 lb (500 g) squash, seeded and cut
    into large pieces
cayenne pepper
ground nutmeg
freshly ground black pepper
4 qt (4 l) water
2 teaspoons salt
12 oz (375 g) dried orzo
3 tablespoons olive oil
2 oz (60 g) pancetta, finely chopped
2 tablespoons unsalted butter
2 leeks, white parts and 2 inches (5 cm)
    green parts, thinly sliced
1 cup (4 oz/125 g) dried bread crumbs
    (see page 294)
¾ cup (3 oz/90 g) grated pecorino
    romano cheese
salt
2 cups (16 fl oz/500 ml) Chicken Stock
    (recipe on page 30)

Preheat an oven to 325°F (165°C). Thinly coat a baking sheet with olive oil or nonstick cooking spray.

❧ Place the squash on the baking sheet, cut side down, and bake until the squash is soft and tender, about 45 minutes. Let cool until cool to the touch, remove the pulp, place in a small bowl and mash. Discard the skins. Add the cayenne, nutmeg and pepper to taste.

❧ In a large pot over high heat, bring the water to a boil. Add the 2 teaspoons salt and the orzo and cook according to the package directions or until al dente, 5–10 minutes. Drain, rinse in cool water and drain again. Place in a bowl and immediately toss with 1 tablespoon of the olive oil.

❧ In a medium frying pan over medium heat, heat the remaining 2 tablespoons olive oil, add the pancetta and sauté, stirring occasionally until it is just crisp, about 10 minutes. Drain on paper towels.

❧ Melt the butter in the pan and add the leeks. Reduce the heat to medium-low and sauté, stirring occasionally until the leeks are completely wilted and tender, about 20 minutes.

❧ In a small bowl, combine the bread crumbs, pecorino romano cheese and salt to taste.

❧ To the orzo, add the squash, pancetta and leeks and toss to mix well. Transfer to a 2-qt (2-l) baking dish. Add the Chicken Stock and top with the bread crumb mixture.

❧ Bake until the crumbs just begin to color, about 20 minutes.

❧ To serve, divide among plates.

❧ Serve hot.

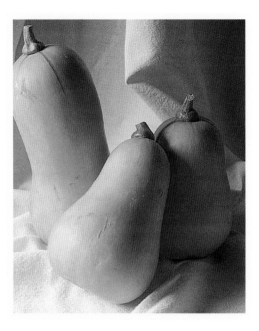

When gourd-shaped butternut squashes arrive in markets, you know that short days and cool weather are not far behind. Purchase these and other winter squashes early in the season and save for a rainy day. Uncut winter squashes stored in a cool, dry place will keep for several months. Include butternut squash in pasta and risotto dishes or halve, seed and bake them as a side dish. Toast the seeds as you do pumpkin seeds, for a healthy snack.

PASTA CARBONARA SOUFFLÉ

SERVES 6

Based on the "charcoal-maker's" traditional pasta dish, this recipe produces a rich, golden soufflé encasing delicate pasta strands. A Caesar salad, crusty bread and platter of olives and roasted peppers are ideal accompaniments.

4 qt (4 l) water
2 teaspoons salt
5 oz (155 g) dried angel hair pasta, broken into thirds
1 tablespoon extra-virgin olive oil
4 oz (125 g) pancetta, diced
1½ cups (12 fl oz/375 ml) half & half (half cream)
7 eggs, separated
¼ cup (⅓ oz/10 g) minced fresh flat-leaf (Italian) parsley
salt and freshly ground pepper
¾ cup (3 oz/90 g) grated Fontina cheese
½ cup (2 oz/60 g) grated Parmesan cheese
fresh flat-leaf (Italian) parsley sprigs

Preheat an oven to 375°F (190°C). Butter the sides and bottom of a 2-qt (2-l) soufflé dish.

❧ In a large pot over high heat, bring the water to a boil. Add the 2 teaspoons salt and the angel hair pasta and cook according to the package directions or until al dente, about 4 minutes. Drain, place in a large bowl and immediately toss with the olive oil.

❧ In a small, heavy frying pan over medium-low heat, cook the pancetta until crisp, about 10 minutes. Add the half & half and simmer until it is reduced by one-third, about 10 minutes. Cool to room temperature.

❧ In a large bowl, beat the egg yolks until thick. Add the parsley and salt and pepper to taste. Stir the egg mixture into the pancetta mixture. Add the Fontina and Parmesan cheeses. Stir to mix well.

❧ In a large bowl, beat the egg whites until soft peaks form. Fold one-third of the egg whites into the egg yolk mixture, then add the pasta, stirring lightly. Carefully fold in the remaining egg whites. Pour the mixture into the soufflé dish.

❧ Bake until the top is golden brown, 45–50 minutes.

❧ To serve, divide among individual plates. Garnish with a parsley sprig.

❧ Serve hot.

FRITTATA OF CAPELLINI, ONIONS AND PANCETTA

SERVES 6

The key to a successful frittata is to remove it from the oven as soon as the eggs have set; any longer and the eggs will release their liquid and lose their delicate texture.

1 cup (3½ oz/105 g) Caramelized
    Onions (recipe on page 203)
4 qt (4 l) water
2 teaspoons salt
8 oz (250 g) dried angel hair pasta
2 tablespoons olive oil
4 oz (125 g) pancetta, finely chopped
8 eggs
1 cup (4 oz/125 g) grated Parmesan
    cheese
salt and freshly ground pepper
¼ cup (2 oz/60 g) unsalted butter

Make the Caramelized Onions.

❧ Preheat an oven to 325°F (165°C).

❧ In a large pot over high heat, bring the water to a boil. Add the 2 teaspoons

salt and the pasta and cook according to the package directions or until almost al dente, about 4 minutes. Drain, rinse in cool water and drain again.

❧ Place in a large bowl. Add the Caramelized Onions and toss to mix well.

❧ In a small frying pan over medium heat, heat the olive oil. Add the pancetta and sauté, stirring occasionally, until it is just crisp, about 10 minutes. Cool, add to the pasta and toss to mix well.

❧ In a medium bowl, beat the eggs until they are creamy. Add the Parmesan cheese and salt and pepper to taste. Stir to mix well.

❧ In a 10-inch (25-cm) ovenproof frying pan over medium-low heat, melt the butter until it foams. Add the pasta mixture and shake the pan so that the pasta is spread evenly. Sauté until the pasta begins to turn golden, 7–8 minutes. Add the egg mixture, reduce the heat to low and cook until the eggs appear slightly firm, about 5 minutes.

❧ Place in the oven and bake until the eggs just set, about 10 minutes.

❧ To serve, invert onto a large serving plate and divide among individual warmed plates.

❧ Serve hot.

Risotto

☙

Considering the fact that half of the world's population relies
on it as their major source of sustenance, rice—not bread—deserves
pride of place as the true staff of life. Risotto, a northern
Italian specialty, may well present the staple in its most glorious form.
Because risotto is based on a starchy ingredient that provides
the same latitude for creative elaboration, Italians usually include it in
the category of pasta. Short, plump grains of Arborio rice are
slowly simmered and stirred in hot liquid until they are chewy and
tender—*al dente,* as they describe it in Italy—and their surface
starch has dissolved to form a thick, creamlike sauce. Along the way,
a wide range of other ingredients, seasonings and garnishes may
be added. Recognizing the widespread popularity risotto has gained
in recent years, the recipes in this chapter celebrate the dish in its
varied forms: as an appetizer, a side dish and an entree, prepared with
utter simplicity and elaborated with vegetables, meat, poultry
or seafood. Recipes for Spanish paella, a related dish,
are included as well.

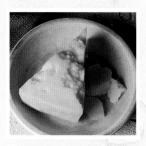

Risotto Appetizers

The purpose of any appetizer is captured in the very word itself: to entice the appetite, to begin a meal with tastes and textures that are intriguing in their own right while providing an appropriate prelude to the courses that follow. Risotto appetizers fulfill that goal by combining creamy-textured, medium-grain rice with combinations of tender-crisp vegetables, fresh herbs and flavorful cheeses to create dishes that are light on the palate and yet full of excitement and satisfaction.

Within such simply defined boundaries, you'll find a wealth of diversity. While designed in portions for starting a meal, all of these recipes make wonderful vegetarian entrees as well.

From the elegantly spare combinations of rice, cheese and herbs, ideal before mild-tasting fish or poultry, to the slightly more complex arrangements that include vegetables, which make a great introduction to robust entrees, risotto appetizers will get any meal off to an exciting start.

FRESH HERB AND PARMESAN RISOTTO

SERVES 6

Simple and pure, this recipe benefits greatly from being made with the best Parmesan cheese available. Look for a block of the imported Italian cheese designated Parmigiano-Reggiano®. Serve the risotto before an equally straightforward main course such as roast chicken or grilled fish. Or substitute it in any recipe that calls for Classic Risotto, such as Chicken Livers with Peas (recipe on page 284) or Osso Buco (recipe on page 290).

5 cups (40 fl oz/1.25 l) Chicken Stock (recipe on page 30) or Vegetable Stock (recipe on page 238)
3 tablespoons olive oil
½ large onion, chopped
1½ cups (10½ oz/330 g) Arborio or medium-grain rice
½ cup (4 fl oz/125 ml) dry white wine
¾ cup (3 oz/90 g) freshly grated Parmesan cheese, plus additional freshly grated Parmesan cheese
⅓ cup (½ oz/15 g) finely chopped mixed fresh herbs such as basil, arugula, chives and flat-leaf (Italian) parsley
salt and freshly ground pepper

In a small saucepan over high heat, bring the Chicken or Vegetable Stock to a simmer. Reduce the heat to low and keep the liquid hot.

👉 In a heavy medium saucepan over medium-low heat, heat the olive oil and sauté the onion, stirring frequently, until the onion is translucent, about 8 minutes.

👉 To the onion, add the rice and stir until a white spot appears in the center of the grains, about 1 minute. Add the wine and stir until it is absorbed, about 2 minutes. Add ¾ cup (6 fl oz/180 ml) of the stock, adjust the heat to simmer, if needed, so that the liquid bubbles and is absorbed slowly. Stir until the liquid is absorbed. Continue cooking, adding the liquid ¾ cup (6 fl oz/180 ml) at a time and stirring almost constantly, until the rice starts to soften, about 10 minutes.

👉 Continue cooking, adding the liquid ½ cup (4 fl oz/125 ml) at a time and stirring almost constantly, until the rice is just tender but slightly firm in the center and the mixture is creamy, about 10 minutes longer.

👉 Add the ¾ cup (3 oz/90 g) Parmesan cheese, herbs and salt and pepper to taste. Stir to mix well.

👉 To serve, spoon into shallow bowls or onto plates. Pass the additional Parmesan cheese separately.

👉 Serve hot.

MOZZARELLA AND DRIED TOMATO RISOTTO

SERVES 6

The fresh mozzarella cheese will melt into threads, giving this risotto an intriguing texture. For a change of pace, try using smoked mozzarella. If you use oil-free, vacuum-packed dried tomatoes, first soften them in hot water to cover before draining and chopping.

5½ cups (44 fl oz/1.4 l) Chicken Stock (recipe on page 30) or Vegetable Stock (recipe on page 238)

⅓ cup (3 oz/90 g) oil-packed sun-dried tomatoes

1 onion, chopped

2 cups (14 oz/440 g) Arborio or medium-grain rice

1 cup (4 oz/125 g) finely shredded mozzarella cheese (preferably fresh, packed in water)

1 cup (4 oz/125 g) freshly grated Parmesan cheese

¼ cup (⅓ oz/10 g) finely chopped fresh basil

basil leaves

In a small saucepan over high heat, bring the Chicken or Vegetable Stock to a simmer. Reduce the heat to low and keep the liquid hot.

❧ Drain the sun-dried tomatoes and reserve the oil. Add more oil from the jar to equal 4 tablespoons (2 fl oz/ 60 ml). Chop the sun-dried tomatoes and set aside.

❧ In a heavy medium saucepan over medium-low heat, heat 2 tablespoons of the oil and sauté the onion, stirring frequently, until it is translucent, about 8 minutes.

❧ To the onion, add the rice and stir until a white spot appears in the center of the grains, about 1 minute. Add

¾ cup (6 fl oz/180 ml) of the stock, adjust the heat to simmer, if needed, so that the liquid bubbles and is absorbed slowly. Stir until the liquid is absorbed. Continue cooking, adding the liquid ¾ cup (6 fl oz/180 ml) at a time and stirring almost constantly, until the rice starts to soften, about 10 minutes.

❧ Continue cooking, adding the liquid ½ cup (4 fl oz/125 ml) at a time and stirring almost constantly, until the rice

is just tender but slightly firm in the center and the mixture is creamy, about 10 minutes longer.

❧ Add the cheeses, sun-dried tomatoes, chopped basil and remaining 2 table-spoons oil. Stir to mix well.

❧ To serve, spoon into shallow bowls. Garnish with the basil leaves.

❧ Serve hot.

RISOTTO WITH GREENS, GORGONZOLA AND WALNUTS

SERVES 6

The combination of robust greens, tangy cheese and toasted nuts makes this an ideal prelude to a simple roast poultry dinner. Substitute Roquefort, Danish blue or another blue-veined cheese for the Gorgonzola.

5 cups (40 fl oz/1.25 l) Chicken Stock (recipe on page 30) or Vegetable Stock (recipe on page 238)
3 tablespoons olive oil
½ large onion, chopped
1½ cups (10½ oz/330 g) Arborio or medium-grain rice
½ cup (4 fl oz/125 ml) dry white wine
3 cups (6 oz/180 g) thinly sliced greens such as escarole, Swiss chard (silverbeet), kale or beet
¾ cup (4 oz/125 g) crumbled Gorgonzola cheese
½ cup (2 oz/60 g) walnuts, toasted and coarsely chopped (see page 297)
salt and freshly ground pepper

In a small saucepan over high heat, bring the Chicken or Vegetable Stock to a simmer. Reduce the heat to low and keep the liquid hot.

❧ In a heavy medium saucepan over medium-low heat, heat the olive oil and sauté the onion, stirring frequently, until it is translucent, about 8 minutes.

❧ To the onion, add the rice and stir until a white spot appears in the center of the grains, about 1 minute. Add the wine and stir until it is absorbed, about 2 minutes. Add ¾ cup (6 fl oz/180 ml) of the stock, adjust the heat to simmer, if needed, so that the liquid bubbles and is absorbed slowly. Stir until the liquid is absorbed. Continue cooking, adding the liquid ¾ cup (6 fl oz/180 ml) at a time and stirring almost constantly, until the rice starts to soften, about 10 minutes.

❧ Add the sliced greens and continue cooking, adding the liquid ½ cup (4 fl oz/125 ml) at a time and stirring almost constantly, until the rice is just tender but still slightly firm in the center and the mixture is creamy, about 10 minutes longer.

❧ Add the Gorgonzola cheese, walnuts and salt and pepper to taste. Stir to mix well.

❧ To serve, spoon into shallow bowls.

❧ Serve hot.

Vegetable Stock

MAKES ABOUT 7 CUPS (56 FL OZ/1.75 L)

This simple stock is suitable for vegetarian risottos. Canned, bottled or frozen chicken or vegetable broth may be substituted.

3 large onions, cut into 1-inch
    (2.5-cm) pieces
4 large carrots, peeled and cut into
    1-inch (2.5-cm) pieces
4 celery stalks with leaves, cut into
    1-inch (2.5-cm) pieces
4 fresh parsley sprigs
1 bay leaf
3 qt (3 l) water

In a large pot over medium heat, combine all the ingredients. Bring to a boil. Reduce the heat and simmer uncovered for 1 hour.

❧ Using a strainer, strain the stock into a large bowl. Store in a tightly covered container in the refrigerator for up to 3 days or in the freezer for up to 1 week.

PORCINI RISOTTO

SERVES 6

Italy's beloved dried porcini mushrooms, the sweetness of onions and the sharp perfume of sage add up to a new classic.

¾ oz (20 g) dried porcini mushrooms
1 cup (8 fl oz/250 ml) hot water
5½ cups (44 fl oz/1.4 l) Chicken
    Stock (recipe on page 30) or
    Vegetable Stock
2 tablespoons unsalted butter
2 tablespoons olive oil
2 onions, quartered lengthwise and
    sliced crosswise
2 cups (14 oz/440 g) Arborio or
    medium-grain rice
¾ cup (6 fl oz/180 ml) dry white wine
1 tablespoon finely chopped fresh sage
    or 1 teaspoon dried
1½ cups (6 oz/185 g) freshly grated
    Parmesan cheese
salt and freshly ground pepper
fresh sage leaves

In a small bowl, combine the mushrooms and hot water. Soak for 30 minutes to soften. Drain the mushrooms, reserving the soaking liquid. Chop the mushrooms.

❧ In a small saucepan over high heat, bring the Chicken or Vegetable Stock to a simmer. Reduce the heat to low and keep the liquid hot.

❧ In a heavy medium saucepan over medium-high heat, melt the butter with the olive oil and sauté the onions, stirring frequently, until brown, about 10 minutes.

❧ To the onions, add the rice and mushrooms and stir until a white spot appears in the center of the grains, about 1 minute. Add the wine and stir until it is absorbed, about 2 minutes. Add the chopped sage, reserved mushroom soaking liquid (discarding any sediment at the bottom) and ¾ cup (6 fl oz/180 ml) of the stock. Adjust the heat to simmer, if needed, so that the liquid bubbles and is absorbed slowly. Stir until the liquid is absorbed. Continue cooking, adding the liquid ¾ cup (6 fl oz/180 ml) at a time and stirring almost constantly, until the rice starts to soften, about 10 minutes.

❧ Continue cooking, adding the liquid ½ cup (4 fl oz/125 ml) at a time and stirring almost constantly, until the rice is just tender but slightly firm in the center and the mixture is creamy, about 10 minutes longer.

❧ Add the Parmesan cheese and salt and pepper to taste. Stir to mix well.

❧ To serve, spoon into a shallow serving bowl or individual plates. Garnish with the sage leaves.

❧ Serve hot.

Fresh vegetable stock provides a clean-tasting base for any meat-free risotto dish. Making it at home allows you to season it to your liking, adding salt, black pepper, lemon pepper or even hot red pepper flakes to suit your taste.

ASPARAGUS RISOTTO

SERVES 6

Prepare this dish when springtime aspara-gus is at its best.

5½ cups (44 fl oz/1.4 l) Chicken Stock
   (recipe on page 30) or Vegetable
   Stock (recipe on page 238)
1¼ lb (625 g) asparagus, cut into
   1½-inch (4-cm) lengths
¾ cup (6 fl oz/180 ml) dry white wine
2 tablespoons olive oil
1 onion, chopped
2 cups (14 oz/440 g) Arborio or
   medium-grain rice
1 cup (4 oz/125 g) freshly grated
   Parmesan cheese
1 tablespoon finely chopped fresh
   tarragon or 1 teaspoon dried
fresh tarragon sprigs

In a small saucepan over high heat, bring the Chicken or Vegetable Stock to a boil. Add the asparagus and boil until just tender-crisp, about 2 minutes.

❧ Using a slotted spoon, transfer the asparagus to a bowl and set aside.

❧ Add the wine to the stock and bring to a simmer. Reduce the heat to low and keep the liquid hot.

❧ In a heavy large saucepan over medium-low heat, heat the olive oil and sauté the onion, stirring frequently, until it is translucent, about 8 minutes.

❧ To the onion, add the rice and stir until a white spot appears in the center of the grains, about 1 minute. Add ¾ cup (6 fl oz/180 ml) of the stock, adjust the heat to simmer, if needed, so that the liquid bubbles and is absorbed slowly. Stir until the liquid is absorbed. Continue cooking, adding the liquid ¾ cup (6 fl oz/180 ml) at a time and stirring almost constantly, until the rice starts to soften, about 10 minutes.

❧ Continue cooking, adding the liquid ½ cup (4 fl oz/125 ml) at a time and stirring almost constantly, until the rice is just tender but slightly firm in the center and the mixture is creamy, about 10 minutes longer.

❧ Add the asparagus, Parmesan cheese, chopped tarragon and salt and pepper to taste. Stir to mix well.

❧ To serve, spoon onto plates. Garnish with the tarragon.

❧ Serve hot.

RED WINE AND PARMESAN RISOTTO

SERVES 6

This risotto gains vibrant color and pungent flavor from the red wine used as part of its cooking liquid. Serve it with the same wine before a beef or veal course. For the best flavor, choose a full-bodied wine.

4 cups (32 fl oz/1 l) Chicken Stock
   (recipe on page 30) or Vegetable
   Stock (recipe on page 238)
2 cups (16 fl oz/500 ml) dry red wine
3 tablespoons unsalted butter
1 onion, chopped
2 cups (14 oz/440 g) Arborio or
   medium-grain rice
1 cup (4 oz/125 g) freshly grated
   Parmesan cheese
salt and freshly ground pepper
finely chopped fresh flat-leaf (Italian)
   parsley
fresh flat-leaf (Italian) parsley leaves

In a small saucepan over high heat, combine the Chicken or Vegetable Stock and wine and bring to a simmer. Reduce the heat to low and keep the liquid hot.

❧ In a heavy medium saucepan over medium-low heat, melt 2 tablespoons of the butter and sauté the onion, stirring frequently, until it is translucent, about 8 minutes.

❧ To the onion, add the rice and stir until a white spot appears in the center of the grains, about 1 minute. Add ¾ cup (6 fl oz/180 ml) of the stock, adjust the heat to simmer, if needed, so that the liquid bubbles and is absorbed slowly. Stir until the liquid is absorbed. Continue cooking, adding the liquid ¾ cup (6 fl oz/180 ml) at a time and stirring almost constantly, until the rice starts to soften, about 10 minutes.

❧ Continue cooking, adding the liquid ½ cup (4 fl oz/125 ml) at a time and stirring almost constantly, until the rice is just tender but slightly firm in the center and the mixture is creamy, about 10 minutes longer.

❧ Add the Parmesan cheese, the remaining 1 tablespoon butter and salt and pepper to taste. Stir to mix well.

❧ To serve, spoon into shallow bowls or onto plates. Garnish with the chopped parsley and parsley leaves.

❧ Serve hot.

Strange to see how a good dinner and feasting reconciles everyone.

—SAMUEL PEPYS

PEA, TARRAGON AND GOAT CHEESE RISOTTO

SERVES 6

Enjoy this contemporary version of the Venetian specialty known as risi e bisi, *a cross between risotto and soup.*

5½ cups (44 fl oz/1.4 l) Chicken Stock (recipe on page 30) or Vegetable Stock (recipe on page 238)
3 tablespoons olive oil
½ large onion, chopped
1½ cups (10½ oz/330 g) Arborio or medium-grain rice
½ cup (4 fl oz/125 ml) dry white wine
1½ cups (7½ oz/235 g) shelled fresh peas (see page 298) or frozen peas
2 teaspoons finely chopped fresh tarragon or ¾ teaspoon dried
½ cup (2½ oz/75 g) crumbled mild goat cheese
salt and freshly ground pepper
fresh tarragon sprigs

In a small saucepan over high heat, bring the Chicken or Vegetable Stock to a simmer. Reduce the heat to low and keep the liquid hot.

❧ In a heavy medium saucepan over medium-low heat, heat the olive oil and sauté the onion, stirring frequently, until it is translucent, about 8 minutes.

❧ To the onion, add the rice and stir until a white spot appears in the center of the grains, about 1 minute. Add the wine and stir until absorbed, about 2 minutes. Add ¾ cup (6 fl oz/180 ml) of the stock, adjust the heat to simmer, if needed, so that the liquid bubbles and is absorbed slowly. Stir until the liquid is absorbed. Continue cooking, adding the liquid ¾ cup (6 fl oz/180 ml) at a time and stirring almost constantly, until the rice starts to soften, about 10 minutes.

❧ Add the peas and chopped tarragon and continue cooking, adding the liquid ½ cup (4 fl oz/125 ml) at a time and stirring almost constantly, until the rice is just tender but slightly firm in the center and the mixture is creamy, about 10 minutes longer.

❧ Add the goat cheese and stir until the cheese melts. Add the salt and pepper to taste. Stir to mix well.

❧ To serve, spoon into shallow bowls or onto plates. Garnish with the tarragon sprigs.

❧ Serve hot.

PEPPER RISOTTO WITH FONTINA CHEESE

SERVES 6

This spicy rice dish is a rich-tasting starter that would be good before a main course of roast chicken.

5 cups (40 fl oz/1.25 l) Chicken Stock (recipe on page 30) or Vegetable Stock (recipe on page 238)
2 tablespoons olive oil
1 large onion, chopped
1 each red and yellow bell pepper (capsicum), seeded, deribbed and cut into ½-inch (12-mm) cubes (see page 298)
1 garlic clove, peeled and minced
1½ cups (10½ oz/330 g) Arborio or medium-grain rice
¾ cup (3 oz/90 g) grated Fontina cheese
1 tablespoon chopped fresh thyme or 1 teaspoon dried

In a small saucepan over high heat, bring the Chicken or Vegetable Stock to a simmer. Reduce the heat to low and keep the liquid hot.

❧ In a heavy medium saucepan over medium-low heat, heat the olive oil and sauté the onion, stirring frequently, until it begins to soften, about 5 minutes. Add the bell peppers and garlic and sauté, stirring frequently, until the peppers begin to soften, about 5 minutes.

❧ To the onion mixture, add the rice and stir until a white spot appears in the center of the grains, about 1 minute. Add ¾ cup (6 fl oz/180 ml) of the stock, adjust the heat to simmer, if needed, so that the liquid bubbles and is absorbed slowly. Stir until the liquid is absorbed. Continue cooking, adding the liquid ¾ cup (6 fl oz/180 ml) at a time and stirring almost constantly, until the rice starts to soften, about 10 minutes.

❧ Continue cooking, adding the liquid ½ cup (4 fl oz/125 ml) at a time and stirring almost constantly, until the rice is just tender but slightly firm in the center and the mixture is creamy, about 10 minutes longer.

❧ Add the Fontina cheese and thyme and stir until the cheese melts.

❧ To serve, spoon into shallow bowls.

❧ Serve hot.

RISOTTO WITH RED BELL PEPPER, TOMATO, MINT AND FETA

SERVES 6

Italy's fabled rice dish travels to the eastern Mediterranean with this combination of classic Greek and Turkish ingredients. To achieve the right balance of flavors, seek out a variety of feta cheese that is not overly salty, so that it won't overwhelm the other zesty ingredients. This makes an outstanding first course or side dish with roast or grilled lamb or seafood. Feel free to substitute a little fresh oregano for the fresh mint, if you like a more Italian taste, and to use yellow bell peppers (capsicums) if red bell peppers are unavailable.

5½ cups (44 fl oz/1.4 l) Chicken Stock (recipe on page 30) or Vegetable Stock (recipe on page 238)

2 tablespoons olive oil

1 onion, chopped

1 large red bell pepper (capsicum), seeded, deribbed and cut into ½-inch (12-mm) pieces (see page 298)

1½ cups (10½ oz/330 g) Arborio or medium-grain rice

2 tomatoes, seeded and chopped (see page 299)

¾ cup (4 oz/125 g) crumbled feta cheese

¼ cup (⅓ oz/10 g) finely chopped fresh mint

salt and freshly ground pepper

fresh mint leaves

In a small saucepan over high heat, bring the Chicken or Vegetable Stock to a boil. Reduce the heat to low and keep the liquid hot.

❧ In a heavy medium saucepan over medium-low heat, heat the olive oil and sauté the onion, stirring frequently, until it begins to soften, about 5 minutes. Add the bell pepper and sauté, stirring frequently, until the pepper begins to soften, about 5 minutes.

❧ To the onion mixture, add the rice and stir until a white spot appears in the center of the grains, about 1 minute. Add ¾ cup (6 fl oz/180 ml) of the stock, adjust the heat to simmer, if needed, so that the liquid bubbles and is absorbed slowly. Stir until the liquid is absorbed. Continue cooking, adding the liquid ¾ cup (6 fl oz/180 ml) at a time and stirring almost constantly, until the rice starts to soften, about 10 minutes.

❧ Add the tomatoes. Continue cooking, adding the liquid ½ cup (4 fl oz/125 ml) at a time and stirring almost constantly, until the rice is just tender but slightly firm in the center and the mixture is creamy, about 10 minutes.

❧ Add the feta cheese, mint and salt and pepper to taste. Stir to mix well.

❧ To serve, spoon into shallow bowls or onto plates. Garnish with the mint.

❧ Serve hot.

GORGONZOLA RISOTTO WITH TOMATO TOPPING

SERVES 6

If you can't find Gorgonzola, substitute another good-quality blue-veined cheese such as Danish blue, American Maytag blue or English Stilton cheese. During summer, look for the best sun-ripened tomatoes available. At other times of year, Italian-style Roma (plum) tomatoes are your best bet for good flavor and texture. For a change of pace, the tomato mixture may also be stirred into the risotto just before serving rather than spooned on top of each portion.

3 tomatoes, seeded and chopped
    (see page 299)
1 cup (3 oz/90 g) chopped green
    (spring) onions, green and white
    parts (about 9 total)
3 tablespoons olive oil
1½ teaspoons balsamic vinegar
5½ cups (44 fl oz/1.4 l) Chicken Stock
    (recipe on page 30) or Vegetable
    Stock (recipe on page 238)
1½ cups (10½ oz/330 g) Arborio or
    medium-grain rice
½ cup (2½ oz/75 g) crumbled
    Gorgonzola cheese

To make the tomato topping, in a bowl, mix the tomatoes, ¼ cup (¾ oz/20 g) of the green onions, 1½ tablespoons of the olive oil and the vinegar.

❧ In a small saucepan over high heat, bring the Chicken or Vegetable Stock to a simmer. Reduce the heat to low and keep the liquid hot.

❧ In a heavy medium saucepan over medium-low heat, heat the remaining 1½ tablespoons olive oil. Add ½ cup (1½ oz/50 g) of the green onions and stir for 2 minutes.

❧ To the saucepan, add the rice and stir until a white spot appears in the center of the grains, about 1 minute. Add ¾ cup (6 fl oz/180 ml) of the stock, adjust the heat to simmer, if needed, so that the liquid bubbles and is absorbed slowly. Stir until the liquid is absorbed. Continue cooking, adding the liquid ¾ cup (6 fl oz/180 ml) at a time and stirring almost constantly, until the rice starts to soften, about 10 minutes.

❧ Continue cooking, adding the liquid ½ cup (4 fl oz/125 ml) at a time and stirring almost constantly, until the rice is just tender but slightly firm in the center and the mixture is creamy, about 10 minutes longer.

❧ Stir in the remaining ¼ cup (¾ oz/20 g) green onions and cheese.

❧ To serve, spoon into shallow bowls. Top with the tomatoes.

❧ Serve hot.

Risotto Side Dishes

All too often, side dishes do not get the attention or credit they deserve, being regarded as little more than something to add a bit of color or fill the empty space on a dinner plate. That is not the case, however, with risotto side dishes, which can be every bit as spectacular as the main courses they accompany.

Take a look at the recipes that follow for stellar examples of how interesting such accompaniments can be. At its most basic, Classic Risotto (recipe on page 20) fashioned into pancakes makes a wonderful side dish or brunch, lunch or light dinner entree. Many side-dish risottos include fresh seasonal produce: from the all-time favorite artichokes for spring (recipe on page 251) to the zesty zucchini of summer (recipe on page 255).

Risotto side dishes can be served as a course alone, plated with other food or shaped into supplì (recipe on page 261). Whether at their utter simplest or in more unusual forms, risotto side dishes are guaranteed to win well-deserved kudos.

BUTTERNUT SQUASH, SAGE AND HAZELNUT RISOTTO

SERVES 6

With its autumnal colors and flavors, this risotto is ideal served alongside a main course of grilled pork chops. If you're out of hazelnuts (filberts), use toasted blanched almonds instead.

5½ cups (44 fl oz/1.4 l) Chicken Stock (recipe on page 30) or Vegetable Stock (recipe on page 238)
2 tablespoons unsalted butter
1 large onion, chopped
1 butternut squash or other orange-fleshed squash, peeled and cubed (see page 299)
5 teaspoons chopped fresh sage or 1 teaspoon dried
1½ cups (10½ oz/330 g) Arborio or medium-grain rice
½ cup (4 fl oz/125 ml) dry white wine
⅓ cup (1 oz/30 g) freshly grated Parmesan cheese
4 tablespoons (1 oz/30 g) hazelnuts (filberts), peeled, toasted and coarsely chopped (see page 297)
1½ teaspoons freshly ground pepper
salt

In a small saucepan over high heat, bring the Chicken or Vegetable Stock to a simmer. Reduce the heat to low and keep the liquid hot.

❧ In a heavy medium saucepan over low heat, melt the butter and sauté the onion, stirring frequently, until it is soft and light brown, about 10 minutes. Add the squash and 4 teaspoons of the fresh sage or all the dried sage and sauté, stirring frequently, for 2 minutes. Cover and cook until the squash is almost tender, about 6 minutes.

❧ Uncover the squash pan, add the rice and stir until a white spot appears in the center of the grains, about 1 minute. Add the wine and stir until absorbed, about 2 minutes. Add ¾ cup (6 fl oz/180 ml) of the stock, adjust the heat to simmer, if needed, so that the liquid bubbles and is absorbed slowly. Stir until the liquid is absorbed. Continue cooking, adding the liquid ¾ cup (6 fl oz/180 ml) at a time and stirring almost constantly, until the rice starts to soften, about 10 minutes.

❧ Continue cooking, adding the liquid ½ cup (4 fl oz/125 ml) at a time and stirring almost constantly, until the rice is just tender but slightly firm in the center and the mixture is creamy, about 10 minutes longer.

❧ Add the Parmesan cheese, 3 tablespoons of the nuts, the pepper and salt to taste. Stir to mix well.

❧ To serve, spoon onto individual plates. Garnish with the remaining 1 teaspoon fresh sage, if using, and the remaining 1 tablespoon nuts.

❧ Serve hot.

FENNEL, LEEK AND PANCETTA RISOTTO

SERVES 6

Three forms of fennel—the bulb vegetable, the dried seeds and the feathery fronds—add the subtly sweet flavor of anise to this risotto. If you can't find the unsmoked Italian bacon called pancetta, substitute another kind of bacon. For a vegetarian version, eliminate the bacon completely or substitute bacon-flavored soy bits.

5 cups (40 fl oz/1.25 l) Chicken Stock (recipe on page 30) or Vegetable Stock (recipe on page 238)

2 tablespoons olive oil

2 leeks, light green and white parts, halved lengthwise and sliced crosswise (see page 297)

1 fennel bulb, quartered lengthwise and sliced crosswise

1½ cups (10½ oz/330 g) Arborio or medium-grain rice

4 oz (125 g) pancetta, chopped

½ teaspoon fennel seeds, crushed

¾ cup (6 fl oz/180 ml) dry white wine

½ cup (2 oz/60 g) freshly grated pecorino romano cheese, plus additional freshly grated pecorino romano cheese

salt and freshly ground pepper

fresh fennel fronds

In a small saucepan over high heat, bring the Chicken or Vegetable Stock to a simmer. Reduce the heat to low and keep the liquid hot.

❧ In a heavy large saucepan over low heat, heat the olive oil and sauté the leeks, stirring frequently, until they begin to soften, about 5 minutes. Add the sliced fennel and sauté, stirring frequently, until the fennel begins to soften, about 5 minutes.

❧ To the leek mixture, add the rice, pancetta and fennel seeds and stir for 1 minute. Add the wine and stir until it is absorbed, about 2 minutes. Add ¾ cup (6 fl oz/180 ml) of the stock, adjust the heat to simmer, if needed, so that the liquid bubbles and is absorbed slowly. Stir until the liquid is absorbed. Continue cooking, adding the liquid ¾ cup (6 fl oz/180 ml) at a time and stirring almost constantly, until the rice starts to soften, about 10 minutes.

❧ Continue cooking, adding the liquid ½ cup (4 fl oz/125 ml) at a time and stirring almost constantly, until the rice is just tender but slightly firm in the center and the mixture is creamy, about 10 minutes longer.

❧ Add the ½ cup (2 oz/60 g) pecorino romano cheese and salt and pepper to taste. Stir to mix well.

❧ To serve, spoon into a serving bowl or onto individual plates. Garnish with the fennel fronds. Pass the additional pecorino romano cheese separately.

❧ Serve hot.

They bring you at dusk a preparation which seems to you to be made of grains of gold, and you are delighted already by nothing more than the sight of those grains of rice…

—EDOUARD DE POMIANE

Rice is a staple food in many parts of the world and has been for thousands of years. Easy to digest, it provides energy and is rich in vitamins and iron.

SAFFRON RISOTTO

SERVES 6

The classic risotto alla milanese *is an easily prepared, golden, aromatic dish traditionally served in Italy with osso buco (braised veal shanks). You'll find, though, that it enhances any meal.*

5½ cups (44 fl oz/1.4 l) Chicken Stock (recipe on page 30) or Vegetable Stock (recipe on page 238)
½ teaspoon saffron threads
4 tablespoons (2 oz/60 g) unsalted butter
½ onion, chopped
2 cups (14 oz/440 g) Arborio or medium-grain rice
¾ cup (6 fl oz/180 ml) dry white wine
¾ cup (3 oz/90 g) freshly grated Parmesan cheese
salt and freshly ground pepper

In a small saucepan over high heat, bring the Chicken or Vegetable Stock to a simmer. Reduce the heat to low, add the saffron and keep the liquid hot.
❧ In a heavy large saucepan over medium-low heat, melt 2 tablespoons of the butter and sauté the onion, stirring frequently, until it is translucent, about 8 minutes.
❧ To the onion, add the rice and stir until a white spot appears in the center of the grains, about 1 minute. Add the wine and stir until it is absorbed, about 2 minutes. Add ¾ cup (6 fl oz/180 ml) of the stock, adjust the heat to simmer, if needed, so that the liquid bubbles and is absorbed slowly. Stir until the liquid is absorbed. Continue cooking, adding the liquid ¾ cup (6 fl oz/180 ml) at a time and stirring almost constantly, until the rice starts to soften, about 10 minutes.
❧ Continue cooking, adding the liquid ½ cup (4 fl oz/125 ml) at a time and

stirring almost constantly, until the rice is just tender but slightly firm in the center and the mixture is creamy, about 10 minutes longer.

❧ Add the Parmesan cheese, remaining 2 tablespoons butter and salt and pepper to taste. Stir to mix well.

❧ To serve, spoon into a serving bowl or onto plates.

❧ Serve hot.

ARTICHOKE RISOTTO

SERVES 6

Using frozen artichoke hearts, widely available in well-stocked food stores, makes it possible to serve this dish at any time of year. Here, it is paired with poached salmon for a summertime feast.

5½ cups (44 fl oz/1.4 l) Chicken Stock (recipe on page 30) or Vegetable Stock (recipe on page 238)
2 tablespoons olive oil
½ onion, chopped
1½ cups (10½ oz/330 g) Arborio or medium-grain rice
9 oz (280 g) frozen artichoke hearts, thawed and halved
1¼ cups (5 oz/155 g) freshly grated Parmesan cheese
1½ oz (45 g) thinly sliced prosciutto, chopped
½ cup (¾ oz/20 g) thinly sliced fresh basil
salt and freshly ground pepper
fresh basil leaves

In a small saucepan over high heat, bring the Chicken or Vegetable Stock to a simmer. Reduce the heat to low and keep the liquid hot.

❧ In a heavy medium saucepan over medium-low heat, heat the olive oil and sauté the onion, stirring frequently, until it is translucent, about 8 minutes.

❧ To the onion, add the rice and stir until a white spot appears in the center of the grains, about 1 minute. Add ¾ cup (6 fl oz/180 ml) of the stock, adjust the heat to simmer, if needed, so that the liquid bubbles and is absorbed slowly. Stir until the liquid is absorbed. Continue cooking, adding the liquid

¾ cup (6 fl oz/180 ml) at a time and stirring almost constantly, until the rice starts to soften, about 10 minutes.

❧ Add the artichoke hearts and continue cooking, adding the liquid ½ cup (4 fl oz/125 ml) at a time and stirring almost constantly, until the rice is just tender but slightly firm in the center and the mixture is creamy, about 10 minutes longer.

❧ Add the Parmesan cheese, prosciutto, sliced basil and salt and pepper to taste. Stir to mix well.

❧ To serve, spoon into a serving bowl or onto plates. Garnish with the basil.

❧ Serve hot.

LIMA BEAN RISOTTO WITH PESTO

SERVES 6

There's nothing fancy here, just simple ingredients that combine to make a risotto with an intriguing color and flavor. Using purchased pesto will make the recipe even easier. Serve with a grilled chicken breast, tomatoes and basil.

Pesto Sauce (recipe on page 36)
5½ cups (44 fl oz/1.4 l) Chicken Stock (recipe on page 30) or Vegetable Stock (recipe on page 238)
2 tablespoons olive oil
1 onion, chopped
2½ cups (17½ oz/545 g) Arborio or medium-grain rice
⅔ cup (5 fl oz/160 ml) dry white wine
10 oz (315 g) frozen baby lima beans, thawed
½ cup (2 oz/60 g) freshly grated pecorino romano cheese
salt and freshly ground pepper

*Cheese, poetry!
Perfume of our meal
What would become of life
if we didn't have you?*

—CHARLES MONSELET

Prepare the Pesto Sauce.

❧ In a small saucepan over high heat, bring the Chicken or Vegetable Stock to a simmer. Reduce the heat to low and keep the liquid hot.

❧ In a heavy large saucepan over medium-low heat, heat the olive oil and sauté the onion, stirring frequently, until it is translucent, about 8 minutes.

❧ To the onion, add the rice and stir until a white spot appears in the center of the grains, about 1 minute. Add the wine and stir until it is absorbed, about 2 minutes. Add ¾ cup (6 fl oz/180 ml) of the stock, adjust the heat to simmer, if needed, so that the liquid bubbles and is absorbed slowly. Stir until the liquid is absorbed. Continue cooking, adding the liquid ¾ cup (6 fl oz/180 ml) at a time and stirring almost constantly for 5 minutes. Add the lima beans and continue cooking, adding the liquid ½ cup (4 fl oz/125 ml) at a time and stirring almost constantly, until the rice is just tender but slightly firm in the center and the mixture is creamy, about 15 minutes longer.

❧ Add the Pesto Sauce, pecorino romano cheese and salt and pepper to taste. Stir to mix well.

❧ To serve, spoon into a serving bowl or onto individual plates.

❧ Serve hot.

Grating hard cheeses just prior to adding them to recipes—and allowing diners to grate cheese at the table—keeps the flavor of the cheese fresh and authentic. There are a variety of small handheld graters for the kitchen and dining table; experiment with different types to find one that is most comfortable for you to use.

ZESTY ZUCCHINI AND BASIL RISOTTO

SERVES 6

Lemon zest and juice contribute a fresh, bright flavor to this risotto. Any leftovers can be thinned with additional Chicken Stock (recipe on page 30) or Vegetable Stock (recipe on page 238), transforming the risotto into a lovely rice soup. This is delicious paired with sautéed or grilled shrimp (prawns).

5 cups (40 fl oz/1.25 l) Chicken Stock (recipe on page 30) or Vegetable Stock (recipe on page 238)
3 tablespoons olive oil
½ large onion, chopped
1½ cups (10½ oz/330 g) Arborio or medium-grain rice
½ cup (4 fl oz/125 ml) dry white wine
2 zucchini (courgettes), sliced lengthwise
1 cup (4 oz/125 g) freshly grated Parmesan cheese
3 tablespoons heavy (double) cream
1 teaspoon grated lemon zest (see page 295)
3 tablespoons fresh lemon juice
⅓ cup (½ oz/15 g) finely chopped fresh basil
salt and freshly ground pepper
fresh basil leaves

In a small saucepan over high heat, bring the Chicken or Vegetable Stock to a simmer. Reduce the heat to low and keep the liquid hot.

❧ In a heavy medium saucepan over medium-low heat, heat the olive oil and sauté the onion, stirring frequently, until it is translucent, about 8 minutes.

❧ To the onion, add the rice and stir until a white spot appears in the center of the grains, about 1 minute. Add the wine and stir until it is absorbed, about 2 minutes. Add ¾ cup (6 fl oz/180 ml) of the stock, adjust the heat to simmer, if needed, so that the liquid bubbles and is absorbed slowly. Stir until the liquid is absorbed. Continue cooking, adding the liquid ¾ cup (6 fl oz/180 ml) at a time and stirring almost constantly, until the rice starts to soften, about 10 minutes.

❧ Add the zucchini and continue cooking, adding the liquid ½ cup (4 fl oz/125 ml) at a time and stirring almost constantly, until the rice is just tender but slightly firm in the center and the mixture is creamy, about 10 minutes.

❧ Add the Parmesan cheese, cream, ¼ teaspoon of the lemon zest, the lemon juice, chopped basil and salt and pepper to taste. Stir to mix well.

❧ To serve, spoon into shallow bowls or onto plates. Garnish with the basil leaves and remaining lemon zest.

❧ Serve hot.

ARUGULA RISOTTO

SERVES 6

Used as both an herb and a salad green, arugula (rocket) has a peppery, slightly bitter taste that adds real distinction to this very simple dish. For the best results, look for the smallest arugula leaves you can find, which have a milder flavor.

5½ cups (44 fl oz/1.4 l) Chicken Stock (recipe on page 30) or Vegetable Stock (recipe on page 238)
2 tablespoons olive oil
½ large onion, chopped
2 cups (14 oz/440 g) Arborio or medium-grain rice
1½ cups (6 oz/185 g) freshly grated Parmesan cheese
1⅓ cups (2 oz/50 g) finely chopped arugula or watercress

In a small saucepan over high heat, bring the Chicken or Vegetable Stock to a simmer. Reduce the heat to low and keep the liquid hot.

❧ In a heavy medium saucepan over medium-low heat, heat the olive oil and sauté the onion, stirring frequently, until it is translucent, about 8 minutes.

❧ To the onion, add the rice and stir until a white spot appears in the center of the grains, about 1 minute. Add ¾ cup (6 fl oz/180 ml) of the stock, adjust the heat to simmer, if needed, so that the liquid bubbles and is absorbed slowly. Stir until the liquid is absorbed. Continue cooking, adding the liquid ¾ cup (6 fl oz/180 ml) at a time and stirring almost constantly, until the rice starts to soften, about 10 minutes.

❧ Continue cooking, adding the liquid ½ cup (4 fl oz/125 ml) at a time and stirring almost constantly, until the rice is just tender but slightly firm in the center and the mixture is creamy, about 10 minutes longer.

❧ Add the Parmesan cheese and arugula. Stir to mix well.

❧ To serve, spoon onto plates.

❧ Serve hot.

BROCCOLI RISOTTO WITH PARMESAN

SERVES 6

You'll get the right amount of florets for this versatile side dish if you purchase about 1 pound (500 g) of broccoli, reserving the stalks for another recipe.

5½ cups (44 fl oz/1.4 l) Chicken Stock (recipe on page 30) or Vegetable Stock (recipe on page 238)
2 tablespoons olive oil
1 onion, chopped
1½ cups (10½ oz/330 g) Arborio or medium-grain rice
4 cups (12 oz/375 g) broccoli florets
1 cup (4 oz/125 g) freshly grated Parmesan cheese plus additional freshly grated Parmesan cheese
salt and freshly ground pepper

In a small saucepan over high heat, bring the Chicken or Vegetable Stock to a simmer. Reduce the heat to low and keep the liquid hot.

✵ In a heavy medium saucepan over medium–low heat, heat the olive oil and sauté the onion, stirring frequently, until it is translucent, about 8 minutes.

✵ To the onion, add the rice and stir until a white spot appears in the center of the grains, about 1 minute. Add ¾ cup (6 fl oz/180 ml) of the stock, adjust the heat to simmer, if needed, so that the liquid bubbles and is absorbed slowly. Stir until the liquid is absorbed. Continue cooking, adding the liquid ¾ cup (6 fl oz/180 ml) at a time and stirring almost constantly, until the rice starts to soften, about 10 minutes.

✵ Add the broccoli and continue cooking, adding the liquid ½ cup (4 fl oz/125 ml) at a time and stirring almost constantly, until the rice is just tender but slightly firm in the center and the mixture is creamy, about 10 minutes.

🕊 Add the 1 cup (4 oz/125 g) Parmesan cheese and salt and pepper to taste. Stir to mix well.

🕊 To serve, spoon into a serving bowl. Pass the additional Parmesan cheese.

🕊 Serve hot.

PROSCIUTTO AND RADICCHIO RISOTTO

SERVES 6

The pairing of two classic Italian ingredients makes this side dish both simple and elegant, a perfect companion to grilled or broiled lamb. If you cannot find prosciutto, substitute another dry-cured raw ham.

5½ cups (44 fl oz/1.4 l) Chicken Stock (recipe on page 30) or Vegetable Stock (recipe on page 238)

2 tablespoons olive oil

½ large onion, chopped

2 cups (14 oz/440 g) Arborio or medium-grain rice

¾ cup (6 fl oz/180 ml) dry white wine

9 oz (280 g) radicchio, thinly sliced

3 oz (90 g) thinly sliced prosciutto, coarsely chopped

¾ cup (3 oz/90 g) freshly grated Parmesan cheese, plus additional freshly grated Parmesan cheese

salt and freshly ground pepper

In a small saucepan over high heat, bring the Chicken or Vegetable Stock to a simmer. Reduce the heat to low and keep the liquid hot.

🕊 In a heavy medium saucepan over medium-low heat, heat the olive oil and sauté the onion, stirring frequently, until it is translucent, about 8 minutes.

🕊 To the onion, add the rice and stir until a white spot appears in the center of the grains, about 1 minute. Add the wine and stir until it is absorbed, about

2 minutes. Add ¾ cup (6 fl oz/180 ml) of the stock, adjust the heat to simmer, if needed, so that the liquid bubbles and is absorbed slowly. Stir until the liquid is absorbed. Continue cooking, adding the liquid ¾ cup (6 fl oz/180 ml) at a time and stirring almost constantly, until the rice starts to soften, about 10 minutes.

🕊 Add the radicchio and continue cooking, adding the liquid ½ cup (4 fl

oz/125 ml) at a time and stirring almost constantly, until the rice is just tender but slightly firm in the center and the mixture is creamy, about 10 minutes.

🕊 Add the prosciutto, the ¾ cup (3 oz/90 g) Parmesan cheese and salt and pepper to taste. Stir to mix well.

🕊 To serve, spoon onto plates. Pass the additional Parmesan cheese.

🕊 Serve hot.

*Rational habits permit of
discarding nothing left over,
and the use to which leftovers
(and their economic allies,
the wild things of nature)
are put is often at the heart
of a cooking's character.*

—RICHARD OLNEY

RISOTTO PANCAKES

SERVES 6

*Resembling small frittatas, these pancakes
make excellent use of leftover risotto. Although they are designed as an appetizer,
consider serving these treats as a breakfast
or brunch item to people who desire a
savory morning meal. For more flavor, stir
in whatever fresh herbs strike your fancy.*

2 cups (10 oz/315 g) Classic Risotto
   (recipe on page 20)
1 egg, lightly beaten
2 tablespoons unsalted butter
6 tablespoons freshly grated Parmesan
   cheese, plus additional freshly grated
   Parmesan cheese

In a medium bowl, gently mix the
Classic Risotto and egg.

☙ In a large nonstick frying pan over
medium heat, melt 1 tablespoon of the
butter. Working in batches and adding
more butter as necessary, drop the
risotto mixture into the pan to make
6 large pancakes.

☙ Using a spatula, gently press the
risotto mixture into rounds. Fry until
the pancakes are light brown on the
bottom, about 3 minutes.

☙ Flip the pancakes. Sprinkle each
with 1 tablespoon of the Parmesan
cheese. Cover and cook until the cheese
melts, about 1 minute. Uncover and
continue frying until the pancakes are
light brown on the bottom, about 2
minutes longer.

☙ To serve, transfer to a heated platter.
Pass the additional Parmesan cheese.

☙ Serve warm.

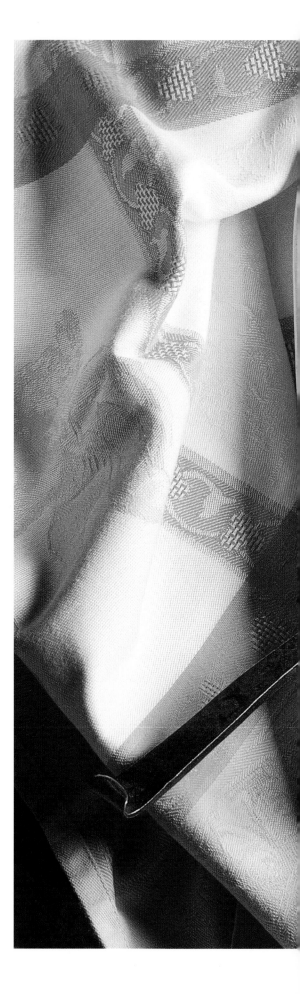

SHIITAKE MUSHROOM AND PEA RISOTTO PANCAKES

SERVES 6

This is a wonderful use of any leftover risotto. Pair these delicious pancakes with a colorful mix of sautéed vegetables for a vegetarian meal. The shiitake mushrooms can be replaced with another variety.

1 cup (5 oz/155 g) shelled fresh peas
   (see page 298) or frozen peas, thawed
3 tablespoons unsalted butter
3 oz (90 g) fresh shiitake mushrooms,
   stemmed and coarsely chopped
2 cups (10 oz/315 g) Classic Risotto
   (recipe on page 20)
2 tablespoons finely chopped fresh
   tarragon or 1½ teaspoons dried
salt and freshly ground pepper
2 eggs, lightly beaten

If using fresh peas, in a medium sauce-pan of boiling salted water, blanch until tender, about 8 minutes. Drain.

❧ In a large nonstick frying pan over medium heat, melt 1 tablespoon of the butter and sauté the mushrooms, tossing frequently, until they brown, about 3 minutes. Remove from the heat.

❧ In a medium bowl, gently mix the Classic Risotto, cooked fresh or thawed frozen peas, sautéed mushrooms, tarragon and salt and pepper to taste. Gently mix in the eggs.

❧ Return the large nonstick frying pan to medium heat and melt 1 table-spoon of the remaining butter. Working in batches and adding more butter as necessary, drop the risotto mixture into the pan to make 12 small pancakes.

❧ Using a spatula, gently press the risotto mixture into rounds. Fry until the pancakes are light brown on the bottom, about 4 minutes on each side.

❧ To serve, transfer to a heated platter or individual plates.

❧ Serve warm.

SUPPLÌ WITH CHEESE AND PORCINI MUSHROOMS

SERVES 6

This traditional Italian preparation is a great way to transform leftover risotto into a fanciful side dish to pair with a salad.

1 oz (30 g) dried porcini mushrooms
2 cups (16 fl oz/500 ml) hot water
2 cups (10 oz/315 g) Classic Risotto
    (recipe on page 20)
2 eggs, lightly beaten
¾ cup (3 oz/90 g) dried bread crumbs
    (see page 294)
3 oz (90 g) Fontina, Gouda or
    mozzarella cheese, cut into 12 strips
vegetable oil for deep-frying

In a small bowl, combine the porcini mushrooms and hot water. Let stand until the mushrooms soften, about 30 minutes. Drain the mushrooms, reserving the soaking liquid.

❧ Chop the mushrooms and place in a small saucepan over medium-high heat. Add the soaking liquid (discarding any sediment in the bottom of the bowl). Boil until all the liquid evaporates, about 8 minutes. Remove from the heat.

❧ In a medium bowl, combine the Classic Risotto and eggs.

❧ To make the supplì, line a baking sheet with waxed paper. Place the bread crumbs in a cake pan. Drop 1 tablespoon of the risotto mixture onto the bread crumbs. Place 1 cheese strip and 1 teaspoon of the porcini mixture in the center of the risotto mound. Top with 1 tablespoon of the risotto mixture. Using your hands, gently form the risotto, cheese and porcini into a cylinder. Roll in the bread crumbs to coat. Transfer to the baking sheet.

Repeat to make 12 supplì. Cover and refrigerate for at least 1 hour and up to 24 hours.

❧ Preheat an oven to 250°F (120°C).

❧ To a large saucepan, add oil to a depth of 2 inches (5 cm). Heat to 350°F (180°C). Working in batches, fry the supplì, turning occasionally, until golden brown, about 3 minutes. Drain on paper towels. Transfer to a baking sheet and keep warm in the oven while cooking the remaining supplì.

❧ To serve, transfer to individual plates.

❧ Serve warm.

ROSEMARY AND WALNUT HERB CROQUETTES

SERVES 6

Just as tasty and satisfying as supplì, these croquettes are a little easier to form. The recipe can be varied in many ways. Replace the rosemary with another herb or substitute pine nuts for the walnuts.

2 cups (16 fl oz/500 ml) Chicken Stock (recipe on page 30) or Vegetable Stock (recipe on page 238)

1 cup (7 oz/220 g) Arborio rice or medium-grain rice

⅓ cup (1 oz/30 g) freshly grated Parmesan cheese

1½ teaspoons finely chopped fresh rosemary or ½ teaspoon dried

⅓ cup (1 oz/30 g) chopped walnuts

salt and freshly ground pepper

1 egg, lightly beaten

½ cup (2 oz/60 g) dried bread crumbs (see page 294)

vegetable oil or olive oil for frying

fresh rosemary sprigs

In a medium saucepan over high heat, bring the Chicken or Vegetable Stock to a boil. Add the rice and bring to a boil, stirring occasionally. Reduce the heat to low, cover and cook until the liquid is absorbed, about 20 minutes. Remove from the heat.

❧ Add the Parmesan cheese, chopped rosemary, walnuts and salt and pepper to taste. Mix in the egg. Refrigerate until the mixture is firm enough to shape, about 2 hours.

❧ To make the croquettes, line a baking sheet with waxed paper. Place the bread crumbs in a cake pan. Form the rice mixture into eighteen 1½-inch (4-cm) balls. Roll them in the bread crumbs to coat. Transfer to the baking sheet. Cover and refrigerate for at least 1 hour or up to 24 hours.

❧ Preheat an oven to 250°F (120°C).

❧ In a heavy large frying pan over medium-high heat, heat enough oil to coat the bottom of the pan. Working in batches, add the croquettes and, using a spatula, flatten each to a ½-inch (12-mm) thickness. Fry until golden brown, about 2 minutes on each side. Using a spatula, remove the croquettes and drain on paper towels. Transfer to a baking sheet and keep warm in the oven while cooking the remaining croquettes.

❧ To serve, transfer the croquettes to a platter. Garnish with the rosemary.

❧ Serve warm.

For ease of serving a multiple-course meal, arrange your place settings with a pile of plates, each designed for a different course. Small decorative plates are the perfect backdrop for appetizer portions of risotto, like the herb croquettes on this page. When the course is finished and you whisk away that plate, the table is still set for the salad course.

Risotto Entrees

When does a risotto take center stage? As the following recipes show in words and pictures, that question can be answered in several distinctive ways.

A risotto is elevated to full dinner entree status when bite-sized vegetables, seafood, poultry or meat join the usual rice, herb and cheese suspects. On other occasions, larger pieces of food may be cooked along with the risotto rice, yielding more substantial fare served together on the plate. In some of the most spectacular featured courses, the risotto becomes a bed upon which separately cooked but harmonious main-course ingredients are presented for delightful results.

Several of these recipes are spectacular examples of the one-dish meal so many meal-planners love. Whichever way you design your entree, the recipes on the following pages employ risotto as a canvas on which you, the cook, create a memorable work of culinary artistry.

SHRIMP AND BROCCOLI WITH SAFFRON RISOTTO

SERVES 6

Saffron, the dried stamens of a variety of crocus flower, infuses this risotto with an intense aroma and flavor as well as a bright golden color. Be sure to use saffron threads, the actual whole stamens, rather than less-expensive powdered saffron, which tends to lose its flavor quickly in storage. If you can't find saffron in your local market, go ahead and make the risotto anyway. Even without the exotic spice, the dish offers a very pleasing combination of tastes and textures. Try substituting scallops or ringlets of squid for the shrimp; snowpeas (mangetout) or fresh asparagus tips for the broccoli; and dice of roasted red bell pepper (capsicum) for the tomatoes. Chopped flat-leaf (Italian) parsley makes a lovely, simple garnish.

6 cups (48 fl oz/1.5 l) Fish Stock (recipe on page 145)
4 cups (12 oz/375 g) broccoli florets
1 teaspoon saffron threads
4 tablespoons (2 oz/60 g) unsalted butter
2 garlic cloves, peeled and crushed
1 onion, chopped
3 cups (1⅓ lb/655 g) Arborio or medium-grain rice
¾ cup (6 fl oz/180 ml) dry white wine
1½ lb (750 g) medium shrimp (prawns), peeled and deveined (see page 299)
4 Roma (plum) tomatoes, seeded and chopped (see page 299)
salt and freshly ground pepper

In a small saucepan over high heat, bring the Fish Stock to a boil. Add the broccoli and boil until it begins to soften, about 3 minutes. Using a slotted spoon, transfer the broccoli to a small bowl. Add the saffron to the stock. Reduce the heat to low and keep the liquid hot.

In a heavy large saucepan over low heat, melt 2 tablespoons of the butter and cook the garlic, stirring frequently, until it is golden brown, about 2 minutes. Discard the garlic. Add the onion and sauté until it is tender, stirring frequently, about 8 minutes.

To the onion, add the rice and stir until a white spot appears in the center of the grains, about 1 minute. Add the wine and stir until it is absorbed, about 2 minutes. Add ¾ cup (6 fl oz/180 ml) of the stock, adjust the heat to simmer, if needed, so that the liquid bubbles and is absorbed slowly. Stir until the liquid is absorbed. Continue cooking, adding the liquid ¾ cup (6 fl oz/180 ml) at a time and stirring almost constantly, until the rice starts to soften, about 10 minutes.

Reserve ½ cup (4 fl oz/125 ml) of the liquid for the following step. Continue cooking, adding the liquid ½ cup (4 fl oz/125 ml) at a time and stirring almost constantly for 6 minutes longer.

Add the shrimp and tomatoes and continue cooking, stirring frequently and adding the reserved liquid, ¼ cup (2 fl oz/60 ml) at a time, until the shrimp are pink, the rice is tender and the mixture is creamy, about 4 minutes.

Add the broccoli, the remaining 2 tablespoons butter and salt and pepper to taste. Stir to mix well.

To serve, spoon into a serving bowl or onto plates.

Serve hot.

CLAMS WITH FRESH LEMON RISOTTO

SERVES 6

The rice absorbs the juices from the steamed clams, and the lemon zest further intensifies the flavor of this dish. Because your guests will be opening their clams at the table, be sure to provide a shell bowl as well as extra napkins or small towels for cleaning up.

strips of zest from 1½ lemons
    (see page 295)
6 cups (48 fl oz/1.5 l) Fish Stock
    (recipe on page 145), or 3 cups
    (24 fl oz/750 ml) bottled clam
    juice mixed with 3 cups (24 fl oz/
    750 ml) water
3 tablespoons vegetable oil
1 large onion, chopped
2 garlic cloves, peeled and minced
60 small clams (about 4½ lb/2.25 kg),
    scrubbed
3 cups (1⅓ lb/655 g) Arborio or
    medium-grain rice
¾ cup (6 fl oz/180 ml) dry white wine
3 large Roma (plum) tomatoes, seeded
    and chopped (see page 299)
½ cup (¾ oz/20 g) chopped flat-leaf
    (Italian) parsley
salt and freshly ground pepper
fresh flat-leaf (Italian) parsley sprigs

In a small saucepan of boiling water, blanch the lemon zest for 30 seconds. Drain. Repeat, using fresh water.

∽ In a small saucepan over high heat, bring the Fish Stock or clam juice and water to a boil. Reduce the heat to low and keep the liquid hot.

∽ In a heavy large dutch oven over medium-low heat, heat the vegetable oil and sauté the onion and garlic for 5 minutes. Add the clams, discarding any open clams, cover and cook until the clams open, about 10 minutes. Using tongs, transfer the clams to a bowl, discarding any that do not open. Cover and keep warm.

∽ To the dutch oven, add the rice and stir over medium heat until a white spot appears in the center of the grains, about 1 minute. Add the wine and stir until it is absorbed, about 2 minutes. Add the tomatoes and ¾ cup (6 fl oz/ 180 ml) of the stock, adjust the heat to simmer, if needed, so that the liquid bubbles and is absorbed slowly. Stir until the liquid is absorbed.

∽ Continue cooking, adding the liquid ¾ cup (6 fl oz/180 ml) at a time and stirring almost constantly, until the rice starts to soften, about 10 minutes.

∽ Continue cooking, adding the liquid ½ cup (4 fl oz/125 ml) at a time and stirring almost constantly, until the rice is just tender but slightly firm in the center and the mixture is creamy, about 10 minutes.

∽ Add the lemon zest, parsley and salt and pepper to taste. Stir to mix well.

∽ To serve, spoon into shallow bowls or onto plates. Top with the clams. Garnish with the parsley sprigs.

∽ Serve hot.

Wine is bottled poetry.

—ROBERT LOUIS STEVENSON

Traditionally, seafood entrees are paired with white wines. When wine is used in cooking a recipe, use the same wine for cooking as you plan to serve with the dish. To keep diners' palates fresh for a white dinner wine, serve a white wine or a sparkling wine with appetizers before the meal. Save red wines for later in the meal or as an after-dinner treat.

LOBSTER, BASIL AND SHALLOT RISOTTO

SERVES 4

In this showstopper entree, risotto gains extraordinary flavor from being cooked in the lobster-poaching liquid. The lobster can be prepared 6 hours ahead, allowing time to prepare the rest of your dinner.

8 cups (64 fl oz/2 l) water
½ onion, cut into large pieces
2 bay leaves
4 fresh parsley sprigs
1 live lobster (about 1½ lb/750 g)
8 tablespoons (4 oz/125 g) unsalted
    butter
4 shallots, finely chopped
2 cups (14 oz/440 g) Arborio or
    medium-grain rice
½ cup (4 fl oz/125 ml) dry white wine
1 cup (1½ oz/40 g) finely chopped
    fresh basil
1½ tablespoons fresh lemon juice

In a large dutch oven over high heat, combine the water, onion, bay leaves and parsley and bring to a boil. Add the lobster, cover, reduce the heat to medium and simmer for 12 minutes.

❧ Using tongs, carefully remove the lobster. Rinse it under cold water. Using a heavy knife, split it down the center. Remove the meat and cube. Return the shells and juices to the cooking liquid and boil to reduce to 5½ cups (44 fl oz/1.4 l), about 10 minutes.

❧ If preparing in advance, cover tightly and refrigerate for up to 6 hours.

❧ Strain the cooking liquid into a small saucepan over high heat and bring to a simmer. Reduce the heat to low and keep the liquid hot.

❧ In a heavy large saucepan over medium heat, melt 3 tablespoons of the butter and sauté the shallots, stirring frequently, until they are translucent, about 5 minutes.

❧ To the shallots, add the rice and stir until a white spot appears in the center of the grains, about 1 minute. Add the wine and stir until absorbed, about 2 minutes. Add ¾ cup (6 fl oz/180 ml) of the cooking liquid, adjust the heat to simmer, so that the liquid bubbles and is absorbed slowly. Stir until the liquid is absorbed. Continue cooking, adding the liquid ¾ cup (6 fl oz/180 ml) at a time and stirring almost constantly, until the rice starts to soften, about 10 minutes.

❧ Continue cooking, adding the liquid ½ cup (4 fl oz/125 ml) at a time and stirring almost constantly, until the rice is just tender but slightly firm in the center and the mixture is creamy, about 10 minutes.

❧ Add the lobster meat, basil, lemon juice and remaining 5 tablespoons (2½ oz/75 g) butter. Stir to mix well.

❧ To serve, spoon into a serving bowl.

❧ Serve hot.

To finish your dinner in fine Italian style, serve biscotti for dessert. These dry cookies are twice baked, and designed to be dunked into coffee, tea or a glass of sweet wine. You can make your own biscotti or purchase commercial varieties in almost every Italian bakery and delicatessan.

GARLIC RISOTTO WITH SWORDFISH TOPPING

SERVES 6

Here are three dining choices from one recipe. Serve as shown, where a fish sauté robust with Sicilian flavors tops a heady risotto. Alternatively, serve the swordfish alone or over pasta. Finally, the garlic risotto alone makes a delicious side dish.

5½ cups (44 fl oz/1.4 l) Fish Stock (recipe on page 145)

7 tablespoons (4 fl oz/100 ml) olive oil

6 garlic cloves, peeled and thinly sliced

2½ cups (17½ oz/545 g) Arborio or medium-grain rice

1⅔ cups (13 fl oz/410 ml) dry white wine

salt and freshly ground pepper

1 large onion, chopped

8 large (1½ lb/750 g) Roma (plum) tomatoes, peeled, seeded and chopped (see page 299)

1½ lb (750 g) swordfish, cubed

3 tablespoons capers, drained

2 teaspoons dried oregano

In a small saucepan over high heat, bring the Fish Stock to a simmer. Reduce the heat to low and keep the liquid hot.

❧ In a heavy large saucepan over medium heat, heat 2 tablespoons of the olive oil and sauté the garlic, stirring frequently, until it begins to color, about 4 minutes.

❧ To the garlic, add the rice and stir until a white spot appears in the center of the grains, about 1 minute. Add ⅔ cup (5 fl oz/160 ml) of the wine and stir until absorbed, about 2 minutes. Add ¾ cup (6 fl oz/180 ml) of the stock, adjust the heat to simmer, if needed, so that the liquid bubbles and is absorbed slowly. Stir until the liquid is absorbed.

❧ Continue cooking, adding the liquid ¾ cup (6 fl oz/180 ml) at a time and stirring almost constantly, until the rice starts to soften, about 10 minutes.

❧ Continue cooking, adding the liquid ½ cup (4 fl oz/125 ml) at a time and stirring almost constantly, until the rice is just tender but slightly firm in the center and the mixture is creamy, about 10 minutes longer. Add 2 tablespoons of the olive oil and salt and pepper to taste.

❧ In a heavy large frying pan over medium heat, heat the remaining 3 tablespoons olive oil and sauté the onion, stirring frequently, until it is translucent, about 8 minutes. Add the tomatoes and simmer until soft, about 5 minutes.

❧ Add the swordfish and stir until it is opaque on the outside, about 2 minutes. Add the remaining 1 cup (8 fl oz/250 ml) wine. Increase the heat to high and boil, stirring frequently, until the fish is opaque throughout, about 3 minutes. Add the capers and oregano.

❧ To serve, spoon the risotto onto plates and top with the swordfish.

❧ Serve hot.

Although it enhances the cuisines of many lands, pungent garlic is practically synonymous with Italian food. A bulb, or head, of garlic is divided into smaller cloves, each wrapped in a papery skin. Choose garlic that looks plump and feels firm. Store garlic heads whole in a cool, dark place, as individual cloves dry out quickly.

ROSEMARY-SCENTED TUNA WITH ROSEMARY RISOTTO

SERVES 6

Risotto forms an aromatic base for quickly grilled fresh tuna in this impressive yet easy summertime dish. Try grilling some bell peppers (capsicums) and eggplant (aubergines) to serve alongside the fish.

3 tablespoons olive oil

3 tablespoons fresh lemon juice

¼ teaspoon red pepper flakes

3 teaspoons finely chopped fresh rosemary

1½ lb (750 g) tuna steaks

6 cups (48 fl oz/1.5 l) Fish Stock (recipe on page 145)

5 tablespoons (3 fl oz/80 ml) olive oil

1 large onion, chopped

2½ cups (17½ oz/545 g) Arborio or medium-grain rice

¾ cup (6 fl oz/180 ml) dry white wine

fresh rosemary sprigs

In a small glass baking dish, combine the olive oil, lemon juice, red pepper flakes and half of the chopped rosemary. Add the tuna and marinate for about 30 minutes.

❧ Prepare a fire in an outdoor charcoal grill or preheat a broiler (griller).

❧ In a small saucepan over high heat, bring the Fish Stock to a simmer. Reduce the heat to low and keep the liquid hot.

❧ In a heavy large saucepan over medium-low heat, heat 2 tablespoons of the olive oil and sauté the onion, stirring frequently, until it is translucent, about 8 minutes.

❧ To the onion, add the remaining chopped rosemary and rice and stir until a white spot appears in the center of the grains, about 1 minute. Add the wine and stir until it is absorbed, about 2 minutes. Add ¾ cup (6 fl oz/180 ml)

of the stock, adjust the heat to simmer, if needed, so that the liquid bubbles and is absorbed slowly. Stir until the liquid is absorbed. Continue cooking, adding the liquid ¾ cup (6 fl oz/180 ml) at a time and stirring almost constantly, until the rice starts to soften, about 10 minutes.

❧ Continue cooking, adding the liquid ½ cup (4 fl oz/125 ml) at a time and stirring almost constantly, until the rice is just tender but slightly firm in the center and the mixture is creamy, about 10 minutes longer. Add the remaining 3 tablespoons olive oil. Stir to mix well.

❧ Grill the tuna over a medium-hot fire or broil (grill) until opaque, about 4 minutes per side. Transfer the tuna to a work surface and cube.

❧ To serve, spoon the risotto onto plates. Top with the tuna. Garnish with the rosemary sprigs.

❧ Serve hot.

Rosemary, the herb of remembrance, is used in many ways. It is lovingly added as a flower in bridal bouquets to signify fidelity. Its culinary use dates back to ancient times. It provides an aromatic touch to recipes and gives the plate visual appeal.

SALMON FILLETS ON ZUCCHINI RISOTTO

SERVES 6

A bouquet of fresh basil, thyme and chive flowers adds an elegant touch to this easy-to-prepare main course. The risotto is delicious enough to serve without the salmon as an appetizer or a side dish.

6 salmon fillets (about 8 oz/250 g each)
5 tablespoons olive oil
3 tablespoons balsamic vinegar
6 cups (48 fl oz/1.5 l) Fish Stock
    (recipe on page 145)
1 onion, chopped
2½ cups (17½ oz/545 g) Arborio or
    medium-grain rice
¾ cup (6 fl oz/180 ml) dry white wine
4 zucchini (courgettes), cubed
1 cup (1½ oz/45 g) finely chopped
    fresh basil
2 tablespoons unsalted butter
salt and freshly ground pepper

In a glass baking dish, arrange the salmon, drizzle with 3 tablespoons of the olive oil and vinegar and marinate for 30 minutes.

❧ Preheat a broiler (griller).

❧ In a small saucepan over high heat, bring the Fish Stock to a simmer. Reduce the heat to low and keep the liquid hot.

❧ In a heavy large saucepan over medium-low heat, heat the remaining 2 tablespoons olive oil and sauté the onion, stirring frequently, until it is translucent, about 8 minutes.

❧ To the onion, add the rice and stir until a white spot appears in the center of the grains, about 1 minute. Add the wine and stir until it is absorbed, about 2 minutes. Add ¾ cup (6 fl oz/180 ml) of the stock, adjust the heat to simmer, if needed, so that the liquid bubbles and is absorbed slowly. Stir until the liquid is absorbed. Continue cooking, adding the liquid ¾ cup (6 fl oz/180 ml) at a time and stirring almost constantly, until the rice starts to soften, about 10 minutes.

❧ Add the zucchini and continue cooking, adding the liquid ½ cup (4 fl oz/125 ml) at a time and stirring almost constantly, until the rice is just tender but slightly firm in the center and the mixture is creamy, about 10 minutes longer. Add half of the basil, the butter and salt and pepper to taste.

❧ Broil (grill) the fish until it is just opaque in the center, about 10 minutes per inch (2.5 cm) of thickness.

❧ To serve, spoon the risotto onto a serving plate. Top with the salmon fillets. Garnish with the remaining basil.

❧ Serve hot.

RISOTTO WITH SMOKED SALMON, SPINACH AND GOAT CHEESE

SERVES 6

The fresh flavors and colors make this a winning choice for brunch or lunch, accompanied with crusty rolls and dry white wine. Avoid salt-cured lox or cold-smoked salmon, which have an oily texture.

6 cups (48 fl oz/1.5 l) Fish Stock (recipe on page 145)

3 tablespoons olive oil

2½ cups (17½ oz/545 g) Arborio or medium-grain rice

¾ cup (6 fl oz/180 ml) dry white wine

5 cups (10 oz/315 g) thinly sliced fresh spinach leaves

1¼ cups (6 oz/185 g) crumbled mild goat cheese

½ cup (1½ oz/45 g) chopped fresh chives or green (spring) onions, green and white parts

4 oz (125 g) smoked salmon, chopped

salt and freshly ground pepper

fresh chives

In a small saucepan over high heat, bring the Fish Stock to a simmer. Reduce the heat to low and keep the liquid hot.

❧ In a heavy large saucepan over medium-low heat, heat the olive oil, add the rice and stir until a white spot appears in the center of the grains, about 1 minute. Add the wine and stir until it is absorbed, about 2 minutes.

❧ Add ¾ cup (6 fl oz/180 ml) of the stock, adjust the heat to simmer, if needed, so that the liquid bubbles and is absorbed slowly. Stir until the liquid is absorbed. Continue cooking, adding the liquid ¾ cup (6 fl oz/180 ml) at a time and stirring almost constantly for about 15 minutes.

❧ Add the spinach and continue cooking, adding the liquid ½ cup (4 fl oz/125 ml) at a time and stirring almost constantly, until the rice is just tender but slightly firm in the center and the mixture is creamy, about 5 minutes longer. Add the goat cheese, chives or green onions, salmon and salt and pepper to taste. Stir to mix well.

❧ To serve, spoon into shallow bowls or onto plates. Garnish with the chives.

❧ Serve hot.

Fish must swim thrice — once in the water, a second time in the sauce, and a third time in wine in the stomach.

—JOHN RAY

MUSSELS, RED BELL PEPPER, CAPER AND OLIVE RISOTTO

SERVES 6

Cooked in Fish Stock and the shellfish broth, this risotto is infused with the rich taste of the sea. If mussels are unavailable, substitute clams. Offer extra napkins and bowls to help guests eat the shellfish neatly at the table. Oyster forks might come in handy as well.

6 cups (48 fl oz/1.5 l) Fish Stock (recipe on page 145)
3 tablespoons vegetable oil
1 large red (Spanish) onion, chopped
1½ large red bell peppers (capsicums), seeded, deribbed and coarsely chopped (see page 298)
red pepper flakes
3 lb (750 g) mussels, scrubbed and debearded
3 cups (1⅓ lb/655 g) Arborio or medium-grain rice
¾ cup (6 fl oz/180 ml) dry white wine
½ cup (3½ oz/105 g) Kalamata olives, pitted and chopped
2 tablespoons capers, drained
salt and freshly ground pepper
fresh flat-leaf (Italian) parsley

In a small saucepan over high heat, bring the Fish Stock to a boil. Reduce the heat to low and keep the liquid hot.

❧ In a heavy large dutch oven over medium-low heat, heat the vegetable oil and sauté the onion, stirring frequently, until it begins to soften, about 5 minutes. Add the bell peppers and sauté until they begin to soften, about 5 minutes. Add the pepper flakes to taste and the mussels, discarding any open mussels. Cover and cook until the mussels open, about 3 minutes. Using tongs, transfer the mussels to a bowl, discarding any that do not open. Cover and keep warm.

❧ To the dutch oven, add the rice and stir over medium heat until a white spot appears in the center of the grains, about 1 minute. Add the wine and stir until it is absorbed, about 2 minutes.

❧ Add ¾ cup (6 fl oz/180 ml) of the stock and adjust the heat to simmer, if needed, so that the liquid bubbles and is absorbed slowly. Stir until the liquid is absorbed. Continue cooking, adding the liquid ¾ cup (6 fl oz/180 ml) at a time and stirring almost constantly, until the rice starts to soften, about 10 minutes.

❧ Continue cooking, adding the liquid ½ cup (4 fl oz/125 ml) at a time and stirring almost constantly, until the rice is just tender but slightly firm in the center and the mixture is creamy, about 10 minutes longer.

❧ Add the olives, capers and salt and pepper to taste.

❧ To serve, spoon onto plates. Top with the mussels and parsley.

❧ Serve hot.

SPANISH PAELLA WITH SEAFOOD

SERVES 6

Spain's national challenger to risotto makes a wonderful main course for a dinner party, especially when paired with ice-cold pitchers of the wine-and-fruit punch known as sangría.

10 cups (2½ qt/2.5 l) Fish Stock
   (recipe on page 145)
1 cup (5 oz/155 g) shelled fresh peas
   (see page 298) or frozen peas, thawed
½ cup (4 fl oz/125 ml) dry white wine
1 teaspoon saffron threads
¼ cup (2 fl oz/60 ml) olive oil
1 large onion, chopped
1 large red bell pepper (capsicum),
   seeded, deribbed and cut into ¾-inch
   (2-cm) pieces (see page 298)
4 large garlic cloves, peeled and finely
   chopped
8 oz (250 g) chorizo or hot Italian
   sausage, casings removed
2 teaspoons paprika
red pepper flakes
4 Roma (plum) tomatoes, peeled,
   seeded and chopped (see page 299)
3 cups (1⅓ lb/655 g) Arborio or
   medium-grain rice
1¼ lb (625 g) medium shrimp (prawns),
   peeled and deveined (see page 299)
24 mussels (about 2 lb/1 kg), scrubbed
   and debearded

Sangría is a party punch that is popular in Spain and Portugal. Made from red wine mixed with club soda and infused with citrus, it's a crowd-pleasing beverage on a summer day. Served in a pitcher or a punch bowl, it provides a festive centerpiece to any meal, but especially one of Spanish derivation like seafood paella.

In a medium saucepan over high heat, bring the Fish Stock to a boil. Add the fresh peas, if using, and cook until tender, about 8 minutes. Using a slotted spoon, remove the peas and reserve.

❧ Reduce the heat to medium and simmer until the liquid is reduced to 5½ cups (44 fl oz/1.4 l), about 15 minutes. Add the wine and saffron and bring to a simmer. Reduce the heat to low and keep the liquid hot.

❧ In a paella pan or heavy large dutch oven over medium heat, heat the oil and sauté the onion, stirring frequently, until it begins to soften, about 3 minutes. Add the bell pepper and cook until it begins to soften, about 3 minutes longer. Add the garlic and sausage and cook, breaking the sausage up with a fork, until it is no longer pink, about 5 minutes.

❧ Add the paprika and red pepper flakes to taste and stir for 30 seconds. Add the tomatoes.

❧ Add the rice and stir until a white spot appears in the center of the grains, about 1 minute. Add the stock mixture. Increase the heat to high and bring the mixture to a boil, stirring constantly.

❧ Reduce the heat to low, cover and simmer for 15 minutes, stirring occasionally.

❧ Add the shrimp, cooked or thawed peas and mussels, discarding any open mussels. Cover and cook until the shrimp are just pink, the mussels open and the liquid is absorbed, about 10 minutes longer. Remove from the heat and let stand, covered, for 10 minutes. Discard any mussels that do not open.

❧ To serve, spoon into a serving bowl.

❧ Serve hot.

ARROZ CON POLLO

SERVES 6

Translated as "rice with chicken," this specialty of Valencia, Spain, is simply a paella without seafood, and resembles Italian risotto in the medium-grain rice that is used and in the robust, creamy texture that develops during cooking. If you like, you can make the dish even easier and more elegant to serve and eat by using boneless and skinless pieces of chicken, left in large portions or cut into bite-sized pieces as you wish. The dish can also be elaborated by adding such popular Spanish ingredients as chunks of spicy chorizo sausage, browned at the same time as the chicken; and pimiento-stuffed green olives or frozen petite peas, folded in to heat through during the last 10 minutes or so of cooking. Saffron threads are an absolute necessity to give this dish its signature bright golden color and heady aroma; although costly, they are very potent, and a little pinch of them goes a long way.

3½ cups (28 fl oz/875 ml) Chicken
   Stock (recipe on page 30)
2 tablespoons olive oil
3¼ lb (1.6 kg) chicken, cut into 8 pieces
salt and freshly ground pepper
1 large onion, chopped
1 each large red and green bell pepper
   (capsicum), seeded, deribbed and
   cut into strips (see page 298)
3 garlic cloves, peeled and minced
1 tablespoon paprika
red pepper flakes
2 large tomatoes, seeded and chopped
   (see page 299)
¼ teaspoon saffron threads
2 cups (14 oz/440 g) medium-grain or
   long-grain rice
½ cup (4 fl oz/125 ml) dry white wine
salt
¼ cup chopped fresh parsley

In a small saucepan over high heat, bring the Chicken Stock to a simmer. Reduce the heat to low and keep the liquid hot.

❧ In a heavy large dutch oven over medium-high heat, heat the olive oil. Season the chicken with salt and pepper to taste. Place in the dutch oven and cook until brown, 5 minutes on each side. Transfer the chicken to a plate.

❧ Pour off all but a thin film of oil from the dutch oven and set the dutch oven over medium heat. Add the onion, bell peppers and garlic and sauté, stirring frequently, until the onion is translucent, about 8 minutes. Add the paprika and red pepper flakes to taste and sauté for 30 seconds. Add the tomatoes and saffron. Cook, stirring frequently, until most of the liquid evaporates, about 5 minutes.

❧ Add the rice and stir until a white spot appears in the center of the grains, about 1 minute. Add the stock and wine and salt to taste. Bring to a boil. Add the chicken and any juices on the plate. Return to a boil.

❧ Reduce the heat to low, cover and cook until the rice is tender and the chicken is opaque throughout, about 30 minutes. Remove from the heat and let stand, covered, for 5 minutes.

❧ To serve, transfer to individual plates. Garnish with the parsley.

❧ Serve warm.

Poultry is for the cook what canvas is for the painter.

—JEAN-ANTHELME BRILLAT-SAVARIN

CHICKEN AND ASPARAGUS RISOTTO

SERVES 6

Perfect for a springtime lunch, this risotto can also be made with baby artichoke hearts or broccoli florets. For an unusual variation, try replacing the Parmesan with crumbled fresh mild goat cheese.

grated zest from 2 lemons
(see page 295)
1 lb (500 g) asparagus, cut into
1½-inch (4-cm) pieces
5½ cups (44 fl oz/1.4 l) Chicken Stock
(recipe on page 30)
4 tablespoons (2 fl oz/60 ml) olive oil
1 whole chicken breast, skinned and
boned (about 1 lb/500 g meat),
cubed
1 onion, chopped
2½ cups (17½ oz/545 g) Arborio or
medium-grain rice
2 cups (16 fl oz/500 ml) dry white
wine
1 cup (4 oz/125 g) freshly grated
Parmesan cheese
½ cup (¾ oz/20 g) finely chopped
fresh flat-leaf (Italian) parsley
strips of zest from 1 lemon
(see page 295)

In a small saucepan of boiling water, blanch the grated zest for 30 seconds. Drain. Repeat, using fresh water, blanching the zest for 30 seconds and draining again.

❧ In a large saucepan of boiling salted water, cook the asparagus until just tender-crisp, about 5 minutes. Drain.

❧ In a small saucepan over high heat, bring the Chicken Stock to a simmer. Reduce the heat to low and keep hot.

❧ In a large saucepan over medium-low heat, heat 2 tablespoons of the olive oil and sauté the chicken, stirring frequently, until it is just opaque throughout, about 3 minutes. Using a slotted spoon, transfer the chicken to a plate.

❧ In the same saucepan over medium-low heat, heat the remaining 2 table-spoons olive oil and sauté the onion, stirring frequently, until it is translucent, about 8 minutes.

❧ To the onion, add the rice and stir until a white spot appears in the center of the grains, about 1 minute. Add the wine and stir until it is absorbed, about 2 minutes. Add ¾ cup (6 fl oz/180 ml) of the stock, adjust the heat to simmer, if needed, so that the liquid bubbles and is absorbed slowly. Stir until the liquid is absorbed. Continue cooking, adding the liquid ¾ cup (6 fl oz/180 ml) at a time and stirring almost constantly, until the rice starts to soften, about 10 minutes.

❧ Continue cooking, adding the liquid ½ cup (4 fl oz/125 ml) at a time and stirring almost constantly, until the rice is just tender but slightly firm in the center and the mixture is creamy, about 10 minutes longer.

❧ Add the chicken, asparagus, lemon zest, cheese and parsley. Garnish with the strips of lemon zest.

❧ Serve hot.

Asparagus—whether simply steamed and served as an appetizer or side dish or added to pasta or risotto dishes—is a springtime delicacy that has been enjoyed since the days of ancient Rome. Nutritious as well as delicious, it is low in calories and high in folate and vitamins A and C.

CHICKEN LIVERS WITH PEAS ON A BED OF RISOTTO

SERVES 6

This casual dish is a rapid sauté of chicken livers, with a sauce made by deglazing the pan with wine that mingles with the risotto over which the sauté is served.

6 cups (48 fl oz/1.5 l) Chicken Stock
    (recipe on page 30)
2 tablespoons unsalted butter
1 onion, chopped
2½ cups (17½ oz/545 g) Arborio or
    medium-grain rice
⅔ cup (5 fl oz/160 ml) dry white wine
1¾ cups (7 oz/220 g) freshly grated
    Parmesan cheese
salt and freshly ground pepper
2 cups (10 oz/315 g) shelled fresh peas
    (see page 298) or frozen peas, thawed
5 tablespoons (2½ oz/75 g) unsalted
    butter
4 shallots, thinly sliced
1½ lb (750 g) chicken livers, trimmed
    and cut into 1-inch (2.5-cm) pieces
12 fresh sage leaves, chopped, or
    ½ teaspoon dried
⅔ cup (5 fl oz/160 ml) Marsala wine

In a small saucepan over high heat, bring the Chicken Stock to a simmer. Reduce the heat to low and keep the liquid hot.

❧ In a heavy large saucepan over low heat, melt the butter. Add the onion and sauté, stirring frequently, until the onion is translucent, about 8 minutes.

❧ To the onions, add the rice and stir until a white spot appears in the center of the grains, about 1 minute. Add the wine and stir until it is absorbed, about 2 minutes.

❧ Add three-fourths of the stock. Increase the heat to high and bring to a boil. Reduce the heat and simmer, uncovered, stirring occasionally and adding the remaining liquid by ¼ cup-fuls (2 fl oz/60 ml) as the mixture thickens, until the rice is just tender but still slightly firm in the center and the mixture is creamy, about 20 minutes.

❧ If using fresh peas, in a large sauce-pan of boiling salted water, blanch the peas until tender, about 8 minutes.

❧ In a large frying pan over medium heat, melt 3 tablespoons of the butter. Add the shallots and sauté, stirring frequently, until they brown, about 5 minutes.

❧ Increase the heat to high. Add the livers and sage and sauté, stirring fre-quently, until the livers are brown on the outside, about 3 minutes. Transfer the livers to a plate.

❧ To the frying pan, add the Marsala wine and bring to a boil, scraping up any browned bits. Boil until syrupy, about 4 minutes.

❧ Add the cooked fresh or thawed peas, the livers and any juice. Stir until heated through and glazed, about 1 minute. Add the remaining 2 table-spoons butter.

❧ To the risotto, add the Parmesan cheese and salt and pepper to taste. Stir to mix well.

❧ To serve, spoon the risotto onto plates. Top with the liver mixture.

❧ Serve hot.

HAM, PEA AND PARMESAN RISOTTO

SERVES 6

A nice variation on the classic pasta dish fettuccine Alfredo, this creamy risotto is especially satisfying on a cold winter's night. For a lighter vegetarian version, leave out the ham and substitute Vegetable Stock (recipe on page 238) for the Chicken Stock.

6 cups (48 fl oz/1.5 l) Chicken Stock (recipe on page 30)
2 tablespoons unsalted butter
1 onion, chopped
12 oz (375 g) ham, cut into ½-inch (12-mm) pieces
2½ cups (17½ oz/545 g) Arborio or medium-grain rice
2 cups (10 oz/315 g) shelled fresh peas (see page 298) or frozen peas
1 cup (4 oz/125 g) freshly grated Parmesan cheese
1 tablespoon finely chopped fresh thyme or 1 teaspoon dried
salt and freshly ground pepper
fresh thyme sprigs

In a small saucepan over high heat, bring the Chicken Stock to a simmer. Reduce the heat to low and keep the liquid hot.

In a heavy large saucepan over medium-low heat, melt the butter and sauté the onion stirring frequently, for 5 minutes. Add the ham and cook until the onion is tender, stirring frequently, about 5 minutes longer.

To the onion mixture, add the rice and stir until a white spot appears in the center of the grains, about 1 minute. Add ¾ cup (6 fl oz/180 ml) of the stock, adjust the heat to simmer, if needed, so that the liquid bubbles and is absorbed slowly. Stir until the liquid is absorbed. Continue cooking, adding the liquid ¾ cup (6 fl oz/180 ml) at a time and stirring almost constantly, until the rice starts to soften, about 10 minutes.

Add the peas and continue cooking, adding the liquid ½ cup (4 fl oz/125 ml) at a time and stirring almost constantly, until the rice is just tender but slightly firm in the center and the mixture is creamy, about 10 minutes.

Add the Parmesan cheese, chopped thyme and salt and pepper to taste. Stir to mix well.

To serve, spoon into bowls or onto plates. Garnish with the thyme sprigs.

Serve hot.

MUSHROOM AND SAUSAGE RISOTTO

SERVES 6

If you prefer a more mild meal, substitute sweet Italian sausage for the spicy, hot variety, as the porcini mushrooms provide plenty of flavor. Garnish with a sprig of fresh rosemary.

1½ oz (45 g) dried porcini mushrooms
3 cups (24 fl oz/750 ml) hot water
2½ cups (20 fl oz/625 ml) Chicken
    Stock (recipe on page 30)
1 tablespoon olive oil
1 large onion, chopped
8 oz (250 g) fresh hot Italian sausages,
    casings removed
12 oz (375 g) button mushrooms, sliced
1½ teaspoons finely chopped fresh
    rosemary or ½ teaspoon dried
2½ cups (17½ oz/545 g) Arborio or
    medium-grain rice
¾ cup (6 fl oz/180 ml) dry white wine
1 bay leaf
⅓ cup (3 fl oz/80 ml) half & half
    (half cream)
2 cups (8 oz/250 g) freshly grated
    Parmesan cheese
salt and freshly ground pepper

In a small bowl, soak the porcini mushrooms in the hot water until soft, about 20 minutes. Drain, reserving the soaking liquid. Chop the porcini mushrooms.

❧ In a small saucepan over high heat, combine the Chicken Stock and mushroom soaking liquid and bring to a simmer. Reduce the heat to low and keep the liquid hot.

❧ In a heavy large saucepan over medium heat, heat the olive oil and sauté the onion, stirring frequently, until it begins to soften, about 5 minutes. Add the sausage meat, increase the heat to high and cook, breaking up the meat with a fork, just until it is no longer pink, about 6 minutes. Add the button mushrooms and chopped rosemary and stir until the mushrooms begin to soften, about 5 minutes.

❧ To the sausage mixture, add the porcini mushrooms and the rice and stir for 1 minute. Add the wine and bay leaf and stir until the wine is absorbed, about 2 minutes. Add ¾ cup (6 fl oz/180 ml) of the stock, adjust the heat to simmer, if needed, so that the liquid bubbles and is absorbed slowly. Stir until the liquid is absorbed. Continue cooking, adding the liquid ¾ cup (6 fl oz/180 ml) at a time and stirring almost constantly, until the rice starts to soften, about 10 minutes.

❧ Continue cooking, adding the liquid ½ cup (4 fl oz/125 ml) at a time and stirring almost constantly, until the rice is just tender but slightly firm in the center and the mixture is creamy, about 10 minutes.

❧ Mix in the half & half, Parmesan cheese and salt and pepper to taste. Remove and discard the bay leaf.

❧ To serve, spoon into bowls.

❧ Serve hot.

LAMB SHANKS IN WINE WITH CLASSIC RISOTTO

SERVES 6

Open your best bottle of full-bodied red wine to pour with this robust winter entree. As an alternative, serve the braised lamb shanks over Lima Bean Risotto with Pesto (recipe on page 252).

4 tablespoons (2 fl oz/60 ml) olive oil
6 lamb shanks (about 1 lb/500 g each)
salt and freshly ground pepper
all-purpose (plain) flour
2 large onions, chopped
3 garlic cloves, peeled and minced
1 large carrot, peeled and chopped
1½ tablespoons tomato paste
2½ cups (20 fl oz/625 ml) dry red wine
2 cups (16 fl oz/500 ml) canned
    reduced-sodium beef broth
2 bay leaves
6 cups (48 fl oz/1.5 l) Chicken Stock
    (recipe on page 30)
2 tablespoons unsalted butter
2½ cups (17½ oz/545 g) Arborio or
    medium-grain rice
⅔ cup (5 fl oz/160 ml) dry white wine
1¾ cups (7 oz/220 g) freshly grated
    Parmesan cheese
salt and freshly ground pepper
3 tablespoons finely chopped fresh
    marjoram or 2 teaspoons dried
fresh marjoram sprigs

In a heavy large dutch oven over high heat, heat 2 tablespoons of the olive oil. Season the lamb with salt and pepper to taste, coat with flour and cook until brown, about 4 minutes on each side. Transfer the lamb to a plate.

☙ Reduce the heat of the dutch oven to medium. Add the remaining 2 tablespoons olive oil, half the onion, the garlic and carrot and sauté until the onion is translucent, about 8 minutes.

☙ Add the tomato paste, red wine and beef broth. Bring to a boil, scraping up any browned bits. Return the lamb to the dutch oven with any juices. Add the bay leaves. Bring to a boil. Reduce the heat, cover and simmer, turning the lamb occasionally, until the lamb is tender, about 1 hour and 45 minutes.

☙ In a small saucepan over high heat, bring the Chicken Stock to a simmer. Reduce the heat to low and keep the liquid hot.

☙ In a heavy large saucepan over low heat, melt the butter. Add the remaining onion and sauté, stirring frequently, until the onion is translucent, about 8 minutes.

☙ To the onion, add the rice and stir until a white spot appears in the center of the grains, about 1 minute. Add the wine and stir until it is absorbed, about 2 minutes.

☙ Add three-fourths of the stock. Increase the heat to high and bring to a boil. Reduce the heat and simmer, uncovered, stirring occasionally and adding the remaining liquid by ¼ cupfuls (2 fl oz/60 ml) as the mixture thickens, until the rice is tender but slightly firm in the center and the mixture is creamy, about 20 minutes.

☙ Uncover the lamb, increase the heat to high and boil until the liquid thickens to sauce consistency, about 15 minutes. Add the chopped marjoram.

☙ To the risotto, add the Parmesan cheese and salt and pepper to taste. Stir to mix well.

☙ To serve, spoon the risotto onto a plate. Top with the lamb shanks and sauce. Garnish with the marjoram sprigs.

☙ Serve hot.

Of all wild or domesticated animals…the lamb is… without exception the most useful to man as food.

—MRS. ISABELLA BEETON

OSSO BUCO ON A BED OF RISOTTO

SERVES 6

Slow simmering gives veal shanks rich, deep flavor, highlighted here by lemon zest and fresh rosemary. For a more traditional presentation, serve the osso buco with Saffron Risotto (recipe on page 250).

4 tablespoons unsalted butter

2 large onions, chopped

2 garlic cloves, peeled and minced

strips of zest from 2 lemons
    (see page 295)

2 teaspoons finely chopped fresh
    rosemary or 1 teaspoon dried

2 bay leaves

1 teaspoon dried sage

2 tablespoons olive oil

6 center-cut veal shanks (about
    12 oz/375 g each)

all-purpose (plain) flour

1⅔ cup (13 fl oz/410 ml) dry white
    wine

6 cups (48 fl oz/1.5 l) Chicken Stock
    (recipe on page 30)

2½ cups (17½ oz/545 g) Arborio or
    medium-grain rice

1¾ cups (7 oz/220 g) freshly grated
    Parmesan cheese

salt and freshly ground pepper

⅓ cup (½ oz/15 g) finely chopped fresh
    flat-leaf (Italian) parsley

1 tablespoon grated lemon zest
    (see page 295)

Crunchy bread sticks, either plain or sprinkled with herbs or seeds, make an excellent textural counterpoint to a creamy pasta or risotto entree.

Preheat an oven to 375°F (190°C).

❧ In a heavy large dutch oven over medium heat, melt half of the butter and sauté half of the onions until they are translucent, about 8 minutes. Add half of the garlic, half of the lemon zest strips, the rosemary, bay leaves and sage. Sauté for 3 minutes. Remove the dutch oven from the heat.

❧ In a heavy large frying pan over medium-high heat, heat the oil. Working in batches, coat the veal with flour and cook until brown, about 4 minutes per side. Place the veal on top of the onions in the dutch oven.

❧ Pour off and discard the drippings from the frying pan. Increase the heat to high, add 1 cup (8 fl oz/250 ml) of the wine and bring to a boil, scraping up any browned bits. Add the wine mixture to the veal in the dutch oven. Add enough Chicken Stock to come to the top of the veal. Bring to a boil.

❧ Cover the dutch oven and place in the oven. Cook, turning the veal and stirring occasionally, until the veal is tender and the sauce is creamy, about 1½ hours.

❧ In a small saucepan over high heat, bring the remaining Chicken Stock to a simmer. Reduce the heat to low and keep the liquid hot.

❧ In a heavy large saucepan over low heat, melt the remaining 2 tablespoons butter. Add the remaining onion and sauté, stirring frequently, until the onion is translucent, about 8 minutes.

❧ To the onions, add the rice and stir until a white spot appears in the center of the grains, about 1 minute. Add the remaining ⅔ cup of wine and stir until it is absorbed, about 2 minutes. Add three-fourths of the stock.

❧ Increase the heat to high and bring to a boil. Reduce the heat and simmer, uncovered, stirring occasionally and adding the remaining liquid by ¼ cup-fuls (2 fl oz/60 ml) as the mixture thickens, until the rice is just tender but still slightly firm in the center and the mixture is creamy, about 20 minutes. Add the Parmesan cheese and salt and pepper to taste. Stir to mix well.

❧ In a small bowl, combine the parsley, grated lemon zest and remaining garlic.

❧ To serve, season the veal sauce with salt and pepper to taste. Spoon the risotto onto individual plates. Top with the veal and sauce. Sprinkle with the parsley mixture. Garnish with the remaining lemon zest strips.

❧ Serve hot.

BEEF BOLOGNESE LAYERED WITH CLASSIC RISOTTO

SERVES 8

The bolognese sauce ordinarily served over spaghetti complements risotto in this easy recipe. For a lighter version, eliminate the pancetta, halve the butter and substitute ground turkey for the beef.

6 tablespoons (3 oz/90 g) unsalted butter

4 oz (125 g) pancetta or bacon, chopped

2 large carrots, peeled and chopped

3 large onions, chopped

1½ lb (750 g) lean ground (minced) beef

1 cup (8 fl oz/250 ml) dry red wine

2 cups (16 fl oz/500 ml) canned reduced-sodium beef broth

1½ cups (12 fl oz/375 ml) milk

8 large Roma (plum) tomatoes, peeled, seeded and chopped (see page 299), or 28 oz (875 g) canned tomatoes with juice

1 cup (8 fl oz/250 ml) tomato juice, if using fresh tomatoes

6 cups (48 fl oz/1.5 l) Chicken Stock (recipe on page 30)

2½ cups (17½ oz/545 g) Arborio or medium-grain rice

⅔ cup (5 fl oz/160 ml) dry white wine

2¼ cups (9 oz/280 g) freshly grated Parmesan cheese

salt and freshly ground pepper

Most pasta and risotto dishes pair beautifully with red wines. To give your meal a European finale, serve a port wine accompanied by fresh fruit.

In a heavy large saucepan over medium heat, melt 4 tablespoons (2 oz/60 g) of the butter. Add the pancetta or bacon, carrots and half the onions. Sauté, stirring frequently, until the mixture begins to brown, about 10 minutes. Add the beef and cook, breaking up the meat with a fork, until it is brown, about 5 minutes.

❧ Add the red wine, reduce the heat and simmer until the wine is absorbed, stirring occasionally, about 5 minutes. Add the broth and simmer, stirring occasionally, until it is almost absorbed, about 15 minutes. Add the milk and simmer until it is almost evaporated, about 15 minutes.

❧ Add the fresh tomatoes and tomato juice or canned tomatoes with their juice, reduce the heat to low and simmer the mixture slowly until it is very thick, stirring occasionally, about 1½ hours. Stir to mix well.

❧ In a small saucepan over high heat, bring the Chicken Stock to a simmer. Reduce the heat to low and keep the liquid hot.

❧ In a heavy large saucepan over low heat, melt the remaining 2 tablespoons butter. Add the remaining onion and sauté, stirring frequently, until the onion is translucent, about 8 minutes.

❧ To the onions, add the rice and stir until a white spot appears in the center of the grains, about 1 minute. Add the white wine and stir until it is absorbed, about 2 minutes. Add three-fourths of the stock.

❧ Increase the heat to high and bring to a boil. Reduce the heat and simmer, uncovered, stirring occasionally and adding the remaining liquid by ¼ cupfuls (2 fl oz/60 ml) as the mixture thickens, until the rice is just tender but still slightly firm in the center and the mixture is creamy, about 20 minutes. Add 1¾ cups (7 oz/220 g) of the Parmesan cheese and salt and pepper to taste. Stir to mix well.

❧ To serve, in a large shallow serving bowl, layer the risotto, beef mixture and the remaining Parmesan cheese. Repeat the layering.

❧ Serve hot.

GLOSSARY

The following entries provide a reference source for this book, offering definitions of essential or unusual ingredients and explanations of fundamental techniques as they relate to the preparation of pasta and risotto recipes.

ANCHOVY FILLETS

These tiny saltwater fish, relatives of sardines, are usually found as canned fillets that have been salted and preserved in oil. Imported anchovy fillets packed in olive oil are the most commonly available.

ASPARAGUS

One of spring's great delicacies, asparagus pairs wonderfully with pasta dishes. Purchase only straight, firm asparagus stalks with compact tips; when you get them home, trim off the base ends of the stalks and wrap them in a damp dishcloth or paper towels, storing the asparagus in the refrigerator. Use within a few days of purchase.

To Peel Asparagus

To use more of each asparagus stalk, peel the skin from the lower ends of the stalk. Using a small, sharp paring knife, carefully cut beneath the thick skin at the base of the stalk; continue cutting upward in the direction of the tip, cutting more thinly as the skin becomes thinner, and ending 2–3 inches (5–7.5 cm) from the tip. Repeat on the other sides of the stalk until it is completely peeled.

BEANS AND LENTILS

All manner of dried beans and lentils may be combined with pasta to make hearty soups or salads. When eaten in combination with pasta, beans and lentils make a complete protein; this is especially important for anyone eating a vegetarian diet.

To Prepare Beans and Lentils

Before use, dried beans and lentils should be carefully picked over to remove any that are discolored or misshapen, or any impurities such as small stones or fibers. Soak

beans in cold water to cover to shorten their cooking time and improve their digestibility, from 3 hours to overnight. Lentils require no presoaking.

BEET GREENS

The slightly bitter leaves of beets have long been enjoyed as a cooked vegetable in their own right. If beet greens are unavailable, spinach or Swiss chard (silverbeet), both related vegetables, may be substituted. Wash all greens thoroughly to remove grit before adding to recipes.

BLANCH

The term blanch describes partially cooking an ingredient, usually a vegetable, by immersing it in a large quantity of boiling water for anywhere from a few seconds to a few minutes, depending upon the ingredient, the size of the pieces and the recipe.

BREAD CRUMBS

Among their many culinary uses, dried bread crumbs form a crunchy, golden coating on supplì. Bread crumbs are an excellent use of day-old bread.

To Make Dried Bread Crumbs

Start with a good-quality country-style loaf made of unbleached wheat flour, with a firm, coarse-textured crumb. Cut away the crusts and crumble the bread by hand, in a blender or in the work bowl of a food processor with the metal blade. Spread the crumbs on a baking sheet and dry them slowly, about 1 hour, in an oven set at its lowest temperature. Store in a tightly covered container at room temperature.

BROCCOLI

This popular green cruciferous vegetable, a relative of the cabbage, finds its way into many rice dishes, most often in the form of its small flowering buds, called florets.

To Cut Broccoli Florets

Cut the flowerlike buds or clusters from the ends of the stalks, including about 1 inch (2.5 cm) of stem with each floret. Reserve

the stalks for another use; they can, for example, be peeled of their tough, fibrous outer layers, then be sliced and stir-fried or steamed until tender.

BUTTER

For the recipes in this book, unsalted butter is preferred. Lacking salt, it allows the cook greater leeway in seasoning recipes to taste and meeting the dietary needs of diners.

Flavored Butters

EACH RECIPE MAKES ½ CUP (4 OZ/125 G)

Add herbs and spices to unsalted butter and use it on pasta, breads and rolls. Make these butters ahead and refrigerate for up to 1 day or freeze for up to 1 month before use.

GINGER BUTTER
½ cup (4 oz/125 g) unsalted butter at room temperature
1 tablespoon grated fresh ginger with its juice
2 teaspoons grated lemon zest
½ teaspoon salt
½ teaspoon sugar
½ teaspoon freshly ground pepper

NASTURTIUM BUTTER
½ cup (4 oz/125 g) unsalted butter at room temperature
40 nasturtium flowers, stemmed and chopped
1 tablespoon chopped flat-leaf (Italian) parsley
2 teaspoons minced shallots
½ teaspoon honey
½ teaspoon salt
½ teaspoon freshly ground pepper

ROASTED GARLIC BUTTER
½ cup (4 oz/125 g) unsalted butter at room temperature
3 tablespoons Roasted Garlic Purée (see page 296)
1 teaspoon minced fresh thyme
½ teaspoon salt
½ teaspoon freshly ground pepper

SAGE AND SHALLOT BUTTER
½ cup (4 oz/125 g) unsalted butter at room temperature
1 tablespoon minced shallots
1 tablespoon minced fresh sage
½ teaspoon salt
½ teaspoon freshly ground pepper

Flavoring Butter

1. *In the work bowl of a food processor with the metal blade or in a blender, combine the butter and flavoring ingredients for each recipe.*

2. *Pulse several times until the mixture is smooth. If necessary, using a rubber spatula, scrape the sides and bottom of the work bowl and pulse again.*

3. *Transfer the mixture to a small container, mold or ice cube tray or roll into a cylinder. Cover and refrigerate up to 1 day or freeze up to 1 month.*

CAPERS

The small, pickled flower buds of a bush native to Asia and common to Mediterranean countries, capers are used whole as a savory flavoring or garnish to add spark to rice and pasta dishes.

CHEESES

Many different types of cheese complement the taste and texture of pasta.

A Guide to Cheeses

For risottos, the cheese is an intricate part of both the flavor and texture of the dish. Cheeses cannot be used interchangeably in recipes. Differences in fat and moisture content cause them to react differently when cooked. If the cheese called for in a particular recipe is not available, substitute one classified as having the same texture, which would be a cheese with a similar fat and moisture content.

Store cheeses sealed in plastic wrap in the refrigerator. Change the wrap every few days to lengthen the storage time.

ASIAGO   Originating in the Italian village of the same name, this firm-textured, piquant cow's milk cheese is sold both fresh and aged for up to 6 months, at which time it is often used in grated form.

FRESH GOAT CHEESE   Most cheeses made from goat's milk are fresh, white and creamy, with a distinctive sharp tang; they are sold shaped into small rounds or logs. Some are coated with pepper, ash or a mixture of herbs, which mildly flavors them. This cheese is also known by the French term *chèvre*.

FONTINA   A semi-firm, creamy, delicate cheese with a slightly nutty taste, made from cow's milk. For the best quality, buy genuine Italian Fontina from the Aosta Valley.

GRUYÈRE   A variety of Swiss cheese, Gruyère has a firm, smooth texture, small holes and a strong, nutty flavor.

GORGONZOLA   A creamy blue-veined Italian cheese. Other creamy blue cheeses may be substituted.

GOUDA   A semi-soft, rich variety of Dutch cheese, yellowish in color and mild to strong. Edam is similar.

MOZZARELLA   A rindless, white, mild-tasting Italian cheese traditionally made from water buffalo's milk and sold fresh, immersed in water. Cow's milk mozzarella is now more common, although it has less flavor. When a recipe calls for whole-milk mozzarella, study the label carefully; some brands may be made at least partly with skim milk.

PARMESAN   A semi-hard cheese made from half skim and half whole cow's milk, with a sharp, salty flavor that results from up to 2 years of aging. In its prime, a good piece of Parmesan cheese is dry but not grainy and flakes easily. For best flavor, buy imported Italian Parmesan in block form and grate or shave just before use.

PECORINO ROMANO   This sheep's milk cheese is sold either fresh or aged.

RICOTTA   A very light and bland Italian cheese traditionally made from twice-cooked sheep's milk, although cow's milk ricotta is now far more common.

To Grate, Shred or Shave Cheese

In most cases, firm- to hard-textured cheeses should be grated with the fine rasps of a cheese grater or cut into thin shreds with the small holes of a shredder; the finer the particles of cheese, the more readily they will melt. Thin shavings of cheese, cut with a cheese shaver or a swivel-bladed vegetable peeler, make an attractive and flavorful garnish.

Zesting Citrus Fruits

1. *Using a zester or fine shredder, carefully draw its thin, sharp-edged holes along the surface of the fruit to remove the zest in fine shreds.*

2. *Alternatively, using a vegetable peeler or a paring knife, carefully remove the zest. Using a small, sharp knife cut it into thin strips.*

3. *For finely grated zest, use a fine hand-held grater. Keeping your fingers out of the way, vigorously rub the fruit against the sharp teeth.*

CITRUS FRUITS

The lively flavor of citrus fruits adds a fresh spark to many recipes. The thin, brightly colored, outermost layer of a citrus fruit's peel is called the zest. It contains most of the fruit's aromatic essential oils, which provide lively flavor to both pasta and risotto dishes. When zesting any citrus fruit, be careful to remove only the colored peel and not the bitter white pith. Use the strips as garnish or mince or grate the zest as directed in the individual recipes. After removing the zest, use the fruit for juice.

CRABMEAT

Find cooked crabmeat in fish markets or the seafood counters of quality food markets. Frequently, it has been frozen; for the best flavor and texture, seek out freshly cooked crabmeat. In season, from September to April, fish markets will usually sell crabs boiled or steamed whole; ask for them to be cracked, so that you can open the shells by hand and remove the meat. Left in coarse chunks, the shelled meat, especially from the body, is sold as "lump" crabmeat; finer particles from the legs or broken down from larger lumps is known as "flaked" crabmeat.

EGGS

Eggs are sold in the United States in a range of standard sizes, the most common being jumbo, extra large, large and medium. The recipes in this book, including those for making fresh pasta, were created using large Grade A eggs.

To Separate an Egg

Crack the shell in half by tapping it against the side of a bowl, then breaking it apart with your fingers. Holding the shell halves over the bowl, gently transfer the whole yolk back and forth between them, letting the clear white drop away into the bowl and taking care not to cut into the yolk with the edges of the shell. Transfer the yolk to another bowl.

Alternatively, gently pour the egg from the shell onto the slightly cupped fingers of your outstretched clean hand, held over a bowl. Let the whites fall between your fingers into the bowl; the whole yolk will remain in your hand.

The same basic function can be performed with an aluminum, ceramic or plastic egg separator placed over a bowl. The separator holds the yolk intact in its cuplike center while allowing the white to drip out through one or more slots in its side into the bowl.

Refrigerate separated eggs in tightly covered containers for up to 4 days.

EMULSIFY

To combine two liquids that would not ordinarily blend, such as vinegar and oil, by causing tiny droplets of one to be suspended in another. In a vinaigrette dressing, for example, an emulsion is made by whisking the vinegar briskly or processing in a food processor or blender while oil is added in a thin, steady stream.

GARLIC

Whether used raw or cooked, this pungent bulb is best purchased in whole heads (or bulbs) composed of individual cloves, to be separated as needed. Purchase no more than you will use within 1 or 2 weeks, as garlic can become bitter with prolonged storage.

To Roast Garlic

Preheat an oven to 325°F (165°C). In a small baking dish with a tight-fitting lid, place 3 garlic bulbs, loose outer skins removed. Add olive oil to a depth of ½ inch (12 mm). Add an equal amount of water. Add 1 teaspoon kosher salt and 2 small sprigs of fresh thyme to the dish, cover and place in the oven until the garlic has the texture of softened butter when a clove is pressed. It will take 45–90 minutes, depending on the size and age of the garlic bulbs. Remove the pan from the oven, remove the garlic from the cooking liquid and let cool. Store in the refrigerator for 4–5 days.

To Make Roasted Garlic Purée

Place a roasted garlic bulb (see above) on a work surface. Using your thumb, pull out the garlic root and discard it. Place the cooked cloves, all in a cluster, on their sides on the work surface and press down on them with the palm of your hand, easing the cooked garlic pulp out the root ends of

Peeling and Mincing Garlic

1. To peel, place the clove on a work surface and cover it with the side of a large knife. Press down to crush the clove slightly. The dry skin should slip off easily.

2. To mince, use a sharp knife to cut the peeled clove into thin slices. Then cut across the slices to make thin strips.

3. Using a gentle rocking motion, move the knife back and forth across the strips to mince the garlic into fine particles.

4. Alternatively, press the peeled clove through a hand-held garlic press.

the cloves. Using a fork, scrape the purée off the work surface and place it in a bowl. Using the fork, mash the pulp to a smooth purée. Occasionally, a root will remain stubbornly in place. In this case, you will need to pull the cloves, gently, one by one, off the root and squeeze the pulp out of each one. One garlic bulb makes 1–3 tablespoons of purée. Store in the refrigerator, covered, for 4–5 days.

GINGER

The rhizome of the tropical ginger plant, strong-flavored ginger is a popular savory and sweet spice. Whole ginger rhizomes, commonly but mistakenly called roots, can be purchased fresh in a food store or vegetable market.

To Prepare Fresh Ginger

Before slicing, chopping or grating, the rhizome's brown, papery skin is usually peeled away from the amount being used. The ginger may then be sliced or minced with a small paring knife or a chef's knife, or grated against the fine holes of a small grater.

HERBS

Many fresh and dried herbs may be used to enhance the flavor of pasta dishes. In general, add fresh herbs toward the end of cooking, as their flavor dissipates with long exposure to heat; dried herbs may be used in dishes that cook longer, and measure for measure are much more concentrated in flavor than their fresh counterparts.

To Store Herbs

Keep fresh herbs in water—as you would cut flowers—awaiting use. They will last up to 1 week if trimmed daily and refrigerated. Store dried herbs in tightly covered containers in a cool dark place and use within 6 months of purchase.

HOT PEPPER SAUCE

This bottled commercial cooking and table sauce made from fresh or dried hot red chilies is an acquired taste. Many varieties are available, but Tabasco is the most commonly known brand.

LEEKS

Grown in sandy soil, these leafy-topped, multilayered vegetables require thorough cleaning before use in any recipe.

To Clean a Leek

Trim the tough ends of the dark green leaves. Trim the roots. If a recipe calls for the white part only, trim the dark green leaves where they meet the slender, pale green part of the stem. Starting about 1 inch (2.5 cm) from the root end, slit the leek lengthwise. Vigorously swish the leek in a basin or sink filled with cold water. Continue rinsing and draining until no dirt remains between the tightly packed pale green portion of the leaves.

MUSHROOMS

With their meaty textures and rich, earthy flavors, mushrooms enrich many pasta and risotto dishes. Eat only mushrooms purchased from a reputable dealer. Never eat mushrooms of unknown origin or those gathered from the wild.

WHITE   Cultivated white and brown mushrooms are widely available in food markets and greengrocers. Your best choice is to buy them in their smallest form, with their caps still closed, when they are often descriptively called button mushrooms.

CREMINI   Similar in size and shape to white mushrooms, cremini mushrooms have a richer flavor and their skin has a darker, rich brown color.

SHIITAKE   This meaty-flavored Asian variety of mushroom has flat, dark brown caps usually 2–3 inches (5–7.5 cm) in diameter and are available fresh with increasing frequency, particularly in Asian food shops; they are also sold dried.

PORCINI   The widely used Italian name for rich, meaty-flavored wild mushrooms, commonly sold in dried form.

To Reconstitute Mushrooms

Put the mushrooms in a large bowl and add water to cover. Leave them until soft, about 20 minutes. Lift them from the water, rinse briefly and trim off any tough stems. If you

wish to use the soaking liquid as a flavoring, strain it through a double layer of cheesecloth (muslin) to remove any grit.

NUTS

Many varieties of nuts may be used to add rich flavor, protein and crunchy texture to pasta and rice dishes. Purchase nuts in quantities that you'll use in a few months. Store in a dry, covered container.

ALMONDS   Mellow, sweet-flavored nuts, an important crop in California and popular throughout the world.

PINE NUTS   Small, ivory seeds extracted from the cones of a species of pine tree, with a rich, slightly resinous flavor. Widely used in Southwestern and Middle Eastern cuisines. Good toasted on pasta and salads.

PISTACHIOS   Slightly sweet, full-flavored nuts with a distinctively green, crunchy meat. Native to Asia Minor, they are grown primarily in the Middle East and California. Often sold roasted.

WALNUTS   Rich, crisp-textured nuts with distinctively crinkled surfaces. English walnuts, the most familiar variety, are grown worldwide, although the largest crops are in California. Good raw and toasted.

To Toast Nuts

Toasting brings out the full flavor and aroma of nuts. To toast any kind of shelled nut, preheat an oven to 325°F (165°C). Spread the nuts in a single layer on a baking sheet and toast in the oven, stirring once, until they just begin to change color, 5–10 minutes. Alternatively, toast nuts in a dry heavy frying pan over low heat, shaking and stirring frequently to prevent scorching.

To Chop Nuts

Spread the nuts in a single layer on a nonslip cutting surface. Using a chef's knife, carefully chop the nuts with a gentle rocking motion. Alternatively, put a handful or two of nuts in the work bowl of a food processor with the metal blade or in a blender and use a few rapid on-off pulses to chop the nuts to the desired consistency. Be careful not to process the nuts too long.

OLIVE OIL

With its rich flavor, its palette of colors from deep green to pale gold and its range of culinary uses, olive oil deserves its reputation as the queen of edible oils. The fruit's first pressing, extra-virgin olive oil is the finest, with a fruity taste and a low acidity that makes it smooth on the palate. Use as a dressing for salads or add to hot dishes at the end of cooking. Later pressings produce pure olive oil, which has a higher acidity level and is fine for a cooking medium. Store all oils in tightly covered containers in a cool, dark place.

OLIVES

A specialty of the cuisines of Mediterranean Europe and popularized by them around the world, ripe black olives—cured in combinations of salt, seasonings, brines, vinegars and oils—make a pungent addition to pasta dishes. Seek out good-quality cured olives, such as Italian Gaeta, Greek Kalamata or French Niçoise varieties.

To Pit an Olive

Use an olive pitter, which grips the olive and pushes out the pit in one quick squeeze. Or, using a small, sharp knife, carefully slit the olive lengthwise down to the pit. Using your fingers, pry the flesh away from the pit.

PANCETTA

Cured simply with salt and pepper, this Italian-style unsmoked bacon may be sold flat or rolled into a large sausage shape. It is most often used finely chopped as a flavoring ingredient. Available in Italian delicatessens and specialty-food stores.

PEAS

Freshly shelled sweet garden peas are one of the great delicacies of early summer. At other times of year, frozen peas—particularly the very small ones often labeled petite peas—are an acceptable substitute. To purchase whole fresh peas, seek out bright green, unblemished, well-filled pods that snap when bent.

To Shell Fresh Peas

Grasp the pea pod at the stem end and snap it, pulling along the pod to string it. With your thumbs, press down on the seam of the pod to pop it open, exposing the peas.

PEPPERS

The widely varied pepper family ranges in form and taste from large, mild bell peppers (capsicums) to small, spicy-hot chilies and may be used as colorful accents in a wide range of salads, pastas and risottos.

Fresh, sweet-fleshed bell peppers are most common in the unripe green form, although ripened red or yellow varieties are also available. Better produce departments and specialty stores often display creamy pale yellow, orange and purple-black types.

Red chilies are sold fresh and dried. Fresh green chilies include the mild-to-hot dark green poblano, which resembles a tapered, triangular bell pepper; the long, mild Anaheim, or New Mexican; and the smaller, fiery jalapeño and serrano.

When handling any chilies, wear rubber gloves to prevent any cuts or abrasions on your hands from contacting the peppers' volatile oils, which will sting. Wash your hands well with warm, soapy water and take special care not to touch your eyes or other sensitive areas.

To Seed and Derib Peppers

Cut the pepper in half lengthwise with a sharp knife. Pull out the stem section from each half, along with the cluster of seeds attached to it. Remove any remaining seeds, along with any thin white membranes, or ribs, to which they are attached. Cut the pepper halves into quarters, strips or thin slices, as called for in the specific recipes.

PROSCIUTTO

A specialty of Parma, Italy, this variety of raw ham is cured by dry-salting for 1 month, followed by air-drying in cool curing sheds for half a year or more. It is cut into tissue-thin slices, the better to appreciate its intense flavor and deep pink color.

Roasting and Peeling Peppers

1. Preheat a broiler (griller). Cut the peppers in half lengthwise and remove the stems, seeds and ribs as directed above.

2. Place the pepper halves on a broiler pan, cut side down, and broil (grill) until the skins are evenly blackened.

3. Transfer the peppers to a paper bag, close the bag and let it stand until the peppers soften and are cool to the touch, about 10 minutes.

4. Using your finger or a small knife, peel off the blackened skins. Then tear or cut the peppers as directed in the individual recipe.

RADICCHIO

A leaf vegetable related to Belgian endive, the most common variety has a spherical head, reddish purple leaves with creamy white ribs and a mildly bitter flavor. Other varieties are slightly tapered and vary a bit in color.

REDUCE

To boil or briskly simmer a liquid until it partially evaporates, thus concentrating its flavor and thickening its consistency. The wider the diameter of the pan being used, the more quickly a liquid will reduce. Judge the degree to which a liquid has been reduced by noting its level on the side of the pan, or carefully pour it into a heatproof glass measuring cup.

SHALLOTS

These small members of the onion family have brown skins, white-to-purple flesh and taste like a cross between a sweet onion and garlic. They are an interesting, versatile seasoning in pasta and rice dishes.

SHELLFISH

Purchase all shellfish fresh and in season from a reputable merchant. They should give off only a fresh clean scent of the sea. Bivalves and other mollusks should be alive when purchased. Discard any with shells not tightly closed before cooking as well as those that remain shut after cooking. Refrigerate until use.

CLAMS Prized for their sweet, tender flesh, these bivalve mollusks must first be scrubbed under cold running water with a small, stiff-bristled brush, then soaked in a mixture of ⅓ cup salt to 1 gallon of water for 1 hour. Rinse well before using. Check all the clams carefully, discarding any with shells not tightly closed.

MUSSELS These popular, bluish black–shelled bivalves require special cleaning. Rinse the mussels thoroughly under cold running water. One at a time, hold them under the water and scrub with a firm-bristled brush to remove any stubborn dirt. Just before cooking, firmly grasp the fibrous beard attached to the side of each mussel and pull it off. Check all the mussels carefully, discarding any with shells not tightly closed.

SHRIMP (PRAWNS) Fresh, raw shrimp are generally sold with the heads removed but the shells still intact.

To Peel and Devein Shrimp

Using your thumbs, split open the thin shell along the inner curve, between its two rows of legs. Peel away the shell, taking care—if the recipe calls for it—to leave the last segment with the tail fin intact and attached to the meat. Using a small, sharp knife, carefully make a shallow slit along the back, just deep enough to expose the long, usually dark veinlike intestinal tract. With the tip of the knife or your fingers, lift up and pull out the vein and discard it.

SPICES

A variety of dried spices—derived primarily from aromatic seeds, roots and barks—enhances the flavor of pasta dishes. As their flavor dissipates quickly, buy spices in relatively small quantities. Store spices in tightly covered containers in a cool, dark place.

SQUASHES

Hard, orange-fleshed winter squashes such as acorn and butternut squashes and pumpkin pair well with rice and pasta dishes.

To Prepare Winter Squash

Cut the squash open with a heavy, sharp kitchen knife, using a kitchen mallet, if necessary, to tap the knife carefully once it is securely wedged in the squash. With a sharp-edged spoon, scrape out all seeds and fibers from the squash's flesh before cutting it as directed in the recipe.

SWISS CHARD

A leafy dark green vegetable with thick, crisp white or red stems and ribs, Swiss chard is also known as silverbeet. The green part may be cooked like spinach, and has a somewhat milder flavor.

TOMATOES

During summer, when tomatoes are in season, use the best red or yellow vine-ripened tomatoes you can find. At other times of year, plum tomatoes, sometimes called Roma or egg tomatoes, are likely to have the best flavor and texture. For cooking, canned whole, diced or crushed plum tomatoes are also good. Both small red cherry tomatoes and small yellow pear-shaped tomatoes have a pronounced flavor during their peak summer season. Store fresh tomatoes of any kind in a cool, dark place; refrigeration causes them to break down quickly. Use within a few days of purchase.

Peeling and Seeding Tomatoes

1. Bring a saucepan of water to a boil. Wash and stem each tomato. Using a small, sharp knife, cut out the core of the tomato. Remove any blemishes.

2. Using a slotted spoon, submerge the tomato for about 10 seconds in the boiling water. Then immediately dip in a bowl of cold water.

3. Starting at the core hole, peel the skin, using your fingertips and, if necessary, the knife blade. Cut the tomatoes in half crosswise.

4. To seed, hold the tomato upside down and squeeze it gently to force out the seed sacs. Alternatively, use a small spoon to scoop out the seeds. Discard the seeds.

INDEX

CREDITS

Front Cover: Enjoy Linguine Tapenade with Basil and Tomatoes (recipe on page 186) in summer, when fresh basil is abundant. Pair this colorful dish with a glass of wine and some crusty bread for an elegant yet casual meal.

RECIPES
Kristine Kidd: Pages 20, 21, 234, 237, 238, 240, 241, 242, 243, 245, 246, 249, 250, 251, 252, 255, 256, 257, 258, 260, 261, 263, 264, 267, 268, 271, 272, 275, 276, 279, 280, 283, 284, 286, 287, 289, 290, 293

Michele Anna Jordan: Pages 12, 26, 29, 30, 32, 33, 35, 36, 38, 39, 40, 43, 44, 45, 46, 49, 50, 53, 54, 55, 56, 59, 60, 62, 63, 65, 66, 69, 70, 71, 72, 75, 76, 77, 78, 81, 82, 83, 84, 87, 88, 91, 92, 95, 96, 99, 108, 109, 115 (left), 170, 172, 173, 175, 176, 178, 179, 180, 181, 183, 184, 185, 186, 188, 189, 190, 191, 192, 195, 196, 199, 200, 203, 204, 207, 208, 210, 213, 214, 217, 218, 221, 222, 225, 226, 227, 229, 230, 231, 294

Joanne Weir: Pages 102, 104, 105, 107, 110, 112, 113, 115 (right), 116, 118, 119, 121, 122, 124, 125, 126, 127, 129, 130, 133, 134, 135, 136, 139, 140, 142, 143, 145, 146, 147, 148, 150, 151, 152, 153, 155, 156, 158, 159, 161, 162, 165, 166, 167, 168

PHOTOGRAPHY
Joyce Oudkerk Pool: Front Cover, Recipes, Back Cover, Pages 2 and 4, Step-by-Step, Section Openers

Stylists: Carol Hacker, Andrea Lucich, Susan Massey, Rebecca Stephany

Assistants: Arjen Kammweraad, Geri Lesko, Elisabet der Nederlanden, Vickie Roberts-Russel, Myriam Varela

Hand Model: Tracey Hughes

Peter Johnson: Incidentals
Stylist: Janice Baker

PROPS COURTESY
Biordi, Bryan Meats, Cal-Mart, Pottery Barn, Williams-Sonoma

ILLUSTRATIONS
Nicole Kaufman, Jennie Oppenheimer

SPECIAL THANKS
James Badham, Mick Bagnato, The Becker Family, Mark Becker Design and Construction, John Boland, James Carroll, Betty Ellsworth, Peggy Fallon, William Garry, Janique Gascoigne, Patty Hill, Leisel Hofman, Santiago Homsi Jr., Jane Lawrence, Sarah Lemas, Ginny Stanford, Michael Stong, Jon Stong, Lesa Tanner